Dynamisms, Development, and Dispositions

Essays in Honor of Kazimierz Dabrowski

Salvatore Mendaglio, Ph.D.
University of Calgary

Gifted
UNLIMITED

Edited by: Molly A. Isaacs-McLeod, JD, LL.M.
Interior design: The Printed Page
Cover design: Julee Hutcheson

Published by
Gifted Unlimited, LLC
12340 U.S. Highway 42, No. 453
Goshen, KY 40026
www.giftedunlimitedllc.com

ISBN: 978-1-953360-09-0

Acknowledgments

While on sabbatical and reflecting on Dabrowski's theory, on a whim, I contacted Molly Isaacs-McLeod, publisher, Gifted Unlimited. I wanted to know whether she was interested in publishing a compilation of my articles on the theory of positive disintegration. To my surprise, Molly's response was "Yes!". It was Molly's enthusiastic support for the idea that made this book possible. Therefore, the first person I thank is Molly.

I am also grateful for the encouragement and support I received from the editors of the publications in which the essays were originally published. I want to thank Nancy Miller, *Advanced Development*; the late Franz Monks & Eva Ganzwer, *journal für begabtenförderung*; Karen M. Magro, *International Journal for Talent Development and Creativity*; Todd Kettler and Anne Rinn, *Journal of Advanced Academics*; Tracy L. Cross, (2006), Jennifer Jolly and Jennifer Robins (2012), *Journal for the Education of the Gifted*; Don Ambrose, *Roeper Review*; Susen Smith, *Handbook of Giftedness and Talent Development in the Asia-Pacific*. I also thank the publishers who hold copyright for some of the essays including the late Jim Webb and Molly Isaacs-McLeod, Great Potential Press/Gifted Unlimited, Sage Publications, and Springer Publishing Company.

Table of Contents

Introduction: My virtual journey with Dąbrowski 1

Part I On Matters Theoretical 7

Chapter 1 The theory of positive disintegration (TPD) 9

Chapter 2 Conception of Development: Positive Disintegration 41

Chapter 3 Dynamisms 51

Chapter 4 Intelligence 75

Chapter 5 TPD and Other Personality Theories 89

Chapter 6 Academic Dialogue on Dąbrowski's Theory 121

Part II Commentaries on Research 149

Chapter 7 Overexcitability Research: Conceptual Analysis 151

Chapter 8 Overexcitability Research: Methodological Analysis 173

Chapter 9 Overexcitability Research: International Focus 193

Part III Recent Words on Dąbrowski's Theory and Giftedness 219

Chapter 10 Interviews on TPD 221

INTRODUCTION

My Virtual Journey with Dąbrowski

I am fond of saying that it was not accidental that I became intimately involved with Dąbrowski's theory of positive disintegration. Previously, I have limited my explanation to the fact that my interest in emotion motivated my study of the theory. There is another reason. From my graduate student days, I have been drawn to theories in psychology. My keen interest in theories went beyond those related to counseling and psychotherapy, which were a required part of my education as a counseling and clinical psychologist. I studied, and was influenced by, Freud's (1924/1970) psychoanalytic, Rogers' (1951) client-centered, Ellis's (1973) rational emotive, and Perls' (1973) gestalt therapies. However, my intense interest in matters theoretical was developed by perusing theories outside of my professional area of study—particularly those of J. Piaget (Piaget & Inhelder, 1969), H. S. Sullivan (1953), G.H. Mead (1934), S. Duval and R.A. Wicklund (1972), and R. Lazarus (1991). These theories provided me with compelling explanations for fundamental constructs that were part of my daily work and interest in personal development: cognition (Piaget), development of self (Sullivan, Mead), self-awareness (Duval & Wicklund), as well as emotion and stress (Lazarus). In the final analysis, my interest in such contributors led me to identify myself as a theoretical psychologist. Little wonder, then, that when I discovered the nature of Dąbrowski's theory, I was hooked. I say *discovered*, rather than *introduced to* because my initial encounters with the theory elicited somewhat negative reactions. My response to the theory changed dramatically as I learned about the primacy of emotion and how Dąbrowski used emotion to explain exemplary development.

My journey of understanding of the theory of positive disintegration began with the reading of literature available in the field of gifted education. That is not surprising since, outside of Europe, Dąbrowski's theory is only known in our field. I must say that the terminology was initially a barrier and it created some resistance in me. However, since it was apparent that the theory was gaining prominence in the gifted education literature, I reluctantly persevered with trying to understand this strange-sounding theory. It is important to note the time frame in which my encounters began. The story I am recounting commenced in the early 1980s, sparked by the reading of Michael Piechowski's chapter in Colangelo and Zaffran, (1979), which not only introduced the theory to me but to gifted education generally. As I realized later in my journey, Piechowski's seminal chapter, though, does not provide a detailed representation of the theory of positive disintegration but rather one focused on a single aspect of it: overexcitability. His comprehensive, though concentrated, approach eventually led him, with colleagues, to develop a questionnaire to assess the five overexcitabilities, as they became to be known. Thus began the almost exclusive focus on one aspect of Dąbrowski's complex, intricate theoretical formulation that contains over 50 discrete constructs and various assumptions and propositions. Gifted education's treatment of the theory of positive disintegration continues to focus on overexcitabilities. Naturally, as a novice to the theory, I implicitly accepted—what I later understood to be—a narrow attitude toward the theory.

As I perused original sources of Dąbrowski's theory, I was also examining the empirical and nonempirical literature purporting to research or apply the theory. However, the academic literature revealed a preoccupation with overexcitabilities. I must admit that I became increasingly disturbed by the discrepancy between the portrayal of the theory in Dąbrowski's own writings and that in scholarly publications. References to the theory of positive disintegration were virtually consumed with overexcitability while the theory was concerned with explaining the full range of human functioning. Given my attraction to well-developed and articulate theories, I ultimately found Dąbrowski's theory to be unique among the theories that I espoused; what struck me the most was a difference that I perceived between his and the other theories. Constructs that at first seemed paradoxical became not only comprehensible, but also provided explanatory power, organized in a cohesive whole. I had become a genuine devotee—not a naïve disciple. While the other theories described development or other phenomena, the theory of positive disintegration provided explanations for its propositions.

In time, the discrepancy that I perceived between my understanding of the theory emergent from original sources and its depiction in scholarly journals reached an intolerable level. Though I did not in any way consider myself an expert on the theory, I felt compelled to share my thoughts with my colleagues in gifted education. The first product of that pressure was a co-authored article (included in this volume) with my friend and colleague William Tillier on the subject, appearing in 2006. It was the first attempt "to set the record straight" by emphasizing that there is so much more to the theory of positive disintegration than overexcitability. And further, given the cohesiveness of the theory, that it is difficult to study a Dąbrowskian construct in isolation. This book is a selection of my publications on this theme.

Overview of the Compilation

The selected papers are organized in three parts.

Part I contains publications related directly to the theory. Chapter 1 is my detailed summary of the components of the theory of positive disintegration which was originally published as a chapter in my edited book, *Dąbrowski's Theory of Positive Disintegration* (Mendaglio, 2008). Chapter 2 is an article on positive disintegration, written in English and translated into German for a special issue of the *Journal fur Begabtenforderung* on Dąbrowski's theory. Chapter 3 is an article on dynamisms, a part of the theory that has received little attention in the literature. In addition to providing a detailed discussion on dynamisms, I have included some of my thoughts on aspects of the theory that, in my view, need further elaboration. Chapter 4 is an article on the role of intelligence in the theory. Though Dąbrowski adopted the traditional Wechsler approach to assessing intelligence, he proposed a unique perspective on intelligence which, among other things, designates it as subservient to emotion. Chapter 5 is the second chapter that I contributed to my edited book on the theory, wherein the theory of positive disintegration is compared with other theories of personality. I selected Freud's and Rogers' theories as contrasts. I also included a brief reference to the Five Factor Model, though not a theory, because of its popularity. Chapter 6, which concludes Part 1, is a co-authored article with William Tillier. It is a response to Michael Piechowski's article, which proposed substantive changes to the theory of positive disintegration. We decided to submit a reply to the article because, in our view, it was one of a series of articles in which Piechowski argued for, what amounted to in our opinion, a neo-Dąbrowskian view. I included this article to illustrate that a dispassionate sharing of disagreements regarding matters in gifted education benefits the field.

Part II includes three chapters analyzing research on overexcitability and giftedness. Chapter 7, co-authored with William Tillier, reviewed empirical investigations appearing soon after the introduction of Dąbrowski's theory to our field. I call it a conceptual analysis of the empirical investigations because we contrasted the research approaches with Dąbrowski's conceptualization of the constructs involved. Chapter 8 is my analysis of research on excitability and giftedness, not only from a conceptual point of view but also from a methodological one. I critiqued the research on the basis of mischaracterization of the construct of interest and, primarily, the questionnaire used and appropriateness of data analyses employed. Chapter 9 contains my chapter in Susen Smith's recent edited handbook in gifted education on the same theme as the other two chapters in Part II. The main difference is that its focus is on the overexcitability research in the Asia Pacific region. In addition to a critical review, I also added suggestions for practitioners who are interested in applying overexcitability in their work with gifted students.

Part III consists of a final chapter. Chapter 10 is a recently published interview, in which I was asked my views of the theory as well as my perspective on giftedness. In my responses, my main message was that individuals interested in the theory of positive disintegration should be cautious not to misrepresent it. Regarding giftedness, I discussed what I call the psychology of giftedness.

References

Colangelo, N. & Zaffran, R. T. (Eds.). (1979). New *voices in counseling the gifted.* Dubuque, IA: Kendall/Hunt.

Duval, S., & Wicklund, R. A. (1972). *A theory of objective self-awareness.* NY: Academic Press.

Ellis, A. (1973). *Humanistic psychotherapy: The rational-emotive approach.* NY: Julian Press.

Flavell, J.H. (1963). *The developmental psychology of Jean Piaget.* NY: Van Nostrand.

Freud, S. (1924/1970). *A general introduction to psychoanalysis.* New York: Pocket Books (original work published 1924).

Lazarus, R.S. (1991). *Emotion and adaptation.* New York: Oxford University Press.

Mead, G. H. (1934). *Mind, self, and society.* Chicago: University of Chicago Press.

Piaget, J., & Inhelder, B. (1969). *The psychology of the child.* NY: Basic Books.

Perls, F. (1969). *Gestalt therapy verbatim.* Moab, UT: Real People Press.

Rogers, C.R. (1951). *Client-centered therapy.* Boston: Houghton-Mifflin

Sullivan, H.S. (1953). *The interpersonal theory of psychiatry.* New York: W.W. Norton.

Part I
On Matters Theoretical

Chapter 1

The Theory of Positive Disintegration (TPD)

The first chapter in this compilation aims to provide a comprehensive summary of the theory of positive disintegration complete with assumptions, propositions and constructs, as appeared in my edited book *Dąbrowski's Theory of Positive Disintegration* (Mendaglio, 2008). The book contained chapters by some of Dąbrowski's former students, with the most well-known being William Tillier. It also included works by luminaries in the field of gifted education including Michael Piechowski, Linda Silverman, Nancy Miller and Frank Falk, who were pioneers in the application of the theory of positive disintegration to gifted education.

At the time of writing my chapter summarizing the theory, I observed that the field of psychology was experiencing doldrums in personality. I argued that the innovative ideas in Dąbrowski's theory would have the potential to create a resurgence in interest in personality—only, however, if psychologists were aware of the theory. And so, one objective—idealistic indeed—was to introduce the theory to psychology, specifically to the study of personality. The other objective was to help colleagues in gifted education recognize that Dąbrowski did not propose a theory of overexcitability but rather a theory of personality. Attaining the second objective proved more achievable than the first. The book has been widely referenced in gifted education and may have encouraged my colleagues to see beyond overexcitability and to explore the numerous other constructs of the theory.

Regrettably, I am not aware of any impact it has had in the domain of psychology, incidentally where the theory actually belongs!

In titling the chapter, I declared that Dąbrowski's theory is a personality theory for the 21st century. It seemed to me that, as a theory of personality proposed by a psychologist (who was also a psychiatrist) and based on clinical practice and research, the theory of positive disintegration belongs in the personality domain of psychology. My rationale for the title was based on two observations. Personality theorizing in psychology in the 1990s and early 2000s needed revitalizing. Another observation was the growing emphasis on emotion and its role in personality development. Based on those two observations, it seemed to me that Dąbrowski's theory was a perfect theory for the new century, for psychology and also for gifted education.

Reference

Mendaglio, S. (2008a). Dąbrowski's theory of positive disintegration: A personality theory for the 21st century. In S. Mendaglio (Ed.), *Dąbrowski's Theory of Positive Disintegration* (pp. 13-40). Scottsdale, AZ: Great Potential Press.

Dąbrowski's Theory of Positive Disintegration: A Personality Theory for the 21st Century

Why should a relatively obscure theory of personality, known only in North America in the fields of giftedness and gifted education and whose development began in the 1930s, be proclaimed a theory for the 21st century? In fact, I selected the title for two specific reasons. First, Dąbrowski's theory of positive disintegration (TPD) places emotions in a central role, relegating intelligence to a secondary position of influence on personality development. Dąbrowski's theory does not only state that emotions influence personality development, but it also specifies how this is accomplished. This emphasis on emotion and its relationship to personality, articulated some 60 to 70 years ago, reflects the emphasis on emotions that we have seen in psychology in the 1990s and continue to see in the 2000s. While emotions have always been an important consideration in personality theories, TPD is unique because it assigns an essential role to emotions in personality *development*, something that is now acknowledged in the field (e.g., Izard & Ackerman, 2000).

Second, some believe that there is a decline in interest in theories of personality (Walters, 2004). Dąbrowski's theory, with its unique approach personality, may serve to re-invigorate the field. At first glance, this may seem ambitious; however, Dąbrowski's theory has a track record in vitalizing a field of study. Dąbrowski's theory, after its introduction to the North American study of giftedness by Michael Piechowski (1979a), has significantly influenced research on the social and emotional aspects of giftedness (e.g., Baum, Olenchak, & Owen, 1998; Colangelo & Ogburn, 1989; Fiedler, 1998; Hazell, 1999; Mendaglio, 1998; Morrissey 1996; Piechowski, 1997; Schiever,

1985). For the past 20 years, the theory of positive disintegration has been *the* driving force in this area of study.

In this chapter, I provide an overview of the assumptions and key concepts of the theory of positive disintegration. I have tried to represent accurately Dąbrowski's ideas, though what follows is, of course, my interpretation of the theory. Those familiar with the theory know of its evocative quality; TPD triggers strong emotional reactions when people are first introduced to it. Because of this quality of the theory, I begin with my initial exposure to it and my reactions.

I was introduced to TPD by Piechowski (1979a) in a book on counseling gifted individuals (Colangelo & Zaffran, 1979), and my reaction was not very positive. The theory was filled with strange language (e.g., positive disintegration, overexcitability) and unusual use of common terms.

However, given my interest in counseling gifted individuals, I found that I could not avoid the theory. I kept bumping into Dąbrowski's theory in the counseling literature on giftedness and gifted education. TPD was becoming an influential force in the field, as evidenced by publications (e.g., Miller, Silverman & Falk, 1994; Piechowski, 1986; Silverman, 1993) and an increasing number of presentations at conferences such as the National Association for Gifted Children and the Council for Exceptional Children. In essence, I was forced to take a second look at the theory, and as I did, I became an enthusiastic student of TPD.

As I explain elsewhere (Mendaglio, 1999), one reason for my attitude change was that TPD provided a cogent explanation for a question that had arisen during my graduate student days: How can some intelligent, highly educated individuals be mean-spirited and hold negative attitudes, such as racism? My graduate school days coincided with several well-publicized American events—the Civil Rights movement, the Vietnam War, and the Watergate scandal. In addition, the question arose from some experiences in my daily life.

TPD provided an answer that no other theory that I had encountered provided—intelligence is not a sufficient condition for human development, because development is not equated with academic or material success in life. In TPD, development is equated with becoming truly human, a state accomplished by individuals who struggle to make sense of themselves and society. In the process, they transform themselves from self-serving human animals to altruistic human beings.

Delving further into TPD, I focused on another feature of the theory that was quite relevant to my work in counseling and psychotherapy—emotions. While teaching and practicing counseling, well before I had heard of TPD, I knew that emotions are critical to the practice of counseling and psychotherapy. Responding effectively to clients' emotions is a mainstay of effective counseling practice, especially for those professionals of the humanistic persuasion (e.g., Rogers, 1980). I had also noted that regardless of presenting problems (e.g., relationship issues, academic underachievement, parenting issues), the reason clients sought my services, and perhaps the services of other helping professionals, was because of their inability to cope with intense negative emotions. That determining factor most often tipped the scales for deciding to seek professional help. To capture this reasoning, my slogan became, "It's all about negative emotions"—negative, because clients do not seek counseling because of positive emotions. Implementing this in counseling, I had a twofold objective: (1) to help clients understand and accept their negative emotions, and (2) to reduce, if not eliminate, the distress experienced by my clients.

Dąbrowski similarly focused on helping his patients understand and accept their negative emotions; however, his rationale for doing so was very different from mine. In TPD, experience of negative emotions is essential for advanced psychological development. Therefore, the goal of therapy is not to eliminate negative emotions, because when individuals are on the path of development, negative emotions are essential companions. Dąbrowski taught his patients TPD concepts to help them understand the necessity of emotions in development. In essence, he taught his patients that their experiencing of intense negative emotions was a sign of their development—something to celebrate, not remediate. Specifically, patients were taught to reframe commonly held beliefs about negative emotions and to move from the view that they are symptoms to be eliminated, instead seeing the negative emotions as harbingers of growth and development. Such conceptual reframing is a hallmark of TPD.

The importance of emotions in TPD extends beyond helping patients understand that emotions trigger psychological growth and development. Emotions are essential for personality development. Although Dąbrowski conceived of personality in a unique manner, TPD is surprisingly consistent with current views of the role of emotion in personality development. In the early years of the 21st century, researchers in fields of emotions (Brandstatter & Eliaz, 2001; Izard & Ackerman, 2000) and personality (Eisenberg, Fabes, Guthrie, & Reiser, 2002; Magnavita, 2002) generally agreed that emotions influence the development of personality. Izard (1971, 1977), who was well known for his research on emotion, investigating it when it was not popular to do so, said unequivocally, "That emotions affect the development of personality is a truism…" (Izard & Ackerman, 2000, p. 260).

What I find remarkable is that Dąbrowski said this in his English-language books in the 1960s (1964a; 1967) and earlier in his Polish-language articles and books. Emotion, with a few notable exceptions, was not a popular field of study in the 1960s and 1970s in North American psychology. It was not until the 1990s that interest in emotion burst forth. Although there was some interest in the 1980s [for example, Howard Gardner's multiple intelligences, (1983)], the 1990s saw the emergence of emotional intelligence (Salovey & Mayer, 1990; Goleman, 1995). Emotional Quotient (EQ) was said to be as important, if not more important, than intelligence quotient (IQ) for success (e.g., Lynn, 2002).

The year 2000 saw the first issue of the American Psychological Association journal *Emotion* and a plethora of research investigations. Psychology had rediscovered emotions after years of neglect, even though their importance had been noted more than a century earlier by Darwin (1965/ 1872) and James (1990/1890).

In this history, it is striking that Dąbrowski predated the current interest in emotions and their connection to personality. His first English-language publication appeared 70 years ago (1937). Though he did not use the term EQ, Dąbrowski noted that intelligence was not as important as the emotional domain. Emotions were not a hindrance; they were a powerful influence on daily living, more so than intelligence. One example of this is his unpublished manuscript on his philosophy of education (Dąbrowski, n.d. 1).

In spite of such historical contribution, TPD remains virtually unknown in North American education and psychology. However, there is one notable exception: TPD is very well known in the fields of giftedness and gifted education. Dąbrowski's theory, with particular emphasis on certain of its elements, has been an influential force in these fields of study. TPD, with its emphasis on emotions, has been proposed as a theory to explain the emotional development of gifted individuals and a wide range of issues related to giftedness. The power of the theory has been demonstrated by its significant influence in the multi-disciplinary field of giftedness, in which TPD is used to understand and study a wide range of issues (see Mendaglio & Tillier, 2006).

From a rather unceremonious introduction, TPD has become a mainstay of my own theorizing about personality and counseling, as well as broadening my understanding of giftedness. I believe that psychologists in general will find TPD useful. Whether their interest lies in giftedness, personality theory, counseling and psychotherapy, or research, psychologists will find in TPD a conceptual framework that will spur them to examine their current assumptions about human functioning and possibly spark new, creative approaches.

In presenting the theory, I begin with a synopsis of TPD. Italicized words will be explained in the presentation of the assumptions and key concepts sections.

A Synopsis of TPD: A Grand Theory of Personality

The theory of positive disintegration is in the tradition of grand theories of personality such as Freud's psychoanalysis and Sullivan's interpersonal theory. Grand theories have similarities; they are ambitious attempts aimed at explaining phenomena such as personality development, human functioning, and psychopathology. The grand theories are complex and coherent. Each has a high level of internal consistency, and key concepts are logically anchored to the assumptions of the theories. A final similarity is the language of grand theories, which tends to be rich in meaning but bereft of specificity. The language theorists use to convey their ideas challenges students of such theories, and there are few operational definitions of concepts in these theories. The theorists' language and choice of labels for their concepts sometimes act as a barrier to their acceptance. For example, at one time, Freud's (1970/1924) psychoanalytic terms, such as *ego*, *id*, and *superego*, were novel and strange; they are now familiar throughout our culture. Sullivan (1953), in his interpersonal theory, created neologisms to convey his concepts—for example, *prototaxic*, *parataxic*, and *syntaxic* modes of experiencing—to depict a growing and maturing of experiencing reality. Dąbrowski, too, introduced some new words in the presentation of his theory—for example, *overexcitability*; but his theory presents another type of challenge with respect to language. In Dąbrowski's theory of positive disintegration, common psychological terms, such as *personality*, *disintegration*, *adjustment*, and *development*, are used in idiosyncratic ways. In reading my synopsis of the theory, readers should bear in mind my comments regarding grand theories, especially those to do with language. The words that are in italics are key terms that are defined more fully in a subsequent section.

In Dąbrowski's theory, *personality* is not a fixed, universal attribute; personality must be shaped—created—by an individual to reflect his or her own unique character. *Positive disintegration*, the process by which personality is achieved, is a twofold process of: (1) disintegration of a primitive mental organization aimed at gratifying biological needs and mindlessly conforming to societal norms, and (2) re-integration at a higher level of functioning, in which the individual transcends biological determinism and becomes autonomous. Personality, shaped by positive disintegration, develops primarily as a result of the action of *developmental potential*, which is a constitutional endowment that includes *overexcitability*—a high level of reactivity of the central nervous system, and *dynamisms*—autonomous inner forces, assumed to be normally distributed in the population. Human development is depicted not by stages, but rather by a *multi-level*—hierarchical—continuum; it is a progression from a lower, primitive level to a higher, advanced level. Favorable developmental potential produces crises, characterized by *psychoneuroses*—strong anxieties and depressions—sparking disintegration of an individual's mental organization, the first phase of positive disintegration and the development of personality.

The second phase of positive disintegration—the beginnings of re-integration—includes an individual's creation of a *hierarchy of values*, viewed as a vertical arrangement of his or her *emotional reactions*, which is critical to the development of an individual's personality and *autonomy*. An individual's emotional reactions guide him or her in the creation of an individualized *personality ideal*, an autonomous standard that becomes the goal of an individual's development. Using that personality ideal, an individual examines his or her essence and makes existential choices that emphasize those aspects of essence that are "more myself" and inhibit those aspects that are "less myself." In this way, individuals achieve personality and become integrated at a high level of human functioning; they become truly human.

Assumptions

Four assumptions underlying TPD are key: multilevelness, conflict, psychopathology, and emotions.

Multilevelness: A Hierarchical View of Phenomena

The theme of hierarchy pervades the theory of positive disintegration. As the word suggests, Dąbrowski believed that human development and experience can be arranged in a hierarchical manner, which he termed *multilevelness*. Human development, including neurological development, is assumed to proceed from lower, simple structures to higher, complex ones. In addition to general developmental processes, multilevelness applies to specific concepts including instincts, emotions, and conflict. A multilevel view of instincts applies to individual instincts as well as to classes of instincts. Dąbrowski believed that higher instincts, such as the instincts of creativity and self-perfection, are uniquely human. Humans share lower ones like self-preservation and sexual instincts with animals.

Dąbrowski also viewed each instinct in a multilevel manner. Self-preservation, for example, may exist in a lower form expressed by aggressively protecting one's physical well-being, or self-preservation may be transformed into a higher form, such as the action of preserving one's identity as a unique human being (Dąbrowski, 1973).

Similarly, emotions are multilevel in nature, as characterized by concrete or increasingly abstract referents. For example, joy, at its lowest level, is associated with physical well-being from satisfying one's needs, such as having a great meal, and from satisfying wishes, such as watching one's favorite sports team win an important game. At a higher level, joy loses its physiological anchors, becomes more abstract, and is associated with, for example, successes in one's development.

Conflict also is considered in a hierarchical manner. Conflict produced by frustration of basic needs is primitive. Conflict resulting from an individual's failure to live up to his or her values is more advanced.

TPD assumes that there are "empirically verifiable differences between levels of all mental functions comparable to the difference between levels of intelligence" (Kawczak, 1970, p. 2) observed in individuals. Levels of mental functioning are seen hierarchically; therefore, mental development proceeds from lower to higher levels. A developmental view of empathy can illustrate this view. In its most primitive form, empathy is a process of emotion contagion; a child in a nursery cries, then all children cry. This initial form evolves into a more conscious, vicarious experiencing of others' feelings; a child sees another person in distress and feels that person's suffering as if it were his or her own. Finally, a more mature form of empathy enables an individual to become attuned to others and to appreciate their perspectives, including their thoughts and emotions.

Conflict and Psychopathology: Essential for Development

TPD assumes that individuals can only make the transition from lower levels of mental functioning to higher levels by experiencing inner conflict. Emanating from this assumption is the belief that many disorders found in the current edition of *Diagnostic and Statistical Manual of Mental Disorders* (American Psychiatric Association, 1994), several of which Dąbrowski termed psychoneuroses, are essential for advanced psychological development. Dąbrowski proclaimed in *Psychoneurosis Is Not an Illness* (1972) that symptoms associated with psychoneuroses, and even some psychoses, serve the transition from lower to higher development by generating the disintegration process.

Integration and Disintegration: Negative and Positive

In TPD, harmony and peacefulness are associated with the notion of integration, which consists of two types: primitive or primary, and secondary (Kawczak, 1970). The harmony associated with primary integration is characterized by the lack of multilevel inner conflict; individuals are simply motivated by basic instincts, drives, and conformity to social norms. These persons are so integrated mentally that they are in a semi-conscious state, responding to life with little or no reflection.

At the other extreme—secondary integration—harmony and peacefulness stem from the achievement of personality. The individual is accepting of self and others, autonomous, authentic, and has a daily life directed by a hierarchy of values.

It is the primary or primitive integration that psychoneurotic symptoms act upon. These symptoms emerge with the growing awareness by individuals of a discrepancy between how they ought to be and how they actually are. Such experiencing extends to society; individuals are distressed by the difference between the way the world should be and the reality.

Without such experiencing and the ensuing disintegration of the primary integrated level of mental functioning, development cannot occur.

Emotions: Directing Forces of Development

A final assumption, apparent in the above discussion, is that emotions are essential elements in the process of a transition from lower to higher mental functioning. Inner conflict or psychoneuroses include the experience of emotions such as anxiety, shame, guilt, and despair, and moods such as depression. It appears that, in this regard, Dąbrowski was influenced by the theorizing of Mazurkiewicz, a renowned Polish psychiatrist, who conceived of emotions as "directing forces" (Aronson, 1964, p. xii) of development. Intense negative emotions and moods, typically regarded as impediments to growth and development, actually set the stage for advanced development by their disintegrating power. Intensely negative affective experiences begin the process of loosening a tightly integrated mental organization. Though painful for individuals, negative emotions—a hallmark of inner conflict—allow people to achieve a more advanced level of human development.

Components of the Theory of Positive Disintegration

The main components of TPD are subsumed under the headings of personality, factors of development, integration, disintegration, dynamisms, and levels of development.

Personality

O. Hobart Mowrer noted that Dąbrowski proposed an "extraordinary" (Mowrer, 1967, p. xxvi) conception of personality. Dąbrowski disagreed with "the generally accepted view [that] personality is a structure or organization of mental functions characteristic of every individual" (Dąbrowski, 1973, p. 108). Though not cited, he may have been referring to Allport's definition: "Personality is the dynamic organization within the individual of those psychophysical systems that determined his unique adjustments to his environment" (Allport, 1937, p. 48). It is safe to say that Dąbrowski would disagree with virtually any subsequent definition of personality as well for two reasons. First, he viewed personality as an achievement, not a universal attribute of individuals. Second, in his view, personality is not a neutral construct; it is value laden. In TPD, personality is the product of an individual's struggle to move upward toward an ideal (Mowrer, 1967). Personality is equated with the highest level of human development:

> *Personality, in the context of this work, is a name given to an individual fully developed, both with respect to the scope and level of the most essential positive human qualities, an individual in whom all the aspects form a coherent and harmonized whole, and who possesses, in a high degree, the capability for insight into his own self, his own structure, his aspirations and aims (self-consciousness), who is convinced that his attitude is right, that his aims are of essential and lasting value (self-affirmation), and who is conscious that his development is not yet complete and therefore is working internally on his own improvement and education (self-education).* (Dąbrowski, 1967, p. 5)

That personality includes knowing that one's attitudes are right and that one's aims are valued reflect the value-laden quality of Dąbrowski's definition. Behaviors of individuals who have achieved personality are driven by their positive value systems. Values are categorized into universal human and individual values. Universal human values are positive characteristics that have been recognized by society over time. These include personal and social responsibility and a sense of justice, courage, honesty, religiosity, and discipline. Individual values include the acquisition of personally meaningful interests and capabilities that are deemed essential by the individual, enduring emotional bonds of love and friendship, and spirituality that pervades one's daily life.

Values, for Dąbrowski, were equated with emotional experiencing; affective reactions to society and to oneself thus guide the creation of a hierarchy of values. Whether one's personality emerges depends on, among other things, an individual's hierarchy of values drawing on both universal and individual values. Personality, then, is neither a given nor neutral; it is an achievement and value laden.

Factors of Development

To fully appreciate Dąbrowski's factors of development, it is important to consider how Dąbrowski viewed development. He identified three types of development: (1) biologically determined, (2) autonomous mental, and (3) one-sided (Dąbrowski, 1970). Biologically determined development, as the phrase suggests, is associated with the biological life cycle directed by the universal laws of physical development of the human species. This development shows a gradual integration of functions and a progression through the stages of birth, infancy, childhood, adolescence, adulthood, and death. In addition, biologically determined development includes conformity to the social environment. Adjustment is a theme in biologically determined development; individuals regulate their behaviors in accordance with their biological drives, and social norms control their drive gratification.

In autonomous mental development, individuals' inner mental forces combine with positive values to direct development. This type of development transcends the dictates of biology and society. Autonomous development is typified by frequent disintegration of functions and subsequent reintegration at a higher level. Positive maladjustment is a theme in this type of development; individuals regulate their behaviors by conforming to their personal values, which often conflict with commonly accepted social norms. This form of maladjustment is positive, because individuals reject being driven by basic drives and social norms that contradict universal positive values (Dąbrowski, 1972).

In one-sided development, mental functions and structures are integrated in an egocentric and antisocial way. This type of development is manifested in mental states such as paranoia and behaviors such as criminality. Negative maladjustment is a theme in this type of development; individuals regulate their behaviors by the fulfillment of their own ends, regardless of the cost to others. This maladjustment is negative, because the reason for rejecting societal values is the gratification of primitive drives and egocentric needs (Dąbrowski, 1972).

For Dąbrowski, advanced human development was not simply successfully going through the biological life cycle. Nor was development equated with material success in life, such as high academic achievement, amassing vast amounts of money, or becoming a famous world figure. Development means transcending biological instincts and drives and the need to conform unconsciously to societal norms. A developed human being is characterized by such traits as autonomy, authenticity, and altruism.

Developmental Instinct and Developmental Potential

Within this view of development, Dąbrowski identified three factors of development. The first factor consists of two related, hereditary, constitutional elements: developmental *instinct* and developmental *potential*. The developmental instinct is the "mother instinct" (Dąbrowski, 1970, p. 27), the source of all developmental forces. Individuals inherit varying levels of the developmental instinct. Ironically, the developmental instinct, anchored to the biological makeup of an individual, though "not reducible to it" (Dąbrowski, 1970, p. 27), is ultimately *the* force responsible for the transcendence of biological drives, such as self-preservation. The specific forces of development identified in TPD spring from this primordial instinct.

Developmental potential of individuals is a constitutional element that is different from the developmental instinct. TPD emphasizes the role of various instincts and constitutional elements, which Mowrer attributed to Dąbrowski's lack of acquaintance with learning theory (Mowrer, 1967). The implication is that if Dąbrowski had been familiar with learning theory, he would rely less on instincts in TPD. However, it is more likely that the focus on instinct reflects the importance Dąbrowski placed on constitutional endowment as a major determiner of human development.

Dąbrowski postulated that the developmental instinct manifested in developmental potential casts a powerful influence in mental growth; it is the "constitutional endowment which determines the character and the extent of mental growth possible for a given individual" (Dąbrowski, 1972, p. 303). Developmental potential is seen primarily in a quality he termed *overexcitability*, a property of the central nervous system. Overexcitability is a higher than average responsiveness to stimuli due to heightened sensitivity of nervous system receptors (Dąbrowski, 1972). Because overexcitability is an expression of developmental potential, it is also differentiated from the developmental instinct; whether overexcitability is part of an individual's makeup is ultimately determined by individuals' hereditary endowment. Some individuals' central nervous systems will be excitable, but not overly so. Overexcitability, then, influences how individuals experience internal and external reality. Individuals who are endowed with overexcitability perceive reality in a different, more intense, multifaceted manner than those not so endowed. They are likely to experience surprise and puzzlement at events in their daily lives.

Dąbrowski identified five forms of overexcitability: psychomotor, sensual, imaginational, intellectual, and emotional. Psychomotorically over-excitable individuals tend to be high-energy, curious, have difficulty sitting still, need constant change of scenery, and are generally restless. Sensually overexcitable individuals are generally highly sensitive to sensory perceptions such as sights, smells, tastes, and tactile stimulation. Imaginationally over-excitable individuals are inclined to be daydreamers, have a rich fantasy life, and are often creative. Intellectually overexcitable individuals manifest abilities of analysis and synthesis, ask probing questions, and love learning for its own sake. Emotionally overexcitable individuals are sensitive individuals who experience emotions intensely, tending to take things to heart. They are empathic toward others and feel a strong need for exclusive relationships. Individuals may inherit some, all, or none of the five forms of overexcitability. In TPD, the presence of intellectual, imaginational, and emotional forms (sometimes referred to as "the big three") are deemed essential for advanced psychological development.

The forms of overexcitability are manifested in special interests and abilities, the seeds of which can be observed during early childhood. For example, intellectual overexcitability can be seen in children's sophisticated approach to formulating questions as they attempt to understand events or concepts. Perceptiveness with respect to the world around them and early mathematical ability are other special abilities that are associated with this form of overexcitability. Children with strong imaginational overexcitability show distinct interests in creative pursuits such as poetry, dance, and painting.

Autonomous inner forces are also part of developmental potential. It appears that Dąbrowski was influenced by Jan Mazurkiewicz, with whose theory Dąbrowski was familiar (see Dąbrowski, 1964a, 1967). Mazurkiewicz postulated the existence, in both animals and human beings, of "*own* forces" (emphasis in original, Aronson, 1964, p. xii). These forces stem from within an organism, rather than being responses to external stimuli. Mazurkiewicz proposed that own forces are most operational in human beings. Dąbrowski called this type of force *dynamism* and defined it as a "biological or mental force controlling behavior and its development. Instincts, drives, and intellectual processes combined with emotions are dynamisms" (1972, p. 294).

Social Environment

The social environment is the second factor of development in TPD.

The effects of the social environment on individual development depend on the amount of endowed developmental potential. If an individual's developmental potential is particularly strong, then the quality of the social environment is of secondary importance. Such individuals are innately resilient and largely impervious to their social environment.

At the other extreme, when developmental potential is very weak, development—in the Dąbrowskian sense—will not occur, even if the social environment is highly nurturing. The quality of the social environment is an important factor when developmental potential lies in between these extremes. In those cases, a nurturing social environment will have a beneficial effect and a negative social environment will have a negative effect on individuals' development.

Third Factor Dynamism

The third factor of development, so named by Dąbrowski, is a special type of dynamism. The third factor is a particularly important dynamism that appears only after other dynamisms are activated. Admittedly a difficult concept to define (Dąbrowski, 1973), it is described as the force by which individuals become more self-determined, controlling their behaviors through their inner voices and values. Once the third factor is activated, individuals are no longer at the mercy of biological needs or under the control of societal conventions. Individuals so characterized lead lives consciously and deliberately, selecting courses of action based on values that they have selected. Their approach to daily life is highly moral in nature. At this high level of development, individuals also increasingly engage in self-education and self-help.

Integrations and Disintegrations

Dąbrowski described two types of integration—primary and secondary—and four types of disintegration—positive, negative, partial, and global.

Dąbrowski equated rigidly integrated mental structures with automatic responses, which are associated with lower levels of functioning; Dąbrowski called this state *primary integration*. In contrast, the less organized, volitional behaviors associated with higher levels of functioning are associated with *secondary integration*.

Primary integration characterizes individuals who are largely under the influence of the first factor (biology) and the second factor (environment). These individuals experience the human life cycle and may become very successful in societal terms, but they are not fully developed human beings. Persons characterized by secondary integration are influenced primarily by the third factor; they are inner directed and values driven. As fully human, they live life autonomously, authentically, and altruistically. Biological drives are sublimated into higher modes of expression. Conformity and nonconformity to societal norms are principled. Movement from primary to secondary integration arises from positive disintegration.

Positive disintegration is a twofold process: (1) dissolution of lower mental structures and functions, and (2) creation of higher forms (Dąbrowski, 1970). During the dissolution part of the process, individuals experience intense external and internal conflicts that generate intense negative emotions. Such experiencing may be initially triggered by developmental milestones, such as puberty, or crises, such as the death of a loved one. As a result, individuals become increasingly conscious of self and the world. They become more and more distressed as they perceive a discrepancy between the way the world ought to be and the way it is, which Dąbrowski called the "psychoneurotic conflict" (1973, p. 2). With the onset of awareness of this discrepancy, conflicts and negative experiences become more internally focused. Such experiencing destroys an individual's pre-existing mental organization which guided his or her daily behaviors.

In a sense, the first part of positive disintegration creates a state of ambiguity. Primary integration is a highly structured state that requires little, if any, reflection on the part of individuals. With the dissolution of one's mental organization, a state of high anxiety ensues that can be reduced only by creating some other organization. Higher-level mental organization arises from such forces as self-awareness, self-direction and autonomy, and the selection of values by which one will live his or her life. These and other related forces create a new, higher-level form of integrated mental organization and thus resolve the inner conflict and anxiety created by the dissolving part of the process. When both parts of the process occur, Dąbrowski called it positive disintegration or global disintegration.

Dąbrowski identified other types of disintegration—negative and partial. Negative disintegration occurs when individuals experience only part of positive disintegration: the dissolving part. That is, individuals are in a sense trapped in the dissolution state, experiencing conflicts and negative emotions with no resolution in sight, yet they are unable to return to their previous state of integration. Chronic psychotic illnesses and suicide are likely expressions of negative disintegration. Partial disintegrations do not have such dramatic outcomes. This type of disintegration may result in several outcomes: a return to the lower level of functioning, a partial re-integration at a higher level, or a transformation into global disintegration.

Genetic endowment, according to Dąbrowski, plays an important role in integration and disintegration. Very favorable hereditary endowment is necessary for positive disintegration. Partial disintegration and negative disintegration come from "limited hereditary endowment" (Dąbrowski, 1970, p. 166). Dąbrowski suggested that, in the case of a very favorable hereditary endowment, the quality of the social environment is not a critical factor; the biological substrate is sufficient to propel an individual toward secondary integration. However, for both partial and negative disintegration, the quality of the social environment is an important factor contributing significantly to the individual's experience. Individuals who remain in a primary integrated state do not have a sufficiently favorable genetic endowment to fuel the disintegration process. A favorable genetic endowment contains the nuclei of inner forces, which are not only essential for disintegration, but also define the process.

Inner Psychic Milieu

Dąbrowski extended the idea of inner milieu—the internal physical and physiological environment of individuals—to inner psychic milieu, the internal mental environment (Dąbrowski, Kawczak, & Piechowski, 1970). Inner milieu is the internal physical environment where a collection of processes and forces regulate various bodily functions, such as body temperature. Inner *psychic* milieu is the internal mental environment where cognitive forces, when activated, regulate development—for example, moving from an other-directed to a self-directed approach to life. While the inner milieu is given, the psychic environment is constructed.

The inner mental environment originates from a lack of balance between the parasympathetic and sympathetic nervous systems. Such imbalances create a disturbance in an individual's internal sensations, and he or she becomes aware of what Dąbrowski called organismic "noise" (1972, p. 103). For example, disruption of a sense of well-being may be indicated by difficulties with sleeping, digestion, or energy level; the accompanying pain and anxiety then begin to affect the development of the internal mental environment by turning the individual's attention inward. Remaining at this rudimentary level results in a primitive form of mental environment where conscious activities are temporarily or permanently under the direction of basic drives (sexual, self-preservation, etc.), with little or no consciousness of a distinct self.

The type of mental environment that Dąbrowski associated with positive disintegration is one that encompasses the totality of mental forces that create disintegration of mental structures and functions, forging a personality—the highest mental organization for individuals (1970, p. 64). Forces of the inner psychic milieu are initially disorganized and antagonistic; at times, one force may predominate, only to be replaced by another in a spontaneous manner. Conflict with the internal and external environments results due to the opposing aims of the forces and to the needs of internal and demands of external environments. As development progresses, the inner psychic milieu—the totality of forces—is transformed by the individual into a hierarchically organized complex of forces that are under the control of the individual's inner self and that result in self-directed behavior free of conflict. Dąbrowski called the mental forces of the inner psychic milieu *dynamisms*.

Dynamisms

Dynamisms are autonomous inner forces, which are either biological or mental in nature, controlling individuals' behaviors and development. As noted earlier, Dąbrowski described dynamisms as constellations of "instincts, drives, and intellectual processes combined with emotions" (1972, p. 294).

There are two general categories of dynamisms—dissolving and developmental—which correspond to the two-part process of positive disintegration. Dissolving dynamisms weaken, disrupt, and ultimately destroy primary integration. Among the first set of dynamisms that start the dissolving process are ambivalence and ambitendency. Ambivalence refers to changeable feelings of dislike or like, simultaneous feelings of inferiority and superiority, fluctuations of moods, and approach-avoidance conflicts. Ambitendencies include conflicting courses of action, indecision, and desiring incompatible goals or things. Experiencing such matters as fluctuation of moods and approach-avoidance conflicts, not previously experienced, begins to disrupt the mental balance. Inner forces such as ambivalences and ambitendencies can produce only temporary loosening of mental organization, resulting in a return to primary integration unless accompanied by other dynamisms.

The dynamisms responsible for the ultimate destruction of primary integration are autonomous inner forces that create a discontent with oneself and with society at large. This discontent intensifies as these dynamisms emerge in the person's interactions with the social environment. There are several dissolving dynamisms: astonishment with oneself, disquietude with oneself, feelings of inferiority toward oneself, dissatisfaction with oneself, feelings of shame and guilt, creativity and positive maladjustment.

Astonishment with oneself refers to the feeling that one's own cognitive qualities are unexpected and surprising. This signals the beginning of the individual's becoming an object of his or her awareness. Disquietude with oneself marks the beginning of negative attitudes toward self. To astonishment with oneself, which is largely cognitive in nature, disquietude with oneself adds an emotional component—negative feelings associated with a self-critical attitude. Feelings of inferiority toward oneself refers to the negative emotions one experiences as a result of increased awareness of the discrepancy between where one is and the higher level to which he or she aspires, i.e., between where one is and where one ought to be. This dynamism contributes significantly to the creation of an individual's hierarchy of values.

Dissatisfaction with oneself, one of the strongest dynamisms of this category, is a negative attitude toward oneself that includes not only disapproval and dislike of self, but also self-aggression and attempts to escape oneself. This dynamism produces experiences of intense anxiety and depression. Feelings of shame and guilt reflect an individual's response to external and internal opinions of self. Both shame and guilt result from dissatisfaction with oneself. Shame, a sense of embarrassment and distressful self-consciousness, is connected with others' perceptions of self, whether real or imagined. Blushing and increased pulse rate may be signs of shame. With guilt, the feelings are internalized. Embarrassment is experienced not only in relation to others, but also to oneself and one's ideals. There is an ownership of responsibility for one's own shortcomings or imperfections. Creative instinct, also influenced by dissatisfaction with self, refers to the individual's search for new experiences that are qualitatively different from current ones.

The last dynamism in the dissolving category requires special attention. Positive maladjustment is the rejection of primitive values held by one's social group or society at large. This is similar to Kierkegaard's belief that individuals need to reject anchoring their behaviors on common values. The rejection is conscious and selective, and it reflects an individual's hierarchy of values, created based on the way things ought to be rather than how they are.

In Dąbrowski's view, there are both positive and negative forms of adjustment and maladjustment. Negative adjustment is shown by automatic and subservient behavior conforming to the demands of society. Negative maladjustment is reflected in criminal or pathological behaviors. The positive maladjustment dynamism propels the individual past automatic conformity. Positive adjustment is associated with advanced development, reflected in an individual's behavior influenced by a consciously constructed hierarchy of values.

Because of the dissolving dynamisms, individuals experience internal and external conflict characterized by persistent, intense, negative emotions, often described by Dąbrowski by using Kierkegaard's phrase of "fear and trembling." Another classic phrase that comes to mind is G. Stanley Hall's "storm and stress" (Smith, 1993, p. 137), which he used to characterize adolescence.

Developmental dynamisms, which create a new mental organization, include self-awareness and self-control; subject and object in oneself; syntony (sympathy and resonance to others), identification, and empathy; the third factor; inner psychic transformation; education of oneself; and autopsychotherapy. Self-awareness and self-control include awareness of one's mental and behavioral activities, personal identity and uniqueness, and differential stability of personal characteristics. Self-awareness and self-control also include the realization that some personality traits are not only more stable than others, but some are more important. The awareness enables the individual to engage in self-control.

Subject and object in oneself refers to the process of self-observation and examination for the purpose of furthering one's mental development. Through active, constant self-exploration, the individual comprehends the essential elements of one's inner life. Ultimately, through this dynamism, an individual experiences his or her own essence, what he or she truly is.

Syntony, identification, and empathy are progressively more complex modes of relating to other individuals. Syntony refers to spontaneously feeling what others feel, a sympathetic reaction, and a social interest, analogous to what we now call "emotional contagion" (Singer, 2006, p. 859). Identification is more a cognitive and somewhat more conscious form that refers to understanding others. Empathy denotes gaining insight into others' experiences and their emotions, combined with an altruistic attitude toward others.

The third factor is the agent of conscious choice of development, seen as the inner self that coordinates an individual's mental life. This dynamism discriminates among functions and events according to their value for enhancing development; if they are not growth-promoting, they are rejected. Inner psychic transformation sublimates instincts and drives into elements that gradually become incorporated into one's personality. Impulses are not only consciously rejected, but also are transformed. Education of oneself and autopsychotherapy refer to the actualization of personal ideals by engaging in self-improvement, as required, guided by an individual's hierarchy of values. Autopsychotherapy also is the process of educating and guiding oneself during experiences of stress—the ability to cope with distress, whether it originates in external or internal environments. For Dąbrowski, individuals who reach the higher levels of functioning literally become their own teachers and psychotherapists.

Dynamisms associated with the highest level of development include: responsibility for oneself and for others, autonomy, authentism, disposing and directing center, and personality ideal. Responsibility for oneself and for others refers to taking responsibility for one's own actions, thinking, and desires as seen in the context of one's life and in relationships with others. Others are not seen as objects but as subjects; individuals develop an I-thou relationship with other people. The sense of responsibility—that is, the need to take ownership of and improve one's shortcomings—extends to helping others who wish to improve.

Autonomy is the dynamism by which individuals consciously free themselves from lower drives and from aspects of the social environment that contradict positive values. Authentism, based on self-awareness, is the expression of one's emotions, cognitions, and attitudes. It refers to being consistent with one's hierarchy of values. Disposing and directing center determines immediate behavior of an individual, as well as his or her long range planning. At the highest level, this center emerges as a distinct dynamism that works toward harmonizing the unity of personality. The disposing and directing center becomes integrated into the personality ideal. Personality ideal is a standard against which an individual evaluates his or her actual personality. It eventually becomes the highest dynamism that shapes one's personality.

Many of terms that Dąbrowski used to denote dynamisms are encountered in the fields of psychology and psychiatry. There is, however, a significant difference in the interpretation given to them. For example, *autonomy, authentic*, *empathy*, and *self-awareness* are encountered in other personality theories, particularly those of the humanistic tradition (Maslow, 1970; Rogers, 1951). However, Dąbrowski did not simply use these concepts as descriptors of personality; he perceived them as forces allowing for and guiding personality development. A more dramatic illustration of the difference is found in the dissolving dynamisms. For example, *feelings of guilt and shame* and *dissatisfaction with oneself* are likely to be viewed as symptoms, but Dąbrowski considered them to be forces essential for personality development. This perspective is emblematic of how Dąbrowski viewed psychopathology.

Psychopathology

Dąbrowski's view of mental health was anchored to positive disintegration and the development of personality. Being on the path of personality development—with all of the negative emotional experiences and conflicts—signified mental health. Lack of mental health was associated with lack of development of personality and with the complacency and automatic living associated with primary integration (Dąbrowski, 1964a).

Dąbrowski reframed individuals' experiences that are normally considered symptomatic of mental illness. In effect, he proposed that experiences deemed symptoms of disorders are in fact essential for human psychological growth and development (Dąbrowski, 1972). This point of view was not restricted to psychoneuroses, but he also extended it to psychoses as well. He cautioned against the automatic assumption that such symptoms as delusions, anxiety, phobias, and depression are signs of mental illness, because they may be in fact signs of an individual's development (Dąbrowski, 1964a).

Of course, Dąbrowski believed that, at times, symptoms traditionally associated with severe psychopathology could, in fact, be signs of mental illness. However, he believed that symptoms associated with psychoneuroses are positive, because they indicate, at the very least, an individual's potential for advanced development.

Dąbrowski distinguished between neuroses and psychoneuroses. Neuroses, he believed, are rooted in psychophysiological or psychosomatic disorders, i.e, in bodily organs or systems that do not show any sign of physical malfunction. Psychoneuroses, on the other hand, depict syndromes and processes that are expressions of individuals' internal and external conflict. Dissolving dynamisms, such as dissatisfaction with oneself, guilt feelings, feelings of inferiority, and positive maladjustment are examples of such psychoneurotic processes. Far from being mental disorders that need remediation, psychoneuroses are considered "basic constituent[s]" of the process of positive disintegration (Dąbrowski, 1973, p. 149).

An important function served by psychoneurotic conflict is the creation of a hierarchy of values that directs an individual's behavior (Dąbrowski, 1972). Emotions play a critical role in this process. Negative emotions of psychoneurotic conflict create a state of distress that is resolved by the activation of dynamisms such as empathy that lead to the experiencing of higher-level emotions. Individuals' experiencing of negative emotions signals that there is something morally wrong with their current attitudes and behaviors. Negative emotions arise from the awareness of discrepancy between the way such individuals believe they ought to be and the way they actually are. They are then motivated to reduce the distress produced by the discrepancy by moving toward their ideal. As individuals succeed in reducing the discrepancy, they experience higher-level emotions—emotions that flow from the movement toward an ideal—rather than the gratification of a biological need. In essence, it is the experience of higher-level emotions that links emotions to values in TPD and to the creation of a hierarchy of values. For example, if an individual who experiences psychoneurotic conflict *feels good* when helping other people, then helping others is added to his or her set of values. Dąbrowski believed that psychoneuroses play a vital role in propelling individuals toward higher levels of human development.

Levels of Development

The phrase *levels of development* differs conceptually from *stages of development* used in other theories. Stages of development are often sequential, age-related, and universal. For example, in Erikson's (1950) theory, development progresses sequentially from trust vs. mistrust (associated with infancy) to ego integrity vs. despair (associated with old age), and this model is applicable to all individuals. In TPD, development does not occur in a lock-step fashion, in which an individual completes the criteria for one stage and then moves on to the next one. Individuals may be at one level of development for certain aspects and at a different level with respect to other areas. There are no age-related criteria associated with each level; individuals at a young age may manifest advanced development associated with the higher levels. Levels of development are not universal; individuals who reach the highest level of development are rare.

Consistent with his conceptualization of personality, Dąbrowski's levels are imbued with moral dimensions. The five levels of development are modes of being in the world analogous to Kierkegaard's view of development. [Apparently Kierkegaard was one of Dąbrowski's favorite writers (Kawczak, 1970), and the influence of the father of religious existentialism can be seen throughout Dąbrowski's writings (e.g., numerous references to Kierkegaard's "fear and trembling").] Kierkegaard believed that love, particularly love of God, is the cornerstone of faith. Faith was the cornerstone of the highest of three "existential positions" (Carlisle, 2005, p. 93), also known as stages (McPherson, 2001).

Kierkegaard proposed three stages of development: aesthetic, ethical, and religious. Aestheticism, the lowest form, was characterized by hedonism. At this stage, individuals are motivated by satisfaction of basic instincts or drives and conforming to societal standards. Individuals can only progress to the ethical stage by becoming dissatisfied with the sense of self associated with gratification of impulses and conformity. They then choose to create a new self. The old self equated with hedonism is consciously rejected. The newly created self chooses to be ruled by a societal code of ethics. In the religious stage, individuals are neither bound by hedonism nor conventional ethics. Instead, the self is driven by faith in and love of God. Individuals who choose to make the transition from the ethical to the religious do so in fear and trembling. Once the transition is accomplished, their daily behaviors are motivated by their faith in God.

Kierkegaard also emphasized autonomy and authenticity. He believed that individuals create a self through the choices they make in the course of their existence, but the ability to make choices is a double-edged phenomenon. Having the ability to choose creates freedom; however, the ability to choose also leads to anxiety and dread. Such experiences are necessary components of becoming an authentic and personally responsible individual.

The influence of Kierkegaard's modes of being can be seen in Dąbrowski's levels, which describe development as a progression from an initial primitive integrated mode of experiencing, followed by three forms of disintegration, and culminating in a re-integrated mode of experiencing that includes the attainment of personality. The five levels of development represent a movement from an egocentric to an altruistic mode—from behavior being motivated by basic drives and conformity to being motivated by values and autonomy.

Level I: Primary Integration

Primary integration is a cohesive mental organization dedicated to gratifying an individual's biological instincts, drives, and needs, including social needs. Attributes of the individual, such as intelligence, focus on self-interest and self-gratification. Behavioral responses are generally automatic, and there is little, or simply transient, self-consciousness. Little inner conflict is associated with this level of development; instead, conflict typically focuses on the external world and reflects a frustration of drives or needs or a lack of social approval. Primary integrated individuals experience crises and challenges associated with the life cycle, but they are not transformed by them.

Dąbrowski noted that some individuals at this level are under the influence of the second factor of development, the social environment. In other words, some individuals characterized by primary integration are overly socialized; their way of being in the world is highly socially conforming. Such individuals may be, for example, primarily driven by a high need for approval from others. They may be "the salt of the earth" and successful materially.

In contrast, there is a second subgroup under the influence of the first factor of development (biology) that is sociopathic. Such individuals are motivated primarily by gratification of their needs and use others for that end. This subgroup includes those engaged in criminal activity. Though both of these subgroups represent a rigidly integrated mental organization, Dąbrowski depicted primary integration as existing in varying degrees in individuals. One characteristic of primary integration is clear in TPD: it is antithetical to mental health:

> *The state of primary integration is a state contrary to mental health. A fairly high degree of primary integration is present in the average person; a very high degree of primary integration is present in the psychopath. The more cohesive the structure of primary integration is, the less the possibility of development; the greater the strength of automatic functioning, stereotypy, and habitual activity, the lower the level of mental health.* (Dąbrowski, 1964a, p. 121)

Level I for Dąbrowski did not represent psychological development. Development requires disintegration of the mental organization of primary integration.

Level II: Unilevel Disintegration

This level represents the first instance of disintegration, hence the first indication that development is occurring. The disintegration process is triggered by the onset of conflict, which is caused by developmental milestones such as puberty and menopause, and crises such as failures in school, work, or relationships. Experiencing such events creates intense negative emotions such as frustration, anxiety, and despair. Such intense emotions lead to uncertainty. The dynamisms of ambivalence and ambitendencies arise, and mental integration is loosened. Manifestations of Level II include identity confusion and moodiness.

Level II is a transition phase from integration to disintegration and is not sustainable: "Prolongation of unilevel disintegration often leads to reintegration on a lower level, to suicidal tendencies, or to psychosis" (Dąbrowski, 1964a, p. 7). In the absence of mental structures to deal with the conflict, the individual either regresses to the primary integrated state, experiences further disintegration, or suffers some very drastic consequences.

Individuals have no readily available means of dealing effectively with the intense emotions associated with the novel experience of conflict. Some individuals cope with these experiences by turning to self-medication using alcohol, drugs, or in extreme cases, suicide. Other individuals become motivated to find more effective solutions to the distress caused by events that are not under their control. Such motivation places them on the path of further disintegration and the possibility for advanced development. The outcomes of Level II—regression to a lower level or further disintegration—depend on the interplay of the three factors of development: constitutional endowment, quality of the social environment, and the third factor.

Crises cannot be addressed by drawing upon what individuals have learned in the socialization process. As individuals try to deal with their conflicts by drawing upon previous learning, they come to realize that nothing appears applicable or helpful. Social norms and values that they were exposed to are questioned and ultimately rejected. Behaviors automatically motivated by one's biological drives and needs are also scrutinised and questioned. Consequently, the experience of distress increases. Dąbrowski postulated that when crises have the effect of loosening the integrated mental organization of individuals, they have limited choices. Individuals either return to previous integrated state, or they move to the next level. Remaining in Level II may lead to dire consequences such as psychoses or suicide.

Level III: Spontaneous Multilevel Disintegration

Dąbrowski noted that the transition from a unilevel to a multilevel phase of development is both crucial for advanced development and unexpected as an event in human development (1996a). In other words, movement from Level II to Level III is not a smooth transition; rather, it is a quantum leap with a multilevel experiencing of reality that cannot be predicted from a unilevel mode. To illustrate this point, Dąbrowski posed the question: "[H]ow is a butterfly logically implied in the larva?" (1996a, p. 26). His response: The potential for the butterfly already exists in the larva. Analogously, the potential for multilevelness must be present in the individual's constitutional endowment—i.e., developmental potential—and specifically in the presence of a high level of overexcitability and the existence of the third factor.

The loosening of primary integration begun in Level II is transformed into a spontaneous and involuntary examination of beliefs, attitudes, and emotions, followed by a repudiation of those deemed lower in value by the individual. Various forms of negative emotions and self-critical attitudes, exemplified in the dissolving dynamisms (e.g., feelings of shame, dissatisfaction with self) begin the process of creating an inner psychic milieu, increasing an individual's awareness of self. These dynamisms represent intense negative emotions, which serve the processes of disintegration and promote an increasing awareness of self-as-object. Inner conflict arises from the individual's growing awareness that the way personal and social phenomena ought to be is discrepant with the way they are. This ideal-real discrepancy intensifies as the individual becomes increasingly self-aware and aware of societal values.

The emergence of multilevelness results in a revolution in how individuals perceive themselves and the world. Individuals are no longer content with meeting biological needs and automatically adhering to societal norms. Self-critical attitudes follow when individuals perceive themselves, for example, succumbing to gratification and self-interest in their relations with others. They have begun the process of transcending their biological bases and conformity, and they develop autonomy and authenticity in their dealings with themselves and others. In essence, they have begun creating a hierarchy of values and using it to gauge their mental states, behaviors, and approaches to other people.

Level IV: Organized Multilevel Disintegration

The main feature of this level is the individual's conscious control of the course of development; individuals become self-organizing. Whereas Level III is dominated by disintegrating dynamisms, Level IV sees the rise of developmental dynamisms such as autonomy, authenticity, self-education and autopsychotherapy, and the third factor. Under the direction of the third factor, individuals deliberately select higher values and courses of action, abandoning lower ones. In addition, individuals develop a strong sense of responsibility for self and others. A sense of social justice and empathic connection with others characterize individuals' interactions with others.

Level IV is the beginning of secondary integration as the individual becomes a self-educating and self-correcting person. He or she becomes aware of areas where learning is needed and seeks that information. When crises occur, he or she can help him- or herself, literally becoming his or her own therapist. The hierarchy of values is clearly entrenched and guides daily behavior.

Level V: Secondary Integration

At the apex of human development, personality is achieved. Individuals experience harmony and are at peace with themselves. They conduct their lives by enacting the personality ideal, whereby behavior is directed by their constructed hierarchy of values. Virtually no inner conflict is experienced, since the lower forms of motivations have been destroyed and replaced by the higher forms of empathy, autonomy, and authenticity.

Emotions, Development, and Personality

Dąbrowski would undoubtedly agree with Izard and Ackerman's truism that emotions drive the process of development that culminates in the achievement of personality. However, Dąbrowski would disagree with their contention that the process by which this occurs is not obvious (Izard & Ackerman, 2000). Emotions influence and direct personality development by their disintegrating and reintegrating power—by directing the process of positive disintegration. The disintegrating power of emotions is seen in general by the central role in TPD played by conflict, with its frustration, anxiety, and other intense emotions. Specific directing power of emotions can be seen in the disintegrating dynamisms, which are intense emotional reactions. The reintegrating power is seen in the creation of a hierarchy of values that lead individuals to behaviors resulting in the experience of higher emotions. Positive disintegration, the process responsible for personality achievement, is anchored to emotions.

Conclusion

For Dąbrowski, personality is constructed through the process of positive disintegration. Emotions are forces that direct the process. The theory of positive disintegration not only places emotions in a central role in personality development, TPD specifies how emotions accomplish this. When Mowrer used the word "extraordinary" with reference to TPD, he was commenting on the uniqueness of Dąbrowski's conception of personality. As things have evolved relative to the place of emotions in psychology, Mowrer's comment can be used in another way; it is extraordinary that a theory with origins in the 1930s could reflect thinking about personality development in the 2000s. For those who agree that emotions influence personality development, TPD is a personality theory for the 21st century.

Chapter 2
Conception of Development: Positive Disintegration

This chapter, an article on positive disintegration, was written in response to an invitation from Professor Franz Monks, who edited a special journal issue on Dąbrowski, which included articles by Michael Piechowski and Frank Falk. I found it challenging to focus on positive disintegration because the ideas of the theory of positive disintegration are so interrelated that it is difficult to discuss them as discrete concepts.

As the title chosen by Dąbrowski for his theory, positive disintegration is the first of several oxymorons with which students of Dąbrowski's theory need to contend. With increasing knowledge of it as the process of development, the discrepancy vanishes. For convenience, I say that positive disintegration is the ***process*** of development, without it Dąbrowskian development cannot occur. For the sake of accuracy, I should say: positive disintegration ***is*** development. The general nature of development in the theory of positive disintegration is a necessary context to discuss positive disintegration.

Reference

Mendaglio, S. (2010). Positive disintegration: The process of development in Dąbrowski's theory. Published in German Journal: Positive Desintegration: Der Prozess der Entwicklung in Dąbrowskis Theorie, *journal für begabtenförderung*)

Positive Disintegration: The Process of Development in Dąbrowski's Theory

Dąbrowski's theory of positive disintegration (TPD) is of the same scope as the grand theories of personality such as Freud's (1970/1924) psychoanalysis, Jung's (1933) psychological types and Rogers' (1959) self-theory. Similar to these better-known theories, Dąbrowski's theory (1964) is an ambitious attempt to explain the variety of human experience, with particular emphasis on identifying the mechanisms responsible for development (Mendaglio, 2008). Interestingly, however, Dąbrowski proposed an idiosyncratic view of development. In TPD, development is described as the progression from a lower to a higher level of human functioning, where lower and higher are defined in terms of not only complexity but also intentionality and morality. Lower level is associated with a robotic-egocentric approach to life, in Dąbrowskian terms, lower level is synonymous with the absence of f development. Low level is manifested by a way of life that lacks reflection and that is motivated by satisfaction of biological drives. Higher level development is associated with an autonomous-altruistic approach to living. High level is manifested by a way of life that is permeated with reflection and motivated by a system of values. Dąbrowski asserted that different types of mental organization underlie these different levels of human development. A rigid mental organization is associated with low developmental level and a more flexible, complex organization of mental structures is associated with higher developmental level. The process by which a lower level of human functioning is transformed into a higher level—the process of development—is termed *positive disintegration* (Dąbrowski, 1964, 1967, 1972).

Human Development: From Primary to Secondary Integration

To appreciate the paramount importance Dąbrowski placed on positive disintegration, it is essential to fully understand his view of development. As noted previously, Dąbrowski viewed development as a progression from a low level to a high level of human functioning, where low and high levels refer to both cognition and morality. Regarding cognition, like other theories, TPD proposes a movement from simple to increasingly complex cognitive structures and mental organization. However, while other theories of development are value-free, Dąbrowski's theory is value-laden. Piaget's theory, for example, discusses how cognitive development progresses from an egocentric sensorimotor stage to a decentred formal operation stage. Piagetian theory, though, focuses on what Flavell (1963) called the cold-blooded aspects of cognitive development, with no direct association with an individual's values. Regarding morality, Dąbrowski's theory is like Kohlberg's (1970) theory in describing a hierarchy of moral reasoning capacity but differs from Kohlberg's conception of moral development since Dąbrowski's focus is not merely moral reasoning but also intentional moral behaviours.

Dąbrowski asserted that low and high functioning modes of being in the world are inseparable from mental organization. Low functioning mode is the manifestation of what Dąbrowski called primary or primitive mental integration. In the low functioning mode, individuals are motivated by the satisfaction of drives and needs. Individuals who do so in a socially appropriate way (i.e., individuals who have been socialized), Dąbrowski termed "normal" (Dąbrowski, 1970, p. 21). Most of the thinking done by normal individuals serves two purposes: it directs the satisfaction of drives in a socially acceptable manner and it directs compliance with societal norms. Such thinking manifests little self-awareness or questioning of prevailing social norms. In contrast to normals, Dąbrowski identified a second group of individuals who are characterized by low functioning; namely, psychopaths. Psychopaths use their mental resources to satisfy drives and needs with an important difference from normal individuals: psychopaths do not concern themselves with social norms and values. Drives and needs are met by whatever means are predicted to be successful by these individuals. In primary mental integration, whether normal or psychopathic, Dąbrowski contended that mental organization is simple and inflexible. In my view, primary mental integration may be described as including "black or white" thinking, little or no awareness of self and others, and a lack of persistent reflection. It is egocentric-automatic processing which, in normal people, motivates both selfishness and mindless conformity to social norms. In the case of the psychopath, however, this way of thinking motivates selfishness with a complete disregard for rules and the feelings of others. In TPD, low functioning mode or primary mental integration represents an absence of development.

High functioning mode is the manifestation of what Dąbrowski called secondary or positive mental integration. In the high functioning mode, individuals are motivated by universal values that distinguish right and wrong actions. Individuals at this level have transcended the tyranny of both biology and environment. Drive and need satisfaction do not control these individuals; nor are they controlled by social conventions. Drives become sublimated; sex drive, for example, becomes love. Selfishness is transformed into altruism. Automatic behaviour and mindless conformity are replaced by self-awareness and critical analysis of prevailing societal values. A hallmark of a high level of functioning is the individual's creation of a system of values which serves to direct daily behaviours, according to Dąbrowski. The complex mental organization that is secondary mental integration is characterized by an individual's awareness of self and the world around him or her, as well as by autonomy, authenticity, and altruism. Thinking at this level is concerned with matters such as continuous learning, being one's own psychotherapist, and taking responsibility for self and others. In brief, secondary mental integration means to be truly human, the pinnacle of development (Dąbrowski, 1967).

As in the realm of cognition, there are obvious differences between primary and secondary integrations in the moral arena. However, there is one factor that they share, albeit for contrasting reasons: a lack of inner conflict. In primary integration, an individual experiences external conflict but little or no conflict within the self, due largely to the lack of consciousness or awareness. In secondary integration, an individual is not in conflict within the self but rather is at peace with the self. Secondary integration is achieved through the resolution of inner conflict; such conflict being essential for development. Inner conflict is the awareness of discrepancy between the ideal and the real, both externally and internally. Dąbrowski expressed the realization as being cognizant of how the world *ought to be* and the way it *is* (Dąbrowski, 1972). Awareness of this discrepancy between lower and higher with respect to external reality results in the experience of intense negative emotions. This process extends inward to the self. Through self-awareness and self-analysis, an individual realizes that a discrepancy between lower and higher exists within the self. Realizing that one is not living consistently with one's system of values (the way that life ought to be lived or at a higher level of functioning) results in, among other things, a growing dissatisfaction with self, with accompanying intense negative emotions. These intense emotions, associated with inner conflict, serve to initiate the disintegration process. The cognitive process of awareness of self and others serves as a foundation for the experience of inner conflict necessary for the destruction of primitive mental organization. Dąbrowski (1964) was emphatic that human development is only possible through the disintegration of the low functioning mode or primary mental integration.

Positive Disintegration

Disintegration "involves loosening, dissociation, and even breakdown of the structure and organization of psychic functions" (Dąbrowski, 1970, p. 20). The breakdown of one's mental structure and organization creates disruption and pain. Integral to TPD was Dąbrowski's view is that the outcome of such loosening may be negative or positive. As a response to external or internal events, individuals begin to lose their cognitive foundation, that is, the patterned ways of thinking about the world and the self. Existing thinking patterns afford something important to an individual: the ability to predict reactions to self and others. Disintegration of typical thought processes creates ambiguity, which in turn creates anxiety. Confusion may be among the first negative emotional reactions, any of which may eventually lead to existential depression. The outcome of this dissolution of cognitive organization may be negative, which in Dąbrowskian terms is exemplified by suicide or by psychoses such as schizophrenia. When the outcome of disintegration of primary mental integration is positive, however, an individual is on the path of growth and development. Negative disintegration and positive disintegration thus have one important feature in common: both involve the breakdown of an integrated cognitive organization. They differ significantly, however, in terms of outcomes. The essential difference is that positive disintegration includes a re-integration at a higher level of mental functioning while negative disintegration does not. Positive disintegration, therefore, is a twofold process of a disruption of mental organization and a reintegration at a higher level of mental functioning. It is important to note that, in this process, existing cognitive structures are destroyed, not amended or shaped, but replaced by new structures. Positive disintegration literally changes the quality of an individual's thinking about phenomena such that the individual moves from simple, tightly organized cognitive structures to complex, less organized (i.e., more flexible) cognitive structures and from unconscious to conscious response to self, others and events.

Positive disintegration may be partial or global. In partial positive disintegration only part of the cognitive organization is involved whereas global positive disintegration affects the entire mental system. Partial positive disintegration occurs often in daily life (Dąbrowski, 1970); it is evident, for example, when an individual's behaviors are not driven by a simple stimulus-response process. If the individual is hurt by another person and responds aggressively, then that individual is responding unthinkingly to a stimulus. On the other hand, one may become aware of feelings of aggression and shocked at the intensity of one's response to the other person's action. This awareness is disturbing because it may never have occurred to the individual that he or she could have such a strong desire to retaliate. The aggression felt is alien to one's conception of self because the individual has thought of himself or herself as peaceful and accepting. As a result, the individual feels disappointment with self and feels ashamed (disintegration). Such feelings motivate the individual to attempt to understand the entire incident, including the other person. The individual's analysis of the incident leads to a greater understanding of both self and the other person (reintegration).

"Global disintegration occurs in major life experiences which are shocking; it disturbs the entire psychic structure of an individual and changes the personality" (Dąbrowski, 1964, p. 10). Very intense life experiences are usual triggers for global disintegration. Experiences such as the death of a loved one may serve to shake an individual at the very foundation of the self. The grieving process is experienced so intensely that, added to the feelings of devastation at the loss of the loved one, an individual may experience existential depression and angst in confronting death directly. Existing cognitions including goals, values, self-concept and meaning attributed to life are challenged and destroyed, putting an individual at risk for psychosis. As one plunges into the depths of despair, at some point there is an acute awareness of the full reality of the dangers lurking should this state continue. The individual then begins the arduous process of acceptance of the new reality and begins to examine his or her world view, which is no longer useful in guiding daily life. The individual begins to develop a new way of thinking about everything—a new mental organization—forged by the intense heat of emotional reactions to a paramount life event.

Initially the process of positive disintegration is triggered by events that are not under an individual's control. As in the examples provided above, the process may be sparked by environmental events. Positive disintegration may also be triggered by milestones in physical development such as puberty or menopause (Dąbrowski, 1972) and so such phenomena may serve to begin the developmental process. To achieve the highest level of human functioning—to become truly human—the process of development must come under one's conscious control.

Dąbrowski's five levels of human development depict how positive disintegration becomes increasingly under developing the individual's aegis. Though detailed discussion of the levels of development is beyond the scope of this article, simply listing the levels will illustrate the point: primary integration, unilevel disintegration, spontaneous disintegration, organized multilevel disintegration and secondary integration. The highest form of disintegration is found in level four, organized multilevel disintegration. At this level, individuals take control of their development through the construction of a hierarchy of values, implementing it in daily living, and by dealing with personal difficulties through educating oneself and engaging in autopsychotherapy. We recognize, here, the high functioning mode described earlier in this article. The beginnings of self-directed growth in level four are fully actualized in level five, secondary or positive integration.

Conclusion

Positive disintegration *is* development in the theory of positive disintegration. To fully appreciate this notion, first and foremost we need to appreciate Dąbrowski's use of terminology. Dąbrowski, himself, identified this challenge facing readers regarding the term *positive disintegration* when he noted that it sounds paradoxical. I am hopeful that the reader has found that the paradox is more apparent than real once the term is seen as encompassing a dual process of disintegration and reintegration. I think that there is another challenge posed by TPD that may linger, particularly for psychologists, whose professional predilection is to predict and influence human adjustment. In the full explication of his theory, Dąbrowski outlined the necessary conditions for the process of positive disintegration. However, as Dąbrowski confessed, we cannot predict the outcome of disintegration. Whether disintegration is positive or negative is only known by its result.

References

Dąbrowski, K. (1964). *Positive disintegration.* Boston: Little Brown & Co.

Dąbrowski, K. (1967). *Personality-shaping through positive disintegration.* Boston: Little Brown & Co.

Dąbrowski, K. (1972). *Psychoneurosis is not an illness.* London: Gryf Publications.

Dąbrowski, K. with Kawczak, A., & Piechowski, M.M. (1970). *Mental growth through positive disintegration.* London: Gryf Publications.

Flavell, J. (1963). The developmental psychology of Jean Piaget. New York: VanNostrand.

Freud, S. (1970/1924). *A general introduction to psychoanalysis.* New York: Pocket Books.

Jung, C.G. (1933). *Psychological types.* New York: Harcourt, Brace, & World.

Kohlberg, L. (1970). Moral stages and moralization: The cognitive-developmental approach to socialization. In T. Kickona (Ed.), *Moral development and behaviour: Theory, research, and social issues* (pp. 31-43). New York: Holt, Rinehart & Winston.

Mendaglio, S. (2008). Dąbrowski's theory of positive disintegration: A personality theory for the 21st century. In S. Mendaglio (Ed), Dąbrowski's *theory of positive disintegration*, pp. 13-40. Scottsdale, AZ: Great Potential Press.

Rogers, C.R. (1959). A theory of therapy, personality, and interpersonal relationships. In S. Koch (Ed.), *Psychology: A study of a science* Vol. 3, pp. 184-256. New York: McGraw-Hill.

Chapter 3
Dynamisms

This chapter, an article on dynamisms, is based on my keynote address to the 12th International Dąbrowski Congress in 2016. The title is a combination of Dąbrowski's chapter heading on dynamisms, "Dynamisms: The Shapers of Development" (Dąbrowski, 1991) with my addition of "and psychological constructs". Dynamisms are not only central to understanding development in the theory, but they also lead to questioning of some psychological constructs. In a field in which the theory of positive disintegration is often reduced to overexcitability, it is necessary to draw attention to the other of its components. No other component has been as neglected as dynamisms, which are, ironically, the sine qua non of Dąbrowskian development. In the article, I address both types of dynamisms: disintegrating and developmental, relating them to developmental levels. Adding the dimension of psychological constructs is important because certain common mainstream constructs are incompatible with the notion of dynamisms, particularly with the disintegrating type. Like the terms development and personality, viewing dynamisms through a Dąbrowskian lens requires the reframing of constructs such as self-esteem. I conclude the article with some ideas aimed at refining the theory of positive disintegration.

Reference

Mendaglio, S. (2017). Dąbrowski's dynamisms: Shapers of development and psychological constructs, *Advanced Development, 16*, 1-17.

Dąbrowski's Dynamisms: Shapers of Development and Psychological Constructs1

Along with many individuals who are interested in Dąbrowski's theory of positive disintegration (TPD), I came to it because of my interest in giftedness. My particular interest was, and continues to be, counseling gifted individuals. Serendipity, rather than an outgrowth of my graduate education, led me to my long-standing interest in gifted individuals, and ultimately in TPD. The series of events that led me to TPD began with my initial university teaching duties. I was assigned to teach a graduate level practicum in counseling psychology. Not wanting to simply teach and supervise students "by the book," I initiated an independent counseling practice. My small practice provided fodder for my teaching, while maintaining my skills. In time, I was approached by an educator who was implementing a new program for gifted students in a local school. She asked me whether I would be willing to counsel gifted students, stating that there were no psychologists to whom she could refer students who needed help. Professionally, my education was in counseling and clinical psychology, which contained no preparation in counseling clients who are gifted. Though I made it clear that I had no background knowledge in the area, she encouraged me to accept some referrals. My initial experience was counseling gifted children, whose cognitive characteristics amazed me. Gifted children astonished me; gifted adults challenged me. Feeling professionally inadequate, I turned to the literature, placing me on a path that led me to TPD.

My Journey with TPD: From Rejection to Appreciation

My introduction to the theory differed dramatically from what others recounted of their first encounter with it. For example, Bill Tillier stated that his introduction was life altering (Tillier, 2008). In stark contrast, I reacted negatively to my first encounter with TPD.

I use *reacted* because it was an emotional response, leading to my initial rejection of TPD. Frankly, TPD lexicon was off putting. Terms such as overexcitability, multilevelness, and the juxtaposition of words such as positive and disintegration created a dislike of the theory. Another component was its levels of development which were conceptualized in a manner significantly different from any theory with which I was familiar. Not only were there no ages associated with levels but progression through them was not universal nor linear. My initial reaction was not a harbinger of a later response to TPD.

In hindsight, it seems that I was destined to become a student of TPD for three reasons. While a graduate student I became increasingly aware of a discrepancy between education and behavior. It will likely be interpreted as naivete but I grew up with the impression that educated people, who, to me, were *de facto* highly intelligent, would also be good persons. I was puzzled as I observed individuals around me who were mean spirited in their approach to people. The awareness extended to events in the wider world, as reported in the media. It became clear to me that my association of high intelligence and moral behavior was wrong. As I delved into Dąbrowski's books, I was stunned to learn that he disconnected intelligence from behavior: an individual can be highly intelligent and immoral.

In my counseling, I placed central importance on emotions. Well before, I knew of TPD, I came to believe in the primacy of emotions in human functioning. My rallying cry to my clients was: "It's all about emotions!" It became clear early in my counseling experience that intense negative emotions caused individuals to seek counseling. Regardless of presenting problems, motivation to seek counseling arose from being overwhelmed by negative emotions. Rather than using techniques to help clients deal with their emotions (e.g., relaxation training, cognitive restructuring), my approach was to help them accept rather than cope with emotional experiences. Of course, I learned later that Dąbrowski gave emotions a preeminent position in his theory, while decrying the absence of psychology's neglect of emotions and emotional development.

In the course of counseling an increasing number of gifted individuals, I began to develop my conception of giftedness to guide my counseling practice. At the time, there were virtually no resources available for psychologists working with gifted clients. There was a dearth of books useful in directing a counseling process. In recent years, this has changed significantly with publications such as Silverman (1993), Mendaglio and Peterson (2007), and Pfeiffer (2013). There was, however, a wealth of literature on affective characteristics, which, I thought, would contribute to my understanding of gifted individuals' emotions. My enthusiasm was short lived. *Affective* was not used as a synonym for *emotional*; affective referred essentially to non-cognitive characteristics, which included, for example, leadership ability and keen sense of humor. Two affective characteristics, however, were closely aligned with emotion: intensity and heightened sensitivity. Both characteristics were evident in clients that I counseled. As I began to articulate my thinking about them (Mendaglio, 1995), I was unaware that they were central components of a fundamental TPD concept: overexcitability.

Aspects of my personal and professional experience predisposed me to appreciate Dąbrowski's theory; my desire to become an effective counselor of gifted individuals led me to encounter it. Literature searches using *counseling* and *gifted* yielded the works of Michael Piechowski, Linda Silverman, Nancy Miller, Frank Falk, and others. It was difficult to avoid encountering citations to TPD when searching for information on counseling gifted individuals. This signaled to me that I needed to investigate it thoroughly. A significant milestone in my journey with TPD was the availability of Dąbrowski's English language books, provided by Bill Tillier with the permission of the Dąbrowski family. Reading and re-reading those books completed the transition from rejection to my deep appreciation of the theory.

Appeal of Overexcitability over Dynamisms

Review of research and websites concerned with TPD reveals that there is a virtual exclusive focus on overexcitability (OE). While the Overexcitability Questionnaire (Lysy & Piechowski, 1983) sparked research on OE, the development of the Overexcitability Questionnaire-Two (OEQ-II, Falk, Miller, Piechowski, & Silverman, 2016) significantly increased research on OE. In contrast to the original questionnaire, the OEQ-II is composed of Likert scales to assess the five forms of OE. The fact that research on TPD is focused on OE makes sense-it is the one component of TPD that is operationalized in a manner providing ease of administration and scoring for researchers. Numerous websites dedicated to gifted children and adolescents, often aimed at parents, are replete with discussions of OE. A cursory look at the five forms of OE may offer an explanation for the allure of OE for authors and the parents of gifted children. Psychomotor, sensual, intellectual, imaginational, and emotional are words that individuals can immediately relate to, even though their definitions differ from their common meanings. Further, they have a largely positive tone to them. The descriptions serve to encapsulate what parents see in their gifted children: a bundle of energy, intellectual prowess, constant questioning, daydreaming, and intense emotionality. The popularity of OE among researchers and parents is understandable.

In contrast to the ubiquity of OE, rarity describes discussions of dynamisms. Dynamisms are rarely mentioned in TPD information aimed at parents. Researchers may simply include them in introductions to their studies, but do not investigate them empirically. A reason for the absence of dynamisms in material aimed at parents may lie in the negative valence of some dynamisms. In contrast to the largely positive associations with overexcitability, dynamisms such as dissatisfaction with oneself and feelings of guilt are clearly negative. Parents may be willing to attribute terms that are largely positive to gifted youth, but are reluctant to associate negative terms with them. In the case of researchers, the reason for avoiding dynamisms is different: there is no OEQ-II equivalent for assessing dynamisms. With the negative quality of some dynamisms and lack of operational definitions, dynamisms remain a mysterious construct in TPD.

A Word on Construct

Construct and *concept* are often considered synonyms; in my usage of them, they are different. Unlike concepts, constructs have no referents in the world. Psychological terms, for example, self-esteem, personality, and emotion are constructs. We do not directly observe, for example, self-esteem. On the other hand, table, chair, tree, television, and museum have referents in the world. We can point to a tree or a table. Though there are various instances of a concept, say of a table, we generally recognize them as table. In other words, concepts have consensual validation—there is agreement on what constitutes a concept—constructs do not. There are implications for definition and interpretation of terms that flow from the nature of constructs. That constructs have multiple definitions is confirmed by exploring the definitions of psychological terms: intelligence and emotion, for example, have numerous definitions. Dąbrowski's lexicon adds to the multiplicity of definitions of such terms as personality. Since there are no referents in the world that we can attach to a construct, we cannot dispassionately validate a particular definition of a construct. Only authors of constructs can "validate" their meaning. Dąbrowski, like other theorists such as Freud and H. S. Sullivan, created a system of constructs that made sense to him. Lacking the opportunity to verify our understanding of the meaning of his constructs with Dąbrowski, we are left to interpreting their meaning by studying Dąbrowski's written words available to us. In what follows, I offer my interpretation of the dynamism construct.

Dąbrowski's Dynamisms

Dąbrowski defined dynamism as: "Biological or mental force controlling behavior and its development. Instincts, drives, and intellectual processes combined with emotions are dynamisms" (Dąbrowski, 1972, p. 294). Dynamisms are "intrapsychic factors which shape development" (Dąbrowski, 1996, p. 30). In TPD, positive disintegration represents development (Dąbrowski, 1964). The paramount importance of dynamisms in development is exemplified by Piechowski who stated: "The dynamisms are often referred to as 'forces' which carry out the process of positive disintegration, as if somehow they were apart from it. Actually they are the disintegration" (Piechowski, 1975, p. 277; emphasis in original).

There are two categories of dynamisms: disintegrating and developmental. Disintegrating dynamisms, as the term implies, serve to destroy the lower forms of function; developmental dynamisms create a high level of functioning. The two categories of dynamisms "operationalize" the process of positive disintegration, responsible for achieving advanced development. Positive disintegration is, in effect, a dual process of disintegration, in which lower mental structures reflective of drive satiation and approval seeking are destroyed, and reintegration, in which new mental structures create freedom from biological and societal influences and create behaviors motivated by positive values.

Dynamisms are inextricably bound to levels of development. Since dynamisms are equated with development, there are no dynamisms in Level I, Primary Integration; they are associated with—define—Levels II through V. Disintegrating dynamisms define Levels II and III. Developmental dynamisms define Level N and Level V. I based the following discussion on various descriptions found in the English language books and largely on Dąbrowski (1996).

Level II: Unilevel Disintegration

Dąbrowski proposed only two dynamisms unique to Level II: ambivalences and ambitendencies. These dynamisms begin to loosen the rigid mental structures of Level I, Primary Integration. At this Level, daily living is automatized, guided by habits formed to cope with forces of biology and social norms. Individuals tend to conform to expectations of society regarding satisfaction of basic needs and goal-oriented behaviors. Individuals may question the dictates of society and oneself but these are temporary with a return to the *status quo*. Selfish egocentrism is a prime motivator, leading to the experience of external conflict. Dynamisms of Level II are triggered by age-related milestones, such as puberty, mid-life crisis, menopause, and environmental events, such as academic failure, unemployment, and the death of a loved one.

Ambivalences and ambitendencies serve to create a novel, unpleasant experience for individuals: rudimentary inner conflict. Implicit certainty about their experience of the world, others, and self, is replaced by fluctuation of feelings and behavior. Incompatible feelings of likes and dislike, approach and avoidance conflicts, and contradictory attitudes toward self of inferiority and superiority are expressions of ambivalences. Incompatible desires related to goals and possessions, conflicting courses of actions, and moodiness are manifestations of ambitendencies. It is important to bear in mind that Dąbrowski's ambivalences and ambitendencies are thoughts, feelings, and behaviors which are different from individuals' habitual thought-feeling processes and behaviors. We must avoid reifying dynamisms of any level.

The dynamisms of Level II disrupt the homeostasis of mental organization—created to meet one's biological needs and to avoid social disapproval. The disruption in the balance of mental organization is temporary. From this novel experience of inner conflict, some individuals return to Level I; others may move to the next level. Ambivalences and ambitendencies lead to strange, unpleasant experiences. Becoming aware of dynamic thoughts and feelings and one's behavior is anxiety provoking for individuals. It seems to me that the anxiety stems from a movement from certainty to ambiguity. The dynamisms attack the certainty of the unexamined life and the uncertainty is rather threatening. Dąbrowski noted that an extended period of unilevel disintegration "often leads to reintegration at a lower level to suicidal tendencies, or to psychosis" (Dąbrowski, 1964, p. 7). Individuals will return to Primary Integration, or have devastating experiences, unless other dynamisms emerge, the dynamisms of Level III.

Level III: Spontaneous Multilevel Disintegration

Dąbrowski proposed several dynamisms that replace ambivalences and ambitendencies. While the former initiate the loosening of Primary Integration mental organization: Level III dynamisms destroy it. Destruction of mental structures or schemas—habitual ways of thinking, feeling, and behaving—is accomplished at a heavy psychological cost: intense anxiety and depression.

Hierarchization, the "least specific and the least differentiated multilevel dynamism" (Dąbrowski, 1996, p. 35), because of its general influence on TPD processes, signals the shift from unilevel to multilevel disintegration. Absent in Level II, hierarchization represents individuals' gradually categorizing external and internal phenomena as lower or higher in value, ultimately creating inner conflict. Though Dąbrowski presented it as a discrete dynamism, its experience pervades the other dynamisms. It is also termed multilevel conflict, describing it as the turmoil increasingly experienced by individuals as they become aware of the discrepancy between what is and what ought to be, generally, and specifically, between lower self and higher self. Such discrepancies may be seen in the various dynamisms associated with the self.

With the exception of astonishment with oneself, discrepancy between lower and higher self permeates the dynamisms of dissatisfaction with oneself, disquietude with oneself, and inferiority with oneself. Astonishment with oneself is the beginnings of self awareness, a cognitive process by which individuals become aware of their thinking, which at times surprises them. The experience of the other self-referent dynamisms are not only cognitive but also emotional in nature. Disquietude with oneself is the start of a negative view of self, in which awareness of discrepancy is implicit. Awareness of lower and higher self becomes evident in inferiority toward oneself. Different from Adler's inferiority, Dąbrowski's self referent inferiority refers to the negative feelings individuals experience as they perceive the incongruity between how they currently view themselves versus the persons they aspire to be, between their real and ideal self. An essential factor responsible for this type of inferiority is the presence of individuals' standards or values against which they judge themselves. Inferiority toward oneself implies that individuals have begun the creation of a hierarchy of positive values. Dissatisfaction with oneself is a prime cause of inner conflict because of its powerful discontent with one's thoughts and behaviors. Unhappiness and frustration with oneself, ironically, is one of the most significant predictors of advanced development.

Feelings of shame and guilt are dynamisms related to social interactions. Feelings of shame are equated with self-consciousness and embarrassment. Such feelings are typically connected with inferiority, not toward oneself, but rather toward others. Because of its association with the social environment, Dąbrowski noted that this dynamism may be experienced in Level II, but when it has a moral conflict dimension, then it is akin to inferiority toward oneself. Feelings of guilt also have an interpersonal dimension of social interaction as they are experienced in the context of relationship with others. Feeling badly for having mistreated others or not treating them as one should foreshadows one of the Level IV dynamism (discussed later), namely responsibility.

There is a progression inherent in the dynamisms presented, from the beginnings of self-awareness (astonishment with oneself) and general social focus (feelings of shame) to a highly self-critical (dissatisfaction with self) and a relationship focus (feelings of guilt). Inner conflict becomes more intense in the process. In TPD, inner conflict is always between "what is" and "what ought to be" (Dąbrowski, 1970). However, there is a simultaneous positive process occurring: individuals are gradually developing a set of values. With the identification of values comes a form of conflict that differentiates the lower from the higher. Positive maladjustment produces a change in values "through disintegration of externally acquired values" (D1:1browski, 1970, p. 68). In essence, this dynamism represents individuals' maladjustment to socialized values and adjustment to higher values. More generally, individuals reject "what is" and embrace "what ought to be."

The importance of positive maladjustment in TPD lies in its relation to advanced development in organized multilevel disintegration. Dąbrowski noted that positive disintegration is the "dynamism from which emerge the broader and stronger dynamisms of self-awareness and self-control" (Dąbrowski, 1970, p. 67) and a "prerequisite to the development towards authenticity" (Dąbrowski, 1970, p. 163). Self-awareness, self-control, and authenticity are dynamisms of Level IV. Furthermore, positive maladjustment "acts through loosening or breakdown of lower levels of psychic homeostasis to allow for its reorganization at a higher level" (1970, p. 68). Positive maladjustment, thus, propels individuals into advanced development of Level N.

Summary and Conclusions

Dynamisms of Level II disrupt the mental organization of plimaiy integration. In the process of positive disintegration, these unilevel dynamisms are replaced by multilevel dynamisms of Level III. As noted earlier, Dąbrowski defined dynamisms as instincts, drives, and intellectual processes combined with emotions. The emergence of multilevel dynamisms may begin with those, in which cognitive processes predominate, that is, with astonishment with oneself and hierarchization. Sustained awareness of one's thoughts coupled with behavioral observations trigger experiences of discrepancies between the real and ideal self. Such mental processing creates intense self-criticism with accompanying emotions of disappointment and frustration with oneself. Bouts of depression are not uncommon. Suicide and psychoses—negative disintegration—are possible outcomes, as well as being propelled to higher level of functioning. An indicator of development is the creation of a set of values. Resolution of the inner conflict begins by individuals making a commitment to adopt the way things ought to be—articulation of the values associated with that thought process. One sign of the rise of importance of values is seen in individuals' responses to others, referring to society at large, as well as specific people. Individuals begin to become disturbed by societal norms and people's attitudes and behaviors. Whereas in the inception of Level III, individuals are, at times, amazed at the behavior of others, as a value system develops, individuals criticize and disapprove of others' attitudes and behaviors that are perceived as inconsistent with their values. It is commitment to one's value system that begins the process of reducing inner conflict. Positive maladjustment contributes to the creation of individuals' value systems by a dual process of rejection of societal values and creation of higher values.

The importance of this dynamism cannot be overstated in development.

Level IV Organized Multilevel Disintegration

Level III dynamisms create inner conflict and begin its reduction; Level IV dynamisms resolve it. Dąbrowski proposed several dynamisms at Level IV that replace the dynamisms of the previous Level.

In stark contrast to the disintegrating dynamisms of Level II and III, dynamisms of Level IV are developmental. Dynamisms of this Level represent individuals directing their development.

Subject-object in oneself is described in ways that we commonly associate with self-awareness. However, in TPD, self-awareness is a distinct dynamism. Subject-object in oneself includes the processes of self-observation, introspection, and self-evaluation. It represents a dispassionate look at self, including mental processes, with the aim of self-improvement. Unlike the "self" dynamisms of Level III, subject-object does not produce negative emotions; it is mostly a cognitive process. The dynamism of self-awareness, on the other hand, is reminiscent of the descriptive aspect of self-concept, without the evaluative one which is often termed *self-esteem*. This process of awareness includes continuity of one's identity through the passage of time, individual uniqueness, and differentiation between personal qualities that endure over time and those that are fleeting. Self-awareness, as used in TPD, seems equivalent to self-knowledge.

Third factor represents a process of judging aspects of self and society, determining which are positive and which are negative. This dynamism, as with other Level IV dynamisms, overlaps with other forces. Specifically, the products of subject-object in oneself—the results of a dispassionate assessment of self—are the focus of third factor evaluation. The standards used are the individual's system of value, which the third factor solidifies. Additionally, third factor coordinates the individual's mental environment.

Inner psychic transformation is the application of the decisions made by the third factor. Inner psychic transformation is seen in responses to events that fundamentally change individuals' approaches to life manifested in attitudes, behaviors, and character. Individuals transcend biological phases. Mental and emotional determinants transcend biological ones, for example, continuation of creative productivity despite illness and aging, deepening of emotional experiencing such as love and friendship. Another significant manifestation is the transcending of psychological type, for example, extroversion to introversion, impatience to patience. Unlike temporary states in which individuals manifest type changes (e.g., being patient with others only in specific situations or for a short period of time), inner psychic transformation results in enduring change in individuals.

Self-control refers to a highly conscious process by which individuals create order and unity to their development. As a result, individuals experience increased tranquility and confidence that they are on the right developmental trajectoly.

Autopsychotherapy and education-of-oneself are inter-related forces. Autopsychotherapy is conceived of as a process of education of oneself. Through autopsychotherapy individuals essentially deal with psychological distress by using their own resources. When confronted with crises, individuals use self-therapy to deal with anxieties and tensions associated with them. Moreover, distressful situations are not only dealt with, but also they are transformed into opportunities for enhancing personal development. Education-of-oneself is the dynamism by which individuals identify or produce strategies to direct their personal development. In essence, individuals create or select existing self-help activities that will contribute to their development. Through regular reflection on daily experience and influenced by a hierarchy of values, individuals consciously direct their personal growth.

Dynamisms of Level IV, in contrast to those in Level III, are developmental dynamisms. While Level III dynamisms serve the function of destruction of mental structures, in Level IV, dynamisms are inner forces of development. Disintegrating dynamisms occur spontaneously and act relatively independently; developmental dynamisms occur deliberately and act in an organized, overlapping manner.

Dąbrowski identified several other dynamisms which are located in the borderline of Level IV and V and one at Level V. Empathy, responsibility, authentism, autonomy, and self-perfection, active in Level IV, serve to propel individuals to Level V. The highest level of development, Level V, Secondary Integration, is also called Personality, the pinnacle of human development. Personality is forged by the only dynamism of Level V, the personality ideal. The process by which personality is achieved, Dąbrowski termed *positive disintegration.*

Dynamisms and Positive Disintegration

As noted earlier, positive disintegration is a twofold process of disintegration and reintegration, coinciding with the types of dynamisms. Though its dual components do not proceed in a linear, sequential manner, positive disintegration can be conceptually located in the description of the Levels. In TPD, dynamisms of one level do not emerge from those in the previous Level—developmental dynamisms are not a refinement of the disintegrating type. Level IV, characterized by developmental dynamisms, is a reintegration at a qualitatively different, more autonomous, altruistic level than III.

Both Level III and Level IV are termed multilevel *disintegration*, however, this is inconsistent with the categorization of dynamisms into disintegrating and developmental. Examination of the Level IV dynamisms does not indicate disintegration processes but rather integration. It may be more consistent to refer to Level IV as Organized Integration to contrast it with Level V Secondary Integration.

Dynamisms: Shapers of Personality

The emergence of dynamisms is equated with development, a movement from lower level to a higher level of human functioning. Disintegrating dynamisms destroy the more primitive ways of thinking that are linked to satisfying both instinctive drives and social needs. Emotional pain created by persistent inner conflict leads either to negative or positive disintegration. Negative disintegration in the form of psychoses, clinical depression, or suicide is a potential outcome of individuals' inability to resolve inner conflict produced by the cumulative action of Level III dynamisms. Positive disintegration in the form of individuals' gradual transcendence of the influence of biology and society is produced by the emergence of Level IV dynamisms. Positive disintegration is the process by which personality is achieved. In TPD, a distinction is made between individuality and personality. Individuality is universal; personality is rare. Unlike the term individuality, or its conception in psychology, personality is not a neutral construct. Personality represents the highest form of human functioning. In Dąbrowski's (1967, p. 5) own words:

> *"Personality, in the context of this work, is a name given to an individual fully developed, both with respect to the scope and level of the most essential positive human qualities, an individual in whom all the aspects form a coherent and harmonized whole, and who possesses, in a high degree, the capability for insight into his own self, his own structure, his aspirations and aims (self-consciousness), who is convinced that his attitude is right, that his aims are of essential and lasting value (self-affirmation), and who is conscious that his development is not yet complete and therefore is working internally on his own improvement and education (selfeducation)."*

Developmental dynamisms of Level IV combine to create and shape personality. With the emergence of dynamisms such as the third factor, education-of-oneself, and auto-psychotherapy, individuals direct their development-organized, no longer spontaneous, multi-level disintegration. As noted earlier, I think it more appropriate to use integration, rather than disintegration to refer to Level IV. Personality is the product of directed multi-level integration. Coordinated action of developmental dynamisms enact the sole dynamisms of Level V, Secondary Integration: the personality ideal. Personality is the enactment of personality ideal. Personality represents a congruence among developmental dynamisms, hierarchy of values, and daily behavior. The process of personality shaping—positive disintegration—begins with the actions of the disintegrating dynamisms. Level III dynamisms not only set the stage for personality creation but also lead to our questioning of the accepted conception of some psychological constructs.

Dynamisms: Shapers of Psychological Constructs

Students of TPD understand that Dąbrowski's lexicon is challenging for two reasons. First, he uses terms that are unfamiliar to mainstream psychology, such as multilevelness, overexcitability, and dynamism. Second, Dąbrowski combines terms that are contradictions, such as positive disintegration and positive maladjustment. Third, and for me the most challenging, Dąbrowski uses ordinary psychological terms idiosyncratically, such as development and personality. Inherent in the Dąbrowskian lexicon, in general, is the requirement for us to reconsider our conception of psychological constructs. This requirement is most apparent in Level III dynamisms. This is visible in the constructs of negative emotion, self-concept, personality, and intelligence.

Negative Emotion

With the exception of hierarchization and positive maladjustment the dynamisms unique to Level III represent negative emotional experiences. Inner conflict, the hallmark of this level, is clearly emotional in nature. Mainstream psychology would declare these as symptoms of psychological problems; Dąbrowski proposes that, in the context of his theory, these are signs of development. Such negative emotions, then, need reframing; though the experience is negative, the outcome is positive.

Self-concept

Psychologists, as well as educators and parents, are concerned with self-concept, often used synonymously with selfesteem. Poor self-concept and low self-esteem are constructs used as causes of or responses to adults' and youth's adjustment difficulties. Low self-concept is symptomatic of psychological problems that need intervention. Changes in the quality of self-concept is also a criterion for effectiveness of interventions: increase in self-esteem is interpreted as evidence that interventions are successful.

The activity of dynamisms predicts a rather different scenario with respect to self-concept. Positive self-concept and high self-esteem are incompatible with forces such as dissatisfaction with one's self and the inner conflict that disintegrating dynamisms produce. At first glance, mainstream conceptions of self-concept and self-esteem may apply at Level IV. However, developmental dynamisms are inconsistent with the self-focused aspects of the self constructs. Individuals at Level IV are characterized by a responsible, empathic focus on their fellow human beings. Highly developed individuals do not enact their values to enhance their sense of self; they do so because of the internal need to have their behavior consistent with their values, not for material gain or societal approval.

The matter of social approval is inherent in popular perspectives on self-concept. Most popular among these is the reflected appraisals approach to self-concept development. In essence, the appraisals approach proposes that self-concept is not present at birth but emerges from the internalization of feedback from significant others. From a Dąbrowskian perspective, self-concept is created by the influence of the second factor—the social environment. A cornerstone of advanced development is the decline and ultimate transcendence of society's influence on individuals.

A more theoretically consistent principle is that individuals create their self-concept by dispelling the socially constructed self. A Dąbrowskian self-concept construct replaces self-esteem with self-acceptance.

Personality

There are many different conceptions of personality in psychology, with some similarities. As noted earlier, mainstream personality is universal, assumed, and neutral: everyone has a personality; it has no valence attached to it. In contrast, Dąbrowski proposes that personality is rare, created, and imbued with positive values.

Intelligence

I have found no explicit conception of intelligence in TPD, though similar to mainstream psychologists, Dąbrowski used Wechsler intelligence tests, in practice and research. There are references to the test scores in illustrative case descriptions. Wechsler tests were used in research with gifted youth to categorize gifted and nongifted participants. Where TPD differs from the traditional view of intelligence is in its status as a construct. For Dąbrowski, emotion has the primary role in human functioning, not intelligence. Intelligence is relegated to the status of a tool, not as a dynamism. The role of intelligence is a function of developmental level. At the lower level of development, intelligence is used primarily to satisfy drives; at the higher levels, intelligence is in the service of positive values. TPD, in general, and its dynamisms in particular, reshape some central mainstream constructs.

Dynamisms: Emergent issues

Dąbrowski provided a comprehensive, coherent account of dynamisms and their role in development. Notwithstanding, Dąbrowski hoped that his theory would be scrutinized and refined further. In that vein, I have focused on two issues: the nature of emotions and the rise of dynamisms.

Nature of Emotions

The preeminence of emotion pervades TPD. The dynamisms themselves are either emotions per se or related to emotional development. It is interesting to note that Dąbrowski's emphasis on the importance of emotion predates the recent interest regarding it in psychology. While there were sporadic indications of interest over the years (e.g., Darwin, 1965/1872; Izard, 1977). It was only in the 1990s where we see a dramatic rise in interest on emotion, evident in emotional intelligence and the inauguration of *Emotion*, journal of the American Psychological Association. Meanwhile, Dąbrowski's perspective on the paramount role that emotions plays occurred well before psychology discovered emotion.

Despite the centrality of emotion in TPD, there is no explicit conception of emotion evident in the theory. I have had a longstanding interest in the nature of emotion stemming from my counseling practice. As I noted earlier in this article, it became clear to me that difficulties with emotions is a common theme for individuals seeking counseling, which led me to explore the question: What is emotion? Drawing upon numerous available conceptions, I developed my own view of emotion, influenced by the works of Michael Lewis (Lewis & Michalson, 1983; Lewis, 2000).

Emotions are short term disruptions of mental and physical homeostasis. They are composed of both thoughts and feelings. Though we use *feelings* and *emotions* synonymously, in this context feelings refer to bodily sensations such as increased heart rate. I distinguish between primitive and higher order emotions. Startle response is an example of a primitive emotion: we hear a loud noise and we respond. On the other hand, anxiety and joy are higher order responses. Primitive and higher order emotions are differentiated by the level of cognition involved. With primitive emotions little cognitive processing is involved; significant cognitive processing is involved with higher order emotions. Another distinction between the two categories of emotion is related to innateness versus learned. Common experiences, such as startle response and fear of the dark, seem to be innate. Experiences such as anxiety are learned. Primitive emotions simply require a conscious individual, higher order emotions require appraisals of stimuli or situations. Cognitive appraisal theory of emotions applies here. A fundamental principle of such an approach to emotion is summed up as: Stimulus event—> Interpretation—>Emotion. Emotions are created by individuals' interpretation of a stimulus, which can be a real or mental event.

Level III dynamisms are higher order emotions. Dissatisfaction with oneself, for example, results from individuals' appraising or interpreting self-referent events. Without the interpretation of one's behaviors and attitudes, dissatisfaction with or inferiority toward oneself cannot occur. Cognitive appraisal theory of emotions is compatible with TPD dynamisms.

Rise of dynamisms

Dąbrowski stated that dynamisms emerge from OE:

> *The five forms of overexcitability undergo extensive differentiation in the course of development. One of its products are developmental dynamisms, i.e. the intrapsychic factors which shape and direct development. Emotional and imaginational overexcitability, in cooperation with the intellectual play the most significant role in their formations.* (Dąbrowski, 1996, 16)

However, he did not specify how this occurred. In a sense he left it to us, adherents of TPD, to work this out. Here, I present my theorizing about this. My analysis is based on two assumptions. First, the presence of dynamisms implies that individuals possess the five forms of OE—psychomotor, sensual, imaginational, intellectual, and emotional. Second, the dynamisms of concern are primarily those of III. Dynamisms of Level II are in effect transitory, meaning that individuals may begin experiencing ambivalences and ambitendencies and return to Level I.

The hallmark of Level III, spontaneous multilevel disintegration, is inner conflict—experience of the way the world ought to be versus how it is and discrepancy between higher and lower self. The presence of all forms of OE itself lays the foundation for inner conflict. Innate hyperactivity of psychomotor OE and the intensity of sensory pleasures of sensual OE are in conflict with emotional form of OE, which draws individuals to attachment and concern with others. In essence, by themselves psychomotor and sensual forms tend to be self-focused; emotional form, other focused. Meanwhile, intellectual form of OE raises probing questions not only about the external social and physical environment but also about the self. It is conceivable that individuals with intellectual OE will focus on making self-observations and wonder why they behave the way they do. Finally, imaginational OE is critical to individuals' experiencing of discrepancies; through imaginational OE, individuals can imagine the ideal world and higher self. Imaginational and intellectual work together to create inner conflict. Action of the forms of OE spark the beginnings of multilevel disintegration, a vertical rather than horizontal process. Emotional OE represents the higher form; psychomotor and sensual, the lower form; imaginational OE enables a vision of the ideal.

My identification of two issues related to dynamisms and my cursory explanations are intended to encourage others to refine TPD. It is difficult for me to believe that Dąbrowski believed that his theory was written in stone.

Conclusion

Dąbrowski stated that dynamisms are shapers of development, which is clearly articulated in TPD. I have argued that they also shape om conception of fundamental psychological constructs. Mainstream conceptions of negative emotions and self-concept are incompatible with the concept of dynamisms. To fully appreciate dynamisms, we must divest ourselves of our ingrained beliefs regarding psychological constructs.

As a practicing psychologist, my primary interest in dynamisms rests with those of Level III. Among those clients who seek counseling due to overwhelming emotions, there are some who suffer from the effects of disintegrating dynamisms. Such clients need not only our support but also our judicious sharing of TPD tenets. As a student of TPD, my interest is twofold: to draw attention to the complexity of Dąbrowski's theory and to contribute to its evolution.

References

Dąbrowski, K. (1964). *Positive disintegration.* Boston: Little, Brown.

Dąbrowski, K. (1967). *Personality shaping.* Boston: Little, Brown.

Dąbrowski, K. (with Kawczak, A., & Piechowski, M. M.). (1970). *Mental growth through positive disintegration.* London, England: Gryf.

Dąbrowski, K. (1972). *Psychoneurosis is not an illness.* London, England: Gryf.

Dąbrowski, K. (1996). *Multilevelness of emotional and instinctive functions. Part 1: Theory and description of levels of behavior*: Lublin, Poland: Towarzystwo Naukowe Katolickiego Uniwersytetu Lubelskiego.

Datwin, C.R. (1965\1872). *The expression of the emotions in man and animals.* Chicago: The University of Chicago Press.

Falk, R. F., Miller, N. B., Piechowski, M. M., & Silverman, L. K. (2016). *Overexcitability Questionnaire-Two (OEQ-II): Manual, Scoring System, and Questionnaire* (2nd Ed.) (Available from the Institute for the Study of Advanced Development, 8120 Sheridan Blvd., Suite C-111, Westminster, CO 80003-6146).

Izard, C. E. (1977). *Human emotions.* New York: Plenum.

Lewis, M. (2000). The emergence of human emotions. In M. Lewis & J. M. Haviland-Jones (Eds.). *Handbook of emotions* (2nd ed., pp. 265-280). New York: Guilford.

Lewis, M., & Michalson, L. (1983). *Children—emotions and moods: Developmental theory and measurement.* New York, NY: Plenum.

Lysy, K. Z., & Piechowski M. M. (1983). Personal growth: An empirical study using Jungian and Dąbrowski measures. *Genetic Psychology Monographs,* 108, 267-320.

Mendaglio, S. (1995). Sensitivity among gifted persons: A multi faceted perspective. *Roeper Review,* 17(3), 169-172.

Mendaglio, S., & Peterson, J. S. (2007). *Models of counseling gifted children, adolescents and young adults.* Waco, TX: Prufrock.

Pfeiffer, S. I. (2013). *Serving the gifted: Evidence-based clinical and psychoeducational practice, 15,* 248-268. New York, NY, US: Routledge/Taylor & Francis Group.

Piechowski, M. M. (1975). The theoretical and empirical approach to the study of development. *Genetic Psychology Monographs,* 92, 231-297.

Piechowski, M. M. (2009). Peace Pilgrim, exemplar of Level V. *Roeper Review,* 31, 103-112.

Piechowski, M.M. (1975). The theoretical and empirical approach to the study of development. *Genetic Psychology Monographs,* 92, 231-297.

Silverman, L. K. (1993). *Counseling the gifted and talented.* Denver, CO: Love.

Tillier, W. (2008). Kazimierz Dąbrowski: The man. In S. Mendaglio (Ed.) (pp. 3-12), *Dąbrowski's theory of positive disintegration.* Scottsdale AZ: Great Potential Press.

Chapter 4
Intelligence

In this chapter, consisting of an article on intelligence, I note that there is evidence of a movement in both psychology and in gifted education, away from the pre-eminence of intelligence. In psychology this is manifested in emphasizing effort over ability and of EQ over IQ. In gifted education, the movement away from intelligence is revealed in recent conceptions of giftedness. Terman's initial operationalizing of giftedness as an IQ score has been replaced by the addition of personality criteria and the factor of productivity. Intelligence, though implicit in current definitions of giftedness, has been superseded by prodigious achievement in areas valued by society. In the course of presenting the new wave of conceptions of giftedness, I observe that the movement from Terman's definition is not yet apparent in research in the field of gifted education. Intelligence still prevails in that arena. As a result, there is a conflict evident in gifted education's treatment of intelligence. Research notwithstanding, conceptually there have been attempts to diminish the importance of intelligence. Ultimately, one is left with the impression that intelligence or cognitive ability is no longer enough for an individual to be identified as gifted.

In my view, Dąbrowski has gone much further than scholars in psychology and gifted education. While explicitly retaining the construct, it is dethroned from its lofty position. Intelligence is relegated to its role as a tool of, not as a cause of, development.

Reference

Mendaglio, S. (20). Dąbrowski on intelligence: Dethroning a venerable construct, *International Journal of Giftedness and Creativity, 2* (1), 15-21

Dąbrowski on Intelligence: Dethroning a Venerable Construct

From IQ to EQ

Interest in the construct of intelligence, its nature and measurement, is as old as the field of modern psychology. Conceptions of the nature of intelligence abound and they range from those that are empirically based (e.g., Spearman, 1927) to those that are proposed to be based on a synthesis of scholarly literature (e.g., Gardner, 1983). Spearheaded by the work of Alfred Binet (Binet & Simon, 1905; cited in Nicolas, Andrieu, Croizet, & Burman, 2013) numerous instruments have been developed to measure intelligence. Among the well-known instruments in their original versions are the Stanford-Binet, Binet-Simon's Test revised by Terman (1916; Terman & Merrill, 1937), and Wechslers' Intelligence Scales that include the Wechsler Adult Intelligence Scale (WAIS, Wechsler, 1955) and the Wechsler Intelligence Scale for Children (WISC, Wechsler,1949). A recent addition is the Woodcock Johnson Test of Cognitive Ability (WJTCA; Woodcock, 1993). Such measures yield scores that are normally thought of as IQ. All of these tests have been revised since their original publication, attesting to their popularity. The use of such measures, particularly the Wechsler scales, is commonplace in school settings. When children encounter difficulties or when a program decision arises, these tests are most likely administered and their scores influence intervention and decision making.

It is important to point out that measures of intelligence do not measure academic achievement; they are an indication of potential not production. Even in our field of gifted education, regardless of authors' attempts to distance giftedness from IQ scores, a high level of intelligence, sometimes called cognitive ability, is a core element in virtually all past and current conceptions of giftedness. Furthermore, a perusal of research in gifted education indicates that cognitive ability is commonly the sole criterion used by researchers to recruit participants who are gifted (e.g., Wirthwein, Becker, Loehr, & Rost, 2011; Yakmaci-Guzel & Akarsu, 2006). One does not have to delve too deeply into the scholarly literature, or attend to general discourse, to find evidence of the privileged position that the construct of intelligence holds.

There have been attempts to deemphasize the importance of intelligence as it is commonly conceived. Among the more well-known attempts are found in the writings of Gardner (1983), Gladwell (2008), and Salovey and Mayer (1990). Gardner proposed a theory of multiple intelligences. Gardner argued that intelligence should be broadened beyond the logical mathematical type to include such abilities as artistic and kinesthetic. Gladwell, on the other hand, proposed that effort and opportunity are the predominant contributors to high achievement, not simply intelligence. He proposed that practice, 10,000 hours, and opportunistic factors displace intelligence as the primary contributors to prodigious productivity. In a similar vein, the work of Salovey and Mayer, pioneers of emotional intelligence, was used to place emotional quotient (EQ; Bar-On, 2000) in a preeminent position over IQ. In essence, this position proposes that EQ is a better predictor of success than IQ.

Intelligence and Giftedness: Diminished, not Disposed

The role of intelligence in giftedness differs in the literature in gifted education depending on whether we are dealing with theory, research, or practice. Regarding theory, the primacy of intelligence has declined in conceptions of giftedness. Historically, we see a movement from intelligence, that is, a superior level of intelligence as *the* defining characteristic of giftedness, to an emphasis on prodigious achievement as the defining criterion. In contrast to the area of theory, in the domains of research and practice, intelligence has generally maintained its pre-eminent position.

Theories of Giftedness

Our well-known and often-cited conceptions of giftedness first appeared in the literature in the 1970s. Two of the most popular conceptions are discussed here. To the sole criterion of intelligence evident in the pioneering work of Terman (1925), Marland (1972) added a number of other criteria including specific academic performance and leadership ability. Marland maintained the idea of potential, not only in his retention of intelligence (i.e., potential to achieve at a high level) but also in his statement that a student may be identified as gifted if she or he manifested potential for advanced achievement in any of the criteria listed. While Marland broadened the concept of giftedness beyond intelligence, he retained it as an independent criterion that can be used for identification of giftedness.

Renzulli (1978), on the other hand, proposed a view that intelligence alone was not sufficient: two other factors were essential, namely, task commitment and creativity. To be precise, Renzulli proposed that the interaction of above-average ability, task commitment, and creativity resulted in *gifted behaviour*—not giftedness. That is, intelligence alone, regardless of its magnitude, could not account for gifted behaviour. In retrospect, Renzulli laid the foundation for the emphasis on production rather than potential that can be seen in current conceptions of giftedness. The 1970s, then, represent two dramatic shifts from Terman's exclusive focus on giftedness as superior intelligence. Thus began the diminution of intelligence in theorizing about the nature of giftedness.

Recent theories extend the decreased importance of traditional intelligence and increased emphasis on productivity. To illustrate this trend, I briefly discuss two current theories. Sternberg (Sternberg, Jarvin, & Grigorenko, 2011) proposed a Pentagonal Theory in which five factors are essential for giftedness: excellence, rarity, value, productivity, and demonstrability. Sternberg's Theory of Giftedness does not have intelligence as a criterion. To meet the excellence criterion an individual must be superior in some dimension compared to her or his peers. A very high level of creativity, wisdom, or skill is an example of the domain of excellence. Rarity means that the dimension in which one is superior to others must be scarce. This means that the criterion cannot be met if everyone in a group is demonstrating ability at a very high level. Excellence and rarity have meaning in a social comparison context. The value criterion means that superior performance must be demonstrated in one or more areas valued by society. An individual demonstrating superior performance as a criminal, for example, is not considered gifted since that activity is not valued by society. The criteria of productivity and demonstrability displace potential as an indication of giftedness. Without a manifestation of superior ability by producing something, an individual cannot be termed gifted.

It seems that the Pentagonal Theory is aimed at giftedness in adulthood: "In childhood, of course, it is possible to be labelled as gifted without having been productive. In fact, children are typically judged largely on potential [for productivity] rather than actual productivity" (Sternberg, Jarvin, & Grigorenko, 2011, p. 5). Lest we conclude that intelligence tests may be used to indicate potential for productivity, Sternberg went on to state: "Simply receiving high scores on an IQ test trivializes what it means to be gifted" (p. 5).

Subotnik, Olszewski-Kublius, and Worrell (2011) proposed a talent development model aimed at rectifying, among other things, the disconnect between giftedness in childhood and eminence in adulthood. Here is the conceptual foundation for their model:

Giftedness is the manifestation of performance that is clearly at the upper end of the distribution in a talent domain even relative to other high-functioning individuals in that domain. Further, giftedness can be viewed as developmental in that in the beginning stages, potential is the key variable; in later stages, achievement is the measure of giftedness; and in fully developed talents, eminence is the basis on which this label is granted. Psychosocial variables play an essential role in the manifestation of giftedness at every developmental stage. Both cognitive and psychosocial variables are malleable and need to be deliberately cultivated. (p. 3)

Similar to Sternberg's theory, Subotnik et al. emphasize a superior level of performance or productivity, when compared to other individuals, as an essential criterion for giftedness. In their developmental view of giftedness, they state explicitly that in childhood, cognitive ability as indicating potential to achieve at an extraordinary level is an acceptable criterion for giftedness. General cognitive ability is viewed as an essential factor in what is termed academic giftedness in children. This stance changes with development: "Although general ability and potential may be the hallmarks of academic giftedness in children, domain-specific ability and achievement become increasingly important as individuals develop" (p. 39). With age and particularly in adulthood, cognitive ability is no longer sufficient for giftedness. In other words, one may be gifted in childhood but not in adulthood, unless there is evidence of prodigious achievement.

Research and Practice in Gifted Education

Paradoxically, in our field, a dichotomy is more apparent in theory-research, rather than in the usual research-practice gap. The diminishing of intelligence in theories of giftedness has had little effect on research and practice in gifted education.

Researchers interested in variables related to gifted individuals and school personnel interested in selecting students for gifted education programs use intelligence in their selection of participants and students respectively. Researchers in gifted education use intelligence/cognitive ability as the selection criterion for gifted and non-gifted participants. In essence, this approach to selection of participants is similar if not identical to that used by the pioneer of the study of giftedness, Terman (1925). In the emergence of psychology of giftedness and gifted education, intelligence was paramount in the conception of giftedness. Pioneering the modern empirical study of giftedness in North America in the 1920s, Terman operationally defined giftedness in terms of intelligence as measured by the Stanford-Binet Test, as noted earlier, a measure of potential not achievement. For the purpose of his research, he used an IQ score of 140 or higher on the Stanford-Binet to identify participants as gifted.

Present-day researchers use the intelligence criterion directly through the use of test scores (e.g., Kettler, 2014; Olthouse, 2014; Peterson & Lorimer, 2011; Rubenstein, Siegle, Reis, Mccoach, &

Burton, 2012; Snyder, Nietfeld, & Linnenbrink-Garcia, 2011) or indirectly through the use of enrolment in gifted-education programs as a criterion. However, intelligence test scores are commonly used as a major, if not sole criterion, for selection of students for gifted education programs (Assouline & Luplowski-Shoplik, 2012). Ironically, then, there is a greater degree of similarity between research and practice in the field, than theory and research. Both researchers and practitioners continue to use Terman's approach to identifying gifted individuals, while current theorists proclaim intelligence as only one of several criteria needed for the construct of *giftedness*.

Theory of Positive Disintegration: Dethroning Intelligence

Dąbrowski makes numerous references to intelligence in his exposition of TPD, though I have found no explicit conceptual definition in his books. It seems reasonable to assume that he shares the Wechsler's conception of intelligence because Dąbrowski used the WISC and the WAIS in his research and practice (1972, 1996). Though a high level of intelligence is a prerequisite for advanced development (Dąbrowski, 1970), such intelligence by no means guarantees that individuals reach the pinnacle of human development. In TPD, intelligence plays a subservient role. An examination of intellectual OE (overexcitability) and development in TPD supports this claim; further, such exploration of the theory answers the question: "To what is intelligence subservient?"

Intelligence and Intellectual Overexcitability (OE).

Dąbrowski (1972) describes OE as a property of the central nervous system that produces "higher than average responsiveness to stimuli, manifested either by sensual, psychomotor, emotional (affective), imaginational, or intellectual excitability, or the combination thereof" (p. 303). When all five forms are present, individuals have the potential for accelerated or advanced development. However, when only sensual and psychomotor are present, development may not only be limited but negative outcomes may result (Mendaglio, 2012). Intellectual OE is one of the big three forms of OE because it, along with imaginational and emotional OE, is needed to attenuate the influence of the two lower forms, sparking development in individuals. Intellectual OE is designated as an essential ingredient for advanced development. Though intelligence is part of intellectual OE, Dąbrowski emphasized that the two are not synonymous. Manifestations of intellectual overexcitability include a drive to ask probing questions, hunger for knowledge, theoretical thinking, respect for logic, and preoccupation with theoretical problems (Dąbrowski, 1996). Intellectual OE, then, refers to *actual sophisticated* cognitive processing by an individual, not the cognitive *potential* assessed by operational definitions of intelligence commonly used in research and practice in gifted education.

Intelligence and Development.

Dąbrowski relegated intelligence to a subservient role in daily functioning. Intelligence is simply a tool individuals use to achieve aims and goals. What an individual does with his or her intelligence depends on the type of development involved. Mendaglio (2012) presented the role of intelligence that is associated with *biological* (also termed *normal*), *one sided*, and *accelerated development*. Biological development represents the most common form. It is characterized by the maturational stages of human life; very little inner conflict and transformation are experienced. Disruptions of mental equilibrium are relatively few and short-lived. Intelligence serves individuals' satiation of drives, meeting needs while conforming to social conventions. One-sided development, as the name suggests, refers to development in which only some emotional and intellectual potentials develop. In this form of development, individuals may be endowed with only one or more OEs, but not all five forms.

There is both a positive and a negative version of one sided development (Dąbrowski, 1996). On the positive side, individuals may demonstrate a high level of expression of one of the OEs. For example, individuals with a disproportionately high level of intellectual OE may make significant contributions in a field of study. With lower levels of the other OEs, development is considered limited because of the intense focus on one domain. Individuals who may have a disproportionately high level of emotional OE may become so identified and attached to others that they may lose their sense of self. On the negative side, psychopathy is also considered a form of one sided development. In this case, as with biological development, intelligence is in the service of the individuals' basic drives which may create, for example, master criminals and dictators. Accelerated development requires the presence of high levels of all forms of OEs. In accelerated development, intelligence serves higher aims and values, such as altruism and authenticity. Different levels of intellectual functioning are associated with all three types of mental development. A hallmark of this form of development is individuals' taking control of their development such that they attain significant autonomy from biological instincts and drives and live their lives guided by universal moral values. In this form of development, intelligence is at the service of values such as responsibility for oneself and others.

The subservient role of intelligence can also be seen in the levels of development, which coincide with the types of development. Dąbrowski proposed five levels of development: primary integration, unilevel disintegration, spontaneous multilevel disintegration, organized multilevel disintegration, and secondary integration. Dąbrowski's levels indicate a progression from lower to higher moral human functioning, *though the progression is by no means linear or universal.* Similar to the types of development, the processes to which intelligence is subservient change with the level of development: in the course of development from Level I, primary integration, to Levels IV and V, the role of intelligence changes from serving lower drives and goals to higher aims and values.

Primary integration, Level I, is characterized by cognitive and emotional structures and functions that form a rigid mental organization. There is little evidence of introspection and questioning of one's life and surroundings. Cognitive and emotional structures are impulsive and automatic. Such mental organization leads to behaviour that is controlled by instincts and drives. Individuals are under the influence of the social environment leading to conformity and being concerned with social approval. In Level I, there is also a subset of individuals, presumably a small minority of the population, that are psychopathic, representing an extreme version of the use of intelligence for their egocentric ends. In primary integration, intelligence does not control primitive urges, but rather it "serves as an instrument subservient to the dictates of primitive drives" (Dąbrowski, 1996, p. 78). In primary integration, intelligence is rigidly linked to primitive drives. Primary integration characterized by use of an individuals' resources, including intelligence, to satisfy biological drives and needs, represents a lack of development in Dąbrowskian theorizing.

That intelligence does not reign supreme in TPD is clear in its articulation of the process of development, that is, positive disintegration. Development is triggered not by intellectual but rather by emotional factors. Dynamisms are the mechanisms of positive disintegration, consisting of destruction of lower functions and creation of higher functions. Two classes of dynamisms are essential components of the two aspects of positive disintegration: disintegrating dynamisms and developmental dynamisms. Disintegrating dynamisms are responsible for the loosening of the rigid mental organization of primary integration. Beginning with their emergence in Level II, unilevel disintegration, and continuing in Level III, spontaneous multilevel disintegration, the disintegrating dynamisms not only destroy the linkage of intelligence and drive satisfaction, they create inner conflict, or psychoneurotic conflict, deemed essential for development. The nature of disintegrating dynamisms is obvious in the terminology Dąbrowski used to label them, for example, feelings of shame, feelings of guilt, astonishment with oneself, and dissatisfaction with self. Disintegrating dynamisms are negative emotional experiences and processes.

Developmental dynamisms are responsible for the replacement of lower mental structures with higher ones and culminating in the creation of personality, the apex of development in TPD. The nature of developmental dynamisms is also evident in the labels used to define them, for example, autonomy, authenticity, empathy, and responsibility. Developmental dynamisms are values that individuals at the highest levels of development in TPD use to guide their daily behaviour. The mechanisms of development, then, are emotions and values. Intelligence is an important construct in TPD, however, it is relegated to a servant role; at the most primitive level, intelligence serves drives and needs; at the most advanced level, it serves emotions and values.

Conclusion

Dąbrowski does not reject the construct of intelligence; nor does he diminish its significance in human functioning. Intelligence is important. While other authors lessen the prominence of intelligence by adding other factors or variables, Dąbrowski retains the construct and integrates it into his conception of human development. My understanding of Dąbrowski's view of intelligence can be summed up as follows. Dąbrowski does not say: Intelligence is no longer supreme because drives, needs, emotions and values are just as important in explaining development. He simply dethrones intelligence by saying: Drives and needs dictate what intelligence does at the lowest level of development; emotions and values dictate what it does at the highest levels of development. To what is intelligence subservient? The answer to that depends on the type and the level of development.

References

Assouline, S.G., & Lupkowski-Shoplik, A. (2012). The talent search model of gifted identification. *Journal of Psychoeducational Assessment, 30*(1), 45-59. doi:10.1177/0734282911433946

Bar-On, R. (2000). Emotional and social intelligence: Insights from the Emotional Quotient Inventory (EQ-I). In R. Bar-On & J. D. A. Parker (Eds.). *Handbook of emotional intelligence* (pp. 363-388). San Francisco, CA: Jossey-Bass.

Dąbrowski, K. (1967). *Personality-shaping through positive disintegration.* Boston: Little Brown.

Dąbrowski, K. (1970). *Mental growth through positive disintegration.* London: Gryf.

Dąbrowski, K. (1972). *Psychoneurosis is not an illness.* London: Gryf.

Dąbrowski, K. (1996). *Multilevelness of emotional and instinctive functions. Part 1: Theory and description of levels of behavior.* Lublin, Poland: Towarzystwo Naukowe Katolickiego Uniwersytetu Lubelskiego.

Gardner, H. (1983). *Frames of mind: The theory of multiple intelligences.* New York: Basic Books

Gladwell, M. (2008). *Outliers: The Story of success.* New York: Little, Brown and Company.

Kettler, T. (2014). Critical thinking skills among elementary school students: Comparing identified gifted and general education student performance. *Gifted Child Quarterly, 58*(2), 127-136. doi:10.1177/0016986214522508

Marland, S. P., Jr. (1972). Education of the gifted and talented: Report to the Congress of the United States by the U.S. Commissioner of Education and background papers submitted to the U.S. Office of Education, 2 vols. Washington, DC: U.S. Government Printing Office. (Government Documents Y4.L 11/2: G36)

Mendaglio, S. (2012). Overexcitabilities and giftedness research: A call for a paradigm shift. *Journal for the Education of the Gifted, 35*(3), 207-219. doi:10.1177/0162353212451704

Nicolas, S., Andrieu, B., Croizet, J., Sanitioso, R. B., & Burman, J. (2013). Sick? Or slow? On the origins of intelligence as a psychological object. *Intelligence, 41*(5), 699-711. doi:10.1016/j.intell.2013.08.006

Olthouse, J. M. (2014). Gifted children's relationships with writing. *Journal for the Education of the Gifted, 37*(2), 171-188. doi: 10.1177/0162353214529044

Peterson, J., & Lorimer, M. R. (2011). Student response to a small-group affective curriculum in a school for gifted children. *Gifted Child Quarterly, 55*(3), 167-180. doi:10.1177/0016986211412770

Renzulli, J. S. (1978). What makes giftedness? Reexamining a definition. *Phi Delta Kappan, 60*(3), 180-184. Retrieved from http://eric.ed.gov

Rubenstein, L., Siegle, D., REIS, S. M., Mccoach, D., & Burton, M. (2012). A complex quest: The development and research of underachievement interventions for gifted students. *Psychology in the Schools, 49*(7), 678-694. doi:10.1002/pits.21620

Salovey, P., & Mayer, J. (1990). Emotional intelligence. *Imagination, Cognition and Personality, 9*(3), 185-211. doi:10.2190/DUGG-P24E-52WK-6CDG

Snyder, K. E., Nietfeld, J. L., & Linnenbrink-Garcia, L. (2011). Giftedness and metacognition: A short-term longitudinal investigation of metacognitive monitoring in the classroom. *Gifted Child Quarterly, 55*(3), 181-193. doi:10.1177/0016986211412769

Spearman, C. (1927). *The abilities of man: Their nature and measurement* (2nd ed.). London: Macmillan.

Sternberg, R.J., Jarvin, L., & Grigorenko, E.L. (2011). *Explorations in giftedness.* New York: Cambridge University Press.

Subotnik, R.F., Olszewski-Kublius, P., & Worrell, F.C. (2011). Rethinking giftedness and gifted education: A proposed direction forward based on psychological science, *Psychological Science in the Public Interest, 12*(1), 3-54. doi:10.1177/1529100611418056

Terman, L.M. (1916). *The measurement of intelligence: An explanation of and a complete guide to the use of the Stanford revision and extension of the Binet-Simon Intelligence Scale.* Boston: Houghton Mifflin.

Terman, L.M. (1925). *Genetic studies of genius: Mental and physical traits of a thousand gifted children.* Palo Alto, CA: Stanford University Press.

Terman, L. M., & Merrill, M. A. (1937). *Measuring intelligence: A guide to the administration of the new revised Stanford-Binet tests of intelligence.* Oxford, England: Houghton Mifflin.

Wechsler, D. (1949). Wechsler Intelligence Scale for Children: Manual. New York, NY: Psychological Corporation.

Wechsler, D. (1958). *The measurement and appraisal of adult intelligence.* Baltimore, MD: Williams and Wilkins.

Woodcock, R. W. (1997). The Woodcock-Johnson Tests of cognitive ability—Revised. In D. P. Flanagan, J. L. Genshaft, & P. L. Harrison (Eds.), *Contemporary intellectual assessment: Theories, tests, and issues* (pp. 373-402). New York: Guilford.

Wirthwein, L., Becker, C.V., Loehr, E-V., & Rost, D. H. (2011). Overexcitabilities in gifted and non-gifted adults: Does sex matter? *High Abilities Studies, 22*(2), 145-153. doi: 10.1080/13598139.2011.622944

Yakmaci-Guzel, B., & Akarsu, F. (2006). Comparing overexcitabilities of gifted and non-gifted 10th grade students in Turkey, *High Ability Studies, 17*(1), 43-56. doi: 10.1080/13598130600947002

Chapter 5

TPD and Other Personality Theories

This chapter from Mendaglio (2008) compares Dąbrowski's theory to two other theories of personality, namely, Freud's psychoanalysis and Carl Rogers' self theory. I felt compelled to include, as well, the Five Factor Model (FFM), based on Cattell's lexical approach to personality traits, because of its prominence in personality research. Since FFM is not a theory per se, I primarily compared the theory of positive disintegration to the two theories. Though I wrote the chapter in the early 2000s, the theories I selected for comparison remain mainstays of theories of personality textbooks (e.g., Schultz & Schultz, 2016).

I begin the entry by describing the process by which I arrived at the theories and model that are the contrasts. To present the comparison, I decided to use the organization that S.R. Maddi (cited later in the entry) used in his theories of personality textbook: biological force, social force, personality structure and stages of development. I presented each theory's stance on the four categories. By comparing Dąbrowski's theory with theories familiar to readers, I believed that the contrasts would enhance their greater appreciation of the theory of positive disintegration.

References

Schultz, D.P., & Schultz, S.E. (2016). *Theories of personality* (11th Ed.). Singapore: Cengage Learning.

The Theory of Positive Disintegration (TPD) and Other Approaches to Personality

In planning to write this chapter, I had to decide to which approaches should I compare TPD. An obvious criterion was that the approaches had to be well known; it would not be useful to compare TPD, a theory unknown in American personology, to an accepted but little known personality theory. I perused classic and recent theories of personality texts for ideas. Some of the texts (e.g., Corsini, 1977; Walters, 2004) organize their texts similar to the presentation by Hall and Lindzey (1970)—that is, the theories are presented in more or less chronological order of their publication. Other authors categorize personality theories by a theme—for example, depth psychology and humanism (Massey, 1981). Some depart from the chronological or thematic approach and organize their presentation according to issues (e.g., Magnivita, 2002).

Dissatisfied with the way theories were commonly presented, Maddi (1989) created a unique approach to organizing his text on theories of personality. Unlike other schemes, he classified theories to "capture the essential pattern or overall meaning behind…the theories concerning the nature of human life" (p. 41), and he devised a three-category solution—conflict model, fulfillment model, and consistency model.

Conflict model includes theories that postulate two forces, which interact to produce conflict within individuals. Typically, the two forces are nature and nurture or person and society. For theorists in this category, conflict is universally experienced, and life is seen as a compromise. Individuals either strike a balance between the two forces or deny one of them.

Fulfillment model includes theories that postulate only one force. Development in these theories is premised on the progressive unfolding of one force within an individual. Life is driven by a sole motivation—actualization of inherited potentials. Society may facilitate or impede the spontaneous unfolding of the inherited force.

Consistency model includes theories that postulate no forces resident within individuals. The theories in this category focus on individuals' responses to feedback received from the social environment in daily living. The prime motivation of individuals is to maintain consistency. Self-referent information that is consistent with individuals' expectations produces no change or discomfort. Feedback that is inconsistent with expectations creates tension and, under some circumstances, leads to change.

Maddi's approach made sense to me, and I decided to use the categories to select theories for my purpose. My first task was to decide in which model category TPD should fit. Given its unique approach to personality, I wasn't surprised when I couldn't fit TPD into any one category (Maddi did warn readers that they may find some theories that did not fit any of his models, though he himself had not encountered any).

TPD postulates the existence of two forces, biology and environment, which Dąbrowski called the first factor and second factor, respectively (Dąbrowski, 1970). In addition, conflict is a hallmark of the theory, and so it is a conflict model theory. However, Dąbrowski also postulated the existence of a third factor of development, representing a powerful autonomous inner force which is rooted in the biological endowment of individuals (Dąbrowski, 1973). With this additional force, TPD has elements of the progressive unfolding of a force within individuals, characteristic of Maddi's fulfillment model. After considering the consistency model criteria, I concluded that TPD did not match the main criterion of the consistency model. Theories, in this model, emphasize the role of feedback from the social environment for personality development. In TPD, although developing individuals certainly note the inconsistencies within themselves and society, personality is achieved, in large measure, by the individuals' transcending the influence of the social environment

(Dąbrowski, 1967). It seemed to me that TPD has fundamental elements in common with both conflict model and fulfillment model theories of personality.

Having established the categories where TPD fits, my next task was to select a theory from each model as contrasts. In the conflict model category, Maddi included Freud (1970/1924) and other theorists such as Murray (1959). Rogers (1959) and Maslow (1968) were theorists that fit the fulfillment model category. Using my popularity criterion, I selected Freud over other conflict theorists such as Murray. Deciding between Rogers and Maslow was more difficult. Given the overlap between Rogers and Maslow, I decided that I needed an additional criterion for my decision making; psychotherapy emerged as a new criterion. Dąbrowski not only had extensive psychotherapeutic experience that influenced his theorizing, but also, like Freud and Rogers, had a theory of psychotherapy related to his personality theory. Therefore, I decided to compare TPD to Freud's psychoanalysis and Rogers' self theory.

I could also have considered existential approaches to personality, because they are part of Maddi's fulfillment model. They were not included for two reasons: first, they are not popular approaches, but more importantly, they do not represent a unified theory. However, there is a great deal of similarity between existential psychology and the theory of positive disintegration. Both emphasize similar key concepts such as values, autonomy, authenticity, and existential emotions such as anxiety and depression. A more fundamental similarity is seen in the philosophical underpinnings of TPD, which is in large measure existentialism. Dąbrowski was influenced significantly by the works of Kierkegaard (see Chapters 1 and 5 in this volume). The theory of positive disintegration could serve as an effective conceptual framework to systematize the contributions made by existential psychologists such as Binswanger (1963), Boss (1963), May (1958), and Yalom (1980; 1985). A discussion of this is beyond the scope of this chapter.

While Freud's and Rogers' theories are well known, they are not currently the most popular approaches to personality in psychology. The Big Five, also known as the Five Factor Model (John & Scrivastava, 1999), is the most popular current approach to personality (e.g., Ekehammar & Akrami, 2007). Although the Big Five is not a theory of personality, because of its current influence in the field, I decided to also include this approach to personality. Therefore, in this chapter, I contrast some core elements of psychoanalysis, self theory, the Big Five, and TPD. I discuss the three theories under the headings of biological force, social force, personality structure, and stages of development. After a brief introductory note for each topic, my discussion of the theories proceeds in the following order: psychoanalysis, self theory, and positive disintegration. I contrast the Big Five and TPD in a final, separate section.

Psychoanalysis, Self Theory, and Theory of Positive Disintegration

Biological Force: Instincts

Psychoanalysis, self theory, and the theory of positive disintegration postulate the existence of a biological force that influences personality development. Instincts are a manifestation of this force. Freud, Dąbrowski, and Rogers differ in their representation of instincts. Of the three theorists, Freud presents the most detailed account of the nature of instincts and their function. Dąbrowski recognized the same instincts as Freud, but Dąbrowski interprets them differently and adds some of his own. Rogers' account of the biological force underlying his theory is rather brief. He did not use the term instinct, but his biological force, in my view, is tantamount to an instinct. While their presentation varies, all three theories view a biological force as a *sine qua non* of personality development.

Psychoanalysis

In psychoanalysis, (Freud, 1970/1924; Maddi, 1989; Hall & Lindzey, 1970) instincts are part of the biological makeup of all individuals and dictate daily behavior throughout life. Gratification of instincts is the motivator of human behavior. According to this view, if it weren't for societal prescriptions and prohibitions, individuals would act impulsively, gratifying each biological need as it arises. Freud, in a detailed account of his view of instincts, noted that their source lies in the in somatic process. Energy of the instincts emanates from the organism's experience of a deprivation in some system—both the source and energy of instincts are internal to the organism. Instincts are mental representations of bodily processes. When the body lacks something, a state of tension is created, and there is internal pressure on the individual to act to reduce the tension by eliminating the deprivation. States of bodily deprivation are presumed to occur constantly within organisms, and so instincts are continually influencing individuals' behavior in daily life.

An important aspect of instincts in psychoanalysis is the object needed for gratification. While the source and energy aspects of instincts are constant, objects are variable. For example, when bodily processes result in a lowering of blood-sugar levels, tension is created—interpreted as hunger—and the individual is motivated to seek food, the object that would gratify the need. The type of food used, however, varies and is influenced by other factors such as learning and cultural contexts. An important element in the notion of object is the idea of substitution. In some cases, for example, when the bodily tension called hunger emerges, an individual may not seek out solid food but may have a cup of coffee or seek distraction instead. Such substitutions, of course, have their limitations and potential problems.

Freud proposed three types of instincts: life instinct, sexual instinct, and death instinct. Of the three instincts, he gave the most prominent position in his theory to the sexual instinct. Gratification of the sexual instinct provides the greatest opportunity for individuals to encounter difficulties with societal mores and expectations. Behaviors driven by the life (self-preservation) instinct—that is, seeking food, water, and air for survival—are governed by fewer societal regulations and taboos. Further, food, water, and air are essential for life. Sexual gratification, on the other hand, while essential for the survival of the species, is not essential for the survival of an individual. In addition, mature gratification of the sexual instinct brings individuals into intimate contact with other members of society.

Freud included the death instinct later in his life (Maddi, 1989). It seems that the death instinct is an extension of the organism's need to be at rest, to be in homeostatic balance. Drives and needs create tension—a disruption of homeostasis—and the individual is motivated to engage in activities to reduce tension and restore balance. The death instinct represents the individual's desire to achieve the ultimate reduction of tension. Of the three instincts, it seems logical that Freud gave the sexual instinct the influential role in personality development (Maddi, 1989).

The instincts are subsumed in Freud's structure of personality; they constitute the id. The id is the repository of the instincts, and it is the innate part of the personality—the constitutional endowment of all individuals. There are neither controls nor consciousness in this part of the personality. Organismic tensions rise, and individuals automatically respond to reduce the tension, to gratify a need. The primary function of individuals is the gratification of instinctual drives and needs—to respond to their ids. When this cannot be done, individuals experience negative emotions such as frustration and anger. The primary reason this cannot be done is civilized society, which is ultimately responsible for the experiencing of such negative emotions—and the emergence of the other components of personality.

Self Theory

Self theory (Rogers, 1959; 1961) postulates a universal biological tendency of all living things to actualize their inherited potentialities. This *actualizing tendency* is the "inherent tendency of the organism to develop all its capacities in ways which serve to maintain or enhance the organism" (1959, p. 196). In addition to satisfying biological needs associated with self-preservation, the actualizing tendency includes a movement away from external, social control toward autonomy. Further, actualizing one's potentialities is consistent with, and not in conflict with, others' actualizing their potentials. In self theory, the actualizing tendency is the only motivation, and the organism as a whole exhibits it. While Rogers does not use the word instinct, the actualizing tendency, with its biological nature and universality, could also be called the actualizing instinct. The actualizing tendency is guided by the organismic valuing process, which selects stimuli and behaviors that serve to enhance the organism. Unlike Freud, Rogers did not elaborate on the biologically-based concepts that are of critical importance to his theory of personality.

Rogers also stipulated that individuals have a need for unconditional positive regard. That is, individuals need to be accepted, or prized, for who they are without judgment; they should not be valued based on the quality of their behaviors. It is unclear whether this need is inherited or learned, though for Rogers (1959), this is irrelevant. Unconditional positive regard, or the lack of it, is of paramount importance for personality development in self theory.

Positive Disintegration

Biological endowment also occupies a central role in positive disintegration (Dąbrowski, 1964a; 1967; 1970; 1973). There are countless references to instincts in positive disintegration (e.g., Dąbrowski, 1970). The theory includes a number of instincts: self-preservation, sexual, developmental, death, creative, and self-perfection. Unlike Freud's analysis of the self-preservation and sexual instincts, Dąbrowski believed that, if personality is to develop, these instincts need to be transformed, not simply gratified. Self-preservation instinct transforms to include the preservation of the integrity of the person, not simple biological survival; sexual instinct moves from an indiscriminate drive for gratification to an exclusive loving relationship with another. While psychoanalysis also speaks of transformation of instincts, the process is unconscious, and the motivation is ego defensive. For example, sublimation of the sexual instinct occurs to protect individuals from the anxiety associated with acknowledging socially tabooed sexual impulses into awareness. For Dąbrowski, it is clear that the transformation of instincts is a conscious process motivated by individuals' values; individuals intentionally reject the lower expression of the instincts for a higher form.

In addition to the two basic instincts, Dąbrowski proposed several others. The developmental instinct is the repository of all forces of development and is endowed differentially among individuals. From the developmental instinct, *developmental potential* is differentiated. Dąbrowski included overexcitability, dynamisms, and special abilities and talents in his concept of developmental potential. Overexcitability, a property of the central nervous system, has five forms: psychomotor, sensual, imaginational, intellectual, and emotional. Dynamisms are autonomous inner forces which direct the process of personality development. Dąbrowski proposed that developmental potential is manifested early in life in various forms of special abilities and talents. As an outgrowth of the developmental instinct, level of development also varies among individuals.

Similar to Freud, Dąbrowski included a death instinct, which he depicted as having two directions: external and internal. Externally focused death instinct includes aggression, hatred, and the desire to inflict pain on others. The internally focused form may result in suicide or in the destruction of primitive aspects of mental organization. The latter form, termed "partial death instinct," is positive and contributes to the development of personality.

The instincts of creativity and self-perfection are not instincts in the usual sense of the word. They are not universally endowed, only appearing in some individuals when they are on the path of advanced development. Dąbrowski noted that the creative instinct "discovers and molds new forms of reality" (1973, p. 27). Similarly, the self-perfection instinct appears in the course of advanced development and is described as "the highest instinct of a human being" (1973, p. 32). Both instincts are anchored to biology—that is, their seeds are evident early in life in those individuals endowed with favorable developmental potential. When combined, creative and self-perfection instincts play an essential role in personality development; their combination results not only in novel mental structures, but also in structures characterized by higher values.

There is some similarity between Dąbrowski's and Rogers' theorizing regarding biological forces. Left to their own devices, developmental instinct and actualizing tendency will unfold, revealing individuals' natures. When individuals are favorably endowed with the Dąbrowskian instincts—developmental potential, creative instincts, and self-perfection—the result is movement toward autonomy and authenticity similar to the unimpeded evolution of the actualizing tendency. However, there is major difference: Rogers assumed that all living organisms are equally endowed with an actualizing tendency, while Dąbrowski spoke of variable endowment of his instincts.

Social Force: Socialization

Psychoanalysis and the theory of positive disintegration postulate a social force which interacts with the biological force, producing conflict in individuals. However, Freud and Dąbrowski conceptualized the nature of the conflict and its role in personality development in dramatically different ways. Self theory does not postulate a social force that is in opposition with the biological force. In self theory, conflict occurs, but it is not inevitable nor necessary for personality development. However, all three theories do emphasize the importance of the socialization process in personality development.

Psychoanalysis

For Freud, there is a double-edged quality to civilized society—it is essential for human functioning, and it causes problems. A world in which individuals are continuously and automatically responding to id impulses is untenable. Instinctual needs are never permanently sated; instincts have a continual, moment-to-moment influence on the organism. A primary purpose of society is to create order out of an otherwise chaotic and dangerous world of self-gratifications. Societies specify acceptable and unacceptable modes of gratification with enforcement of these prescriptions, ranging from inducing feelings of embarrassment and guilt to physical punishment and death. This instilling of inhibition of impulses is achieved through the socialization process in the first few years of life. Society, through parents as primary agents of socialization, teaches inhibition through direct instruction and punishment or the threat of it. Through parental instructions, admonishments, criticism, and punishment, children learn self-regulation.

Self Theory

Unlike Freud and Dąbrowski, Rogers did not postulate society as one of two antagonistic forces. An individual's actualizing tendency—the instinct of maintaining and enhancing the organism—does not, in and of itself, run counter to others' actualizing their inherited potentials. In Rogers' approach, actualizing one's potentials is not only good for the individual, it is good for others as well; what's good for an individual is good for society. However, the social environment has a significant influence on the actualizing tendency and on personality development.

The social environment may facilitate or impede the operation of the actualizing tendency. If individuals' need for unconditional positive regard from significant others such as parents is met, then individuals' organismic valuing process occurs, in which "the organism experiences satisfaction in those stimuli or behaviors which maintain and enhance the organism and the self both in the immediate present and in the long range" (Rogers, 1959, p. 210). This process works in concert with the actualizing tendency of the organism. Problems arise if socialization interferes with the organismic valuing process and if young children begin to shift their focus for guiding their actions and experiencing away from the internal to the external world. In essence, problems arise when the need for unconditional positive regard is not met and children are not valued for themselves but rather for the quality of their actions. In this way, individuals learn to evaluate their experiences and actions based on the values and expectations of others rather than their actualizing tendency. Rogers noted that his analysis did not mean that children should not be socialized, but rather that significant others need to do this in a way that communicates acceptance and respect for the personhood of the child.

Positive Disintegration

Dąbrowski proposed that the two forces—nature and nurture—may or may not produce conflict for individuals. For highly socialized individuals, there may be little conflict experienced as they live their lives in robotic compliance with societal demands. When conflict is experienced, it is not simply of the psychoanalytic type. Some individuals experience conflict caused by their exclusive focus on gratification of biological needs, which conflicts with the strictures of society. Other individuals may experience conflict that stems from the discrepancy they experience between the way society ought to be and the way it is. Whether or not conflict is experienced, and its type, depends largely on constitutional endowment. The greater the developmental potential, the more likely individuals are to experience conflict stemming from the discrepancy they perceive between universal values and the actual workings of society.

In positive disintegration, the social environment is also discussed in terms of its role in development. At the extreme levels of developmental potential, high or low levels, the environment has virtually no influence. Those with very high levels will develop psychologically, while those at the other extreme will not, regardless of the quality of the social environment. For levels of developmental potential in between, a nurturing environment will facilitate development; a neglectful or abusive social environment will impede development.

The theory of positive disintegration notes, as does self theory, that socialization of children should be conducted in a sensitive manner. Adults are to accept children's expression of overexcitabilities and nurture their special abilities and talents. However, the goal is not to have highly socialized individuals who are adjusted to society. For Dąbrowski, adjustment to societal expectations did not indicate mental health. Instead, living life by one's constructed system of values, which would at times be in conflict with society, was an important feature of mental health.

Personality Structure

Both psychoanalysis and self theory discuss the structure of personality in varying detail, with Freud's account being more elaborate than Rogers. With his unique approach to personality, Dąbrowski (not surprisingly) does not specify a structure, but rather describes its nature in terms of traits that comprise it.

Psychoanalysis

The structure of personality includes the id, ego, and superego. The id, as previously noted, is part of the universal constitutional endowment of individuals and is the repository of all instincts. Were it not for societal demands, the id would form the entirety of Freudian personality; it is the socialization process that necessitates the Freudian personality structure. Young children learn that when they do what comes naturally, they are likely to experience harsh consequences from significant others. To deal with this eventuality, psychoanalysis postulates the differentiation of the ego from the id. It is important to note that the ego is in the service of the id.

The ego is a mental function that becomes conscious of societal rules and expectations, with its aim being the gratification of id impulses in the external, social world. In order to accomplish this, the ego guides an individual's intelligence and muscles in such a way as to minimizing punishment and defend the individual against anxiety and guilt (Maddi, 1989). The ebb and flow of tension created by instincts and their gratification continually puts the individual at odds with societal rules. Because of the ubiquitousness of the action of instincts, individuals regularly experience conflict with society. They learn to avoid punishment by inhibition of impulses or by using socially prescribed objects for instinctual gratification.

However, whenever these processes cannot be followed or when the intensity of an instinct is too strong, individuals experience anxiety and guilt, and they anticipate punishment. The well-known ego defenses (e.g., denial, sublimation, and projection) spontaneously engage to deal with the conflict and prevent anxiety from coming into awareness. By definition, the defenses are unconscious, and so the process of transforming an original prohibited impulse into an acceptable desire or behavior is not available to individuals. If it were, the individual would experience dire psychological consequences, such as a loss of integrity—disintegration of the personality. According to Freud, we can't handle the truth! Defenses protect us from it.

The superego is a mental process that is differentiated from the ego. Societal rules and expectations are incorporated by children into a set of values, which are used to classify behaviors or thoughts into either "right" or "wrong." With the emergence of the superego, individuals begin to feel guilt. Whereas punishment controls individuals from the outside, guilt is an internal regulator of behavior. Guilt produces tension in individuals equal to that produced by punishment. The superego, as a result, affects ego functioning; the ego now has to include guilt reduction as well as prevention of punishment as factors to manage while it engages in instinctual gratification.

Self Theory

In self theory, the organism is the biological substrate of personality; it is the "locus of experience" (Hall & Lindzey, 1970, p. 528). For Rogers, experiencing is the *sine qua non* of personality, which consists of the phenomenal field and self-concept (Rogers, 1951). The phenomenal field "includes all that is experienced by the organism... whether or not these experiences are consciously perceived" (p. 483). The phenomenal field, also termed the "perceptual field," is dynamic and fluid, representing the variability of moment-to-moment experiencing of the individual. Specific sensations and perceptions continuously move from background to figure in the phenomenal field. Rogers contended that only a small portion of the phenomenal field is consciously experienced at any particular time, though a large portion of it is available to conscious awareness.

Rogers used the term "experience" both as a noun and a verb. Experience, the noun, referred to all the here-and-now processes within the organism that are available to awareness. As such, experience does not refer to the accumulation of an organism's history. Experience as a verb referred to "symboliz[ing] in some accurate form at the conscious level the impact of...sensory or visceral events" (1959, p. 197). Symbolization, awareness, and consciousness were used synonymously by Rogers. Awareness or consciousness is the symbolic representation of one's experience. Symbolizing experience may be accurate or inaccurate. Accurate symbolization results when the symbols we use to represent a sensation accurately reflect external reality. Determination of accuracy for Rogers rests on the individual's use of hypothesis testing of inwardnesses. Inaccurate symbolization of experiences is presumed to create psychological difficulties for individuals.

From a portion of the individual's total experiences emerges an awareness of one's being that Rogers termed "self-experience" (1959, p. 223), and it is from this self-experience that self-concept is constructed. Self-experience, shaped by interaction with significant adults, becomes the self or self-concept—a perceptual object in one's phenomenal field. The self-perceptions that comprise self-concept are not necessarily conscious, though they are available to consciousness. Rogers described self-concept as a gestalt of perceptions that are related to "I" or "me," including any values associated with these perceptions (1959). Self-experiences include an evaluative dimension which is emotionally laden and "may arise directly from organismic responses to experiences, or they may be introjected or borrowed from others, so that the individuals claim them as his or her own, but is really distorting personal experience by imposing another's interpretation on it" (Massey, 1981, p. 310). Rogers also included an ideal self—what the person would like to be—in addition to the self as it is.

Positive Disintegration

Dąbrowski proposed a conception of personality that differs significantly from Freud's and Rogers.' While Freud and Rogers obviously differ in their respective approaches to personality, there is a common element in their theories: universality of personality. All individuals possess an id, ego, and superego, or a phenomenal field and a self-concept. In contrast, positive disintegration views personality as an achievement—and a rare one at that. Personality is a coherent and harmonized mental organization characterized by the most positive of human values. It represents the highest level of human development. Individuals who achieve personality are highly self-aware, autonomous, authentic, and responsible for self and others. They are capable of guiding their own learning and, when confronted with difficulties, can act as their own therapists. Personality consists of a constellation of traits, many of which are encountered in humanistic theories of personality, such as self theory. Dąbrowski's view of personality has some features in common with Rogers' fully functioning person (discussed below); a major difference is that Dąbrowski reserved the term "personality" to denote the highest level of human functioning and not as an attribute of all humanity. Though personality is an organized and harmonized mental organization, it is not static; self-improvement continues, though it is consciously guided by the individual and his or her system of values (Dąbrowski, 1967).

Stages of Personality Development

Both Freud and Dąbrowski articulated stages of personality development. While their thinking on this issue is dramatically different, there is at least one similarity: not all individuals progress through all of the stages. Rogers does not specify stages, but I see a progression, an evolution, in his articulation of self theory, and so I have included that description in this section as well.

Psychoanalysis

As noted earlier, Freud focused his theory of personality on the sexual instinct, because compared with the self-preservation instinct, individuals will experience more conflict in the course of sexual gratification than the other instincts; society simply has more rules and regulations surrounding this area of human nature. The main stages of development are identified by "concrete form[s] of the sexual instinct" (Maddi, 1989, p. 274) and, as such, can be described as particular instances of the general conflict between society and the sexual instinct. Psychoanalysis postulates four major psychosexual stages associated with so-called erogenous—pleasure-producing—zones of the body: oral, anal, phallic, and genital. Stages are associated with physical maturation, ranging from infancy to adolescence, but *"the first few years of life are decisive for the formation of personality"* (italics in original, Hall & Lindzey, 1970, p. 51).

In the oral stage, which is associated with the first year of life, pleasure is primarily associated with the mouth and eating. With the eruption of teeth comes chewing of food and biting. Incorporating of food and biting are said to be prototypical of later traits. Incorporation of food is later transformed, for example, into taking in knowledge—that is, learning. Biting may later be expressed in sarcasm.

In the anal stage, associated with the second year of life, the primary source of pleasure is bowel movements, which eliminate the source of discomfort brought on by the digestive process. Toilet training is the child's first experience with a societally-imposed control over an instinctual impulse. In essence, the child is required to delay gratification of the elimination impulse and the pleasure associated with it. How toilet training is implemented is said to have significant consequences for the development of personality traits. Approached in a strict, punitive manner, this training may result in a child's withholding elimination. Later in life, this may lead to a retentive characteristic, which may express itself in miserliness and stubbornness.

Alternatively, if the training is conducted in a supportive manner including praise, creativity and productivity may ensue in later life.

In the phallic stage, ages three to five, the sex organs are the primary source of pleasure. It is in this phase that the child experiences the Oedipus complex, for males, and the Electra complex, for females. Children want to possess parents of the opposite sex, displacing parents of the same sex. As children resolve these conflicts through such processes as identification with the same-sex parent, they long to be adults.

If individuals' development is not arrested or fixated at any of the first three stages of development, they progress to the genital stage, the apex of personality development. While the erogenous zone is not different from the phallic stage, the genital stage is characterized by complete physical sexual maturation and full adult expression of the sexual instinct. However, the genital stage is not conflict-free; individuals still need to contend with societal taboos.

In psychoanalysis, the pregenital stages represent immaturity; the genital stage represents maturity. Psychological maturity is defined in terms of how successful individuals are in coming to terms with the inevitable conflict stemming from the sexual instinct bumping up against the taboos of society at each stage of development.

Self Theory

Self theory does not include any stages of personality development. However, Rogers did describe a progression beginning with the differentiation of self-concept from the phenomenal field, the development of the needs for positive self-regard, the development of maladjustment and its remediation, and culminating in his pinnacle of development—the fully functioning person.

With the emergence of self-concept, the needs for positive regard from others and positive self-regard appear. These needs, which are considered universal and persistent, refer to needing attitudes such as respect, liking, and warmth from other people. However, for Rogers, to facilitate an individual's growth, the positive regard should be given without conditions. Unconditional positive regard, a key concept in his theory, is synonymous with acceptance and prizing; in this form of positive regard, there is literally no judgment or evaluation of the person or his or her behaviors. As a result of receiving unconditional positive regard, all self-experience is equal and allowed into awareness. The need for positive self-regard is an extension of the need for positive regard by others and is presumed to be learned through the incorporation of positive regard from others. As with positive regard from others, the highest form of positive self-regard is the unconditional type.

Rogers postulated that problems develop when the need for positive regard from significant others overrides the organismic valuing process, which is anchored to experiencing and the actualizing tendency. When children, for example, do not receive unconditional positive regard, they become conditioned to focus their behavior and selectively attend to their experiences that do receive positive regard from parents. This process subverts the naturally occurring organismic valuing process by which the organism attends to stimuli and engages in behaviors that maintain and enhance both the organism and the self—in concert with the actualizing tendency. To illustrate this, Rogers provided an example of an "infant who at one moment values food, and when satiated, is disgusted with it; at one moment values stimulation, and soon after, values only rest; who finds satisfying that diet which in the long run most enhances its development" (1959, p. 210). This example also illustrates the related notion of locus of evaluation. In self theory, this could either be internal or external. The example illustrates internal locus of evaluation. Left to his or her own devices, the infant is the center of the valuing process; what is of importance is determined by sensory experience. When the locus of evaluation is external, the judgment of others becomes the criterion determining the value of an event or object.

Related to external locus of evaluation is the concept of conditions of worth, italicized to indicate its importance in self theory. Conditions of worth are created when positive regard, dispensed by significant others, is contingent on what those significant others perceive to be worthy based on their standards and values. Over time, such feedback from significant others is incorporated into individuals' self-concepts. Assimilated conditions of worth serve to impose values on experiences, not because of their intrinsic value, but because certain experiences and behaviors have satisfied the need for positive regard from significant others. In this way, the locus of evaluation shifts from internal to external—to society—meaning that values are not created by the organismic valuing process but rather by the opinions of others. In the process, conditions of worth interfere with accurate symbolization of experience. Individuals decide upon the value of experiences as positive or negative as if they were applying the actualizing tendency, when they are actually using external criteria that have been introjected. With the valuing process disturbed, individuals' ability to function effectively and freely is reduced.

Conditions of worth, once incorporated into self-concept, produce selective perception of experience, which ultimately has negative psychological consequences for individuals. Experiences that are consistent with the conditions of worth are accurately symbolized; experiences that are inconsistent with the conditions of worth are distorted or denied awareness. What this means is that some of the experiences occurring in the organism are not allowed into awareness; the experiences are not recognized as self-experiences. In this fashion, the conditions of worth, by producing incongruence between self and experience, lead to psychological maladjustment. Incongruence is a state of tension and confusion. For Rogers, as conditions of worth increase, so does incongruence with proportionate increases in psychological maladjustment.

Rogers postulated that the source of maladjustment is internal conflict, because with the incorporation of the conditions of worth, the organism no longer acts as a whole. This fragmentation is reflected in behaviors. Some behaviors will be motivated by the conditions of worth; other behaviors by the actualizing tendency. For Rogers, when conditions of worth are involved, the tendency to self-actualize is a partial actualization of the organism's experiences—only those that have been symbolized as the self-concept will be actualized. Neurotic behavior, which is incomprehensible to the individual him- or herself, is one result of this conflict: "What is commonly called neurotic behavior is one example; the neurotic behavior is incomprehensible to the individual himself, since it is at variance with what he consciously 'wants' to do, which is to actualize a self no longer congruent with experience" (Rogers, 1959, p. 203). This conflict and the severity of the maladjustment intensify as conditions of worth become a greater influence on the self with the ensuing selective handling of one's experiencing.

Some experiences that are inconsistent with the self-concept are subceived—perceived as threatening without symbolizing into awareness (Rogers, 1959). If such experiences were symbolized for what they actually are, they would have a drastic effect on the self-concept. Awareness of such experiences would shatter the organization of the self-concept, because they run counter to the conditions of worth. A state of anxiety would ensue. To counter this eventuality, defenses are activated. For Rogers, defenses included selective perception, distortion, and denial. In the course of protecting the gestalt structure of the self, defensiveness produce rigidity in perception and inaccurate perception of reality.

The description of self theory to this point involves concepts and processes that are universal, but Rogers also included concepts and processes that occur only under certain circumstances. These include disorganization, reintegration, and the fully functioning person.

Disorganization is a rather serious state of distress caused by the failure of defenses. The integrity of self-concept is ruptured by the failure of the individual to deny or distort a threatening experience. The discrepancy between self-concept and the awareness of the experience produces intense anxiety. The state of disorganization manifests in fluctuations of behaviors; some behaviors are motivated by the experience newly admitted into awareness; other behaviors are motivated by the existing self-concept. Disorganization is an extreme form of "the basic estrangement" (Rogers, 1959, p. 226) of humanity, which has its origins in the conditions of worth. Severe maladjustment is associated with disorganization, and Rogers was not optimistic about the prognosis for individuals who experience it.

As one can see, in self theory, the conditions of worth are the cause of psychological maladjustment. The communication of these conditions causes infants to move away from their naturally occurring integrated state, thereby subverting the natural organismic valuing system. Seeking positive regard from others becomes the primary motivation. Attaining positive regard from others requires distortion and denying of experiences that are inconsistent with others' values. The need for positive regard gives rise to defensiveness. Defensiveness creates neurotic and psychotic behaviors. Unlike his view of disorganization representing a failure of defensiveness, Rogers stated that neurotic and some psychotic conditions brought about by defensiveness can be treated successfully. The process by which individuals may approximate the original organismic valuing process and actualizing tendency is reintegration.

Reintegration is a twofold process of elimination of defensiveness and assimilation of a previously threatening experience into the self-structure. For Rogers, reintegration rests on individuals' experiencing an increase of unconditional positive regard with the concomitant reduction in conditions of worth. Empathic understanding is the way that unconditional positive regard is communicated. Through empathic understanding, individuals' perception of threat is reduced, with the concomitant reduction in the need for defense. With a lessening of perception of threat, individuals allow awareness of experience and integrate it into the self-concept. Rogers noted that this process of reintegration rests squarely on feedback from other people:

> *[T]he reintegration or restoration of personality occurs always and only...in the presence of certain definable conditions [unconditional positive regard and empathic communication]. These are essentially the same whether we are speaking of formal psychotherapy continued over a considerable period, in which rather drastic personality changes may occur, or whether we are speaking of the minor constructive changes which may be brought about by contact with an understanding friend or family member* (1959, p. 231).

Reintegration cannot be accomplished through individual effort. This restorative process occurs within a relationship in which an individual experiences unconditional positive regard from a significant other. With ongoing receipt of this acceptance and prizing by another, a series of events is triggered that are necessary for reaching the pinnacle of human development. With the empathically communicated unconditional positive regard, individuals dramatically reduce the perception of threat in their experiences. They significantly reduce the need for defensives, and self and experience become more congruent. Positive regard for others increases with increase in self-regard. In the reintegration process, the person becomes fully functioning.

Rogers used various terms to describe the fully functioning person, including "the goal of social evolution" and "the end point of optimal psychotherapy;" however, I think that the best phrase, congruent with his theory, is "the ultimate in the actualization of the human organism" (1959, p. 234). The fully functioning person is attuned to the actualizing tendency and organismic valuing system. The self-structure is consistent with the individual's experiencing. Such individuals are also open to experience; all experiences are allowed into awareness. With no need for external regard, the individual experiences unconditional positive self-regard, which is also extended to others. Rogers' depiction of optimal psychological adjustment and maturity is not static—that is, the fully functioning person is a "person-in-process" (1959, p. 235). There are certain factors that are absent in the fully functioning person. These include conditions of worth, incongruence, and external locus of evaluation.

Positive Disintegration

Dąbrowski proposed five levels of development representing different forms of integration and disintegration. Progression through the levels is neither universal nor linear. In psychoanalysis, individuals are presumed to experience the three pregenital stages unless fixation occurs, though not everyone reaches the genital stage—the psychoanalytical pinnacle of development. Reaching the genital stage is premised on one's handling of the societal prescriptions; presumably, the less restrictive the social environment is regarding sexual gratification, the better it is for individual development. An environment with fewer taboos seemingly facilitates individuals' achievement of the genital stage and psychological maturity. In self theory, only those who experience sufficient unconditional positive regard by significant others, communicated empathically, will become fully functioning. In both of these theories, advanced development is largely dependent on the social environment. In positive disintegration, advanced development is premised on favorable constitutional endowment. Such endowment, reflected in developmental potential, spurs individuals into the process of development. Personality is achieved through the internal process of positive disintegration, which is responsible for the destruction of an individual's original primitive mental organization, and a reintegration at a higher level of functioning culminating in secondary integration.

The primitive or primary integration, Level I, is not considered healthy, because at this level, individuals are motivated by their biological need and the need to comply with societal norms. Dąbrowski proposed two subgroups of individuals who are at the first level: highly socialized individuals, and sociopaths. Many of the primitively integrated individuals, though potentially successful materially, lead an unexamined life. Such individuals are not considered unworthy or evil by Dąbrowski; in fact, they may be perceived as "the salt of the earth" types. They simply are prisoners either of their biological drives and/or the need to unquestionably conform to societal standards.

The other subgroup, however, is more notorious and dangerous. Such individuals typically use their personal resources, such as intelligence, to take advantage of others to gratify their egocentric needs and, in extreme cases, to gratify their needs regardless of the consequences to others and themselves. Individuals' integrated mental organization is at the service of biological needs and/or compliance with society.

Dąbrowski's view of integration is different from other theorists' (such as Rogers') use of the term. Integration has traditionally been thought of as a positive psychological quality. In positive disintegration, only secondary integration, the final level of development, is seen as positive in terms of psychological health.

The mental organization associated with primary integration needs to be loosened before an individual can move to the next level. The process of undoing and ultimately destroying the existing mental organization is performed by dynamisms, autonomous forces that are part of developmental potential. Initially, dynamisms are triggered by developmental milestones, such as puberty, or crises in the social environment. Such experiences serve to disrupt mental equilibrium, creating a state of ambiguity where structure and predictability once existed. Level II, unilevel disintegration, is in essence a transition level; because of the high anxiety associated with it, individuals either return to primary integration or move to Level III, spontaneous multilevel disintegration.

In contrast to the ambivalences experienced in unilevel disintegration in Level II, disintegration is multilevel and spontaneous in Level III. It is called multilevel because individuals begin to experience phenomena in a hierarchical way: some feelings, attitudes, and behaviors are perceived to be more valuable than others. It is in this phase of development that individuals experience the internal conflict arising from their experiencing the discrepancy between how the world ought to be and the way it actually is. It is called spontaneous because it is not under the direction of the person. A variety of dynamisms operate at this level—including feelings of shame and guilt, astonishment with oneself, and dissatisfaction with self—to extend the loosening of the mental organization begun in Level II and form the disintegration process.

In contrast to the spontaneous quality of the disintegration in Level III, disintegration in Level IV is organized and multilevel—that is, it is under the deliberate control of the individual. At this level, human functioning is driven by dynamisms of empathy, autonomy, authenticity, and the third factor, which coordinates the operation of the dynamisms. In addition, the dynamisms of self-education and autopsychotherapy appear, motivating individuals to identify areas of improvement and to develop their own strategies to meet those needs. Dynamisms at this level begin the reintegration process.

Level V completes the reintegration process with the achievement of personality. The only novel dynamism at this final level is one's personality ideal, which individuals use to guide their daily behaviors. Individuals at Level V have achieved personality and represent the epitome of humanity.

The levels of development represent the process of positive disintegration. Positive disintegration is a combination of disintegration and reintegration at a higher level. It is defined by the positive outcome of the process. In Dąbrowski's theory, there is also negative disintegration—that is, a disintegrative process that ends in negative outcomes, such as suicide. In both cases, however, "disintegration" is different from its use by Freud or Rogers. In both psychoanalysis and self theory, disintegration is always negative, representing a failure of defensiveness. In both of those theories, defensiveness is seen as necessary for psychological adjustment. Implicit in Freud's and Rogers' views is that unconsciousness or lack of awareness is associated with adjustment. With ideal environmental conditions, this would not be the case, but because of societal taboos regarding sex or because of the conditions of worth present in the social environment, a certain amount of unconsciousness is required.

On the other hand, Dąbrowski's disintegration is not the product of a breakdown of defenses, but rather the result of a disruption of mental equilibrium brought about primarily by autonomous inner forces, specifically the dynamisms. Although Dąbrowski uses defensive terms such as "sublimation," their use lacks the unconscious quality associated with their use by Freud or Rogers. In fact, for Dąbrowski, psychological development is a progression from an unconscious approach to life to an increasingly conscious appreciation of self and society. Awareness of one's nature, including self-preservation and sexual instincts, enables its transformation from an animal-like state to one of being truly human.

Similarly, Rogers' use of reintegration is different from Dąbrowski's. For Rogers, reintegration refers to assimilation of a previously threatening experience into the self-structure by the elimination of defensiveness. Reintegration can only occur when individuals experience unconditional positive regard. For Dąbrowski, reintegration, as part of positive disintegration, occurs within an individual and is equated with the acquisition of a higher level of human functioning.

Similar contrasts can be seen in the terminology used by both Rogers and Dąbrowski. "Consistency" or "congruence" appears in both theories. However, Rogers spoke of congruence between self-concept and phenomenal field of experiencing, whereas Dąbrowski referred to consistency of behavior and values. Both use terms such as "autonomy" and "authenticity," and there is some overlap between Dąbrowski's view of personality and Rogers' fully functioning person. However, the process by which these arise and their role in personality development is explained by Dąbrowski and, largely, simply proclaimed by Rogers.

A related difference between positive disintegration and the other theories rests in how it sees psychopathology. This difference is particularly evident in the area of neuroses. What Freud and Rogers saw as something to be remedied, Dąbrowski saw as indicative of the potential for advanced development. To be precise, Dąbrowski spoke of psychoneuroses, which referred to mental processes, rather than neuroses, which he equated with psychosomatic conditions (Dąbrowski, 1972). The disintegration part of positive disintegration—the dynamisms such as shame, guilt, and dissatisfaction with oneself—are psychoneurotic symptoms serving the essential purpose of destroying the existing primitive mental structures. Not only are psychoneuroses not illnesses, they are essential for personality development. Psychoneurotic individuals are not to be treated with the intention of "curing" them; such individuals need to understand the essential contribution of their suffering to their development.

On a final note, unlike psychoanalysis, positive disintegration does not view values and morals as factors to be coped with or denied. They are to be lived. The contents of the superego are not to be rejected because the moral standards may be too high; they are to be scrutinized, and those inconsistent with an individual's hierarchy of values are discarded. Further, the pinnacle of human development is not the satisfaction of sexual instincts in all of its erogenous zones in mature relationships with others, but rather consciously living one's life consistent with one's ideals autonomously, authentically, and altruistically.

The Big Five and Positive Disintegration

The Big Five is a trait approach to personality that has immense popularity among those conducting psychological research in personality. Traits are also mentioned in the theory of positive disintegration, though Dąbrowski typically used "psychological types" to refer to them.

The Big Five

Also known as the Five Factor Model, the Big Five approach has its origin in the lexical approach to personality traits used by Allport and Odbert (1936). In their seminal work, they perused dictionaries to identify words that they deemed to have relevance for describing people. They amassed about 18,000 words, which they presented alphabetically and in four categories: (1) personality traits; (2) states, moods, and activities;(3) judgments of personality conduct and reputation; and (4) physical characteristics, capacities, and talents (John & Scrivastava, 1999). Of relevance to the development of the Big Five are those words categorized as personality traits, which Allport and Odbert defined as "generalized and personalized determining tendencies—consistent and stable modes of an individual's adjustment to his environment"(p. 26). As predicted by Allport and Odbert, their compilation of words did keep researchers busy for many years. Researchers working with the personality traits category ultimately discovered the Big Five trait taxonomy.

Cattell (1959) made a significant contribution to the development of the taxonomy of traits. Using a subset of 4,500 trait terms drawn from Allport and Odbert's list, Cattell extracted 35 variables, and in so doing, eliminated 99% of the terms on the original list (John & Scrivastava, 1999). From his factor analytic research with the variables, Cattell identified 12 personality factors that he included in his Sixteen Personality Factor Questionnaire (Cattell, Eber, & Tatsuoka, 1970). The discovery and clarification of the Big Five were accomplished by several researchers (e.g., Borgatta, 1964; Digman & Takemotto-Chock, 1981; Fiske, 1949, Norman, 1963; Tupes & Christal, 1992) working with Cattell's variable list.

The Big Five taxonomy consists of five higher-order personality traits or factors: Neuroticism, Extroversion, Openness to Experience, Agreeableness, and Conscientiousness (Chamorro-Premuzic, 2005). These factors have been found consistently, regardless of measurement technique used [e.g., self-report or expert rating (McCrae & Costa, 1999)] or specific scales [e.g., California Psychological Inventory (Gough, 1987), *Adjective Check List* (Gough & Heilbrun, 1983),

NEO Personality Inventory Revised (Costa & McCrae, 1992; John & Scrivastava, 1999)].

The best validated measure of the Big Five (John & Scrivastava, 1999), the NEO Personality Inventory Revised (NEO-PI-R) (Costa & McCrae, 1992) operationally defines the five factors with facets. *Neuroticism* consists of the following facets: anxiety, hostility, depression, self-consciousness, impulsiveness, and vulnerability; *Extroversion*: warmth, gregariousness, assertiveness, activity, excitement-seeking, and positive emotions; *Openness*: fantasy, aesthetics, feelings, actions, ideas, and values; *Agreeableness*: trust, straightforwardness, altruism, compliance, modesty, and tendermindedness; *Conscientiousness*: competence, order, dutifulness, achievement-striving, self-discipline, and deliberation.

The Five Factor Model of personality is not a theory of personality (McCrae & Costa, 1999), a fact that has led to some criticism of this approach to personality (e.g. Pervin, 1994). Instead, it is empirically derived and has its origins in words that the general population uses, rather than in the work of experts in psychology and psychiatry. There is a degree of overlap, however, between the terminology of the Big Five and personality theorists. For example, extroversion is part of Jung's (1933) elaborate framework of psychological types; openness to experience is one of Rogers' (1961) characteristics of fully functioning persons.

Positive Disintegration and Traits

For Dąbrowski, traits were inherited, molded by the environment, and included both temperamental qualities and qualities of character. Dąbrowski (1973) recognized others' approaches to traits and specifically referred to Jung's (1933) introversion and extroversion, Kretschmer's cylothymes and schiothymes (Roeckelein, 1998), and Sheldon's somatotypes (Sheldon & Stevens, 1942). Both Kretschmer and Sheldon were interested in relating constitutional types of psychiatric disorders. Jung proposed an elaborate typology that was founded on introversion and extroversion but also included functional modes. Jung's introversion and extroversion were not mutually exclusive categories. For example, when we describe a person as extroverted, in

Jungian terms, it means that extroversion is dominant and conscious within that person, and introversion is nondominant but active at the unconscious level (Maddi, 1989). Jung constructed his psychological types by adding four styles of experiencing, termed "functional modes": thinking, feeling, sensing, and intuiting. As a result, Jung described eight major types by combining the dominant factor with the functional modes.

Apparently borrowing Jung's phrase, Dąbrowski used *psychological types* to refer to all traits, including his own five forms of overexcitability. However, Dąbrowski was not interested in psychological types per se; he was not interested in distinguishing introverts from extroverts, associating body types and psychiatric disorders or body types and temperament. When it came to psychological types, *the* question for him related to transformation: "Is there any possibility of transformation of such psychological types as introverted and extraverted, cyclothymic and schizothymic; types of various kinds of mental hyperexcitability, such as emotional, imaginational, sensual, psychomotor or intellectual?" (Dąbrowski, 1973, p. 136). Transformation referred to both processes of sublimation and the acquiring of other traits, at times polar opposite to the pre-existing ones. Dąbrowski argued that such transformations of psychological types are possible and particularly evident in individuals' possessing favorable constitutional endowment—that is, in individuals who are endowed with the potential for accelerated or advanced development. Hereditary forces, then, provide the substrate for development of traits and, in some cases, the power to change their expression to higher forms (sublimation) and to add traits that are not there and not part of the original endowment (e.g., conscious introverts become both conscious extroverts as well as introverts).

Various facets of the Big Five are similar to concepts used in the theory of positive disintegration—for example, the facets of trust, altruism, tendermindedness, and straightforwardness of Agreeableness; and the warmth of Extroversion. Other traits would be descriptive of some forms of overexcitability—for example, activity and excitement-seeking of the psychomotor form; fantasy and aesthetics of imaginational; ideas of intellectual; and positive emotions, trust, and values of emotional overexcitability. However, value placed on some of the traits would likely differ from the interpretation of the Big Five. Neuroticism, with the exception of the facet of hostility, would be viewed as positive in positive disintegration. Anxiety, depression, self-consciousness, impulsiveness, and vulnerability are viewed as indicators of positive disintegration and as such are reframed as signifying development.

Conclusion

Positive disintegration includes many of the same components as the other approaches to personality, but the components are reframed. The basic instincts are to be transformed, not sated. The prescriptions of the social environment are to be transcended, not complied with. Conflict is rooted in individuals' values, not the product of frustration of needs. Ideals are to be lived, not attenuated. Neurotic symptoms are not to be remedied, but celebrated. Traits are not to be static, but dynamic. Unlike the other approaches, positive disintegration places values and morality front and center. Thoughts, feelings, and behaviors are viewed hierarchically, and development occurs as individuals move from their primitive forms to the more refined ones.

Dąbrowski proposed a distinctive theory of personality. The uniqueness of positive disintegration compels its students to become more aware of their taken-for-granted assumptions regarding personality and its development. Whether one becomes a devotee or not, examination of one's assumption and viewing concepts from a different perspective enhances the prospect of creativity. It may very well be that the process would include the destruction of rigidly held beliefs, causing distress in the reader, with a reintegration at a higher level of thinking about personality.

Reference

Mendaglio, S. (2008b). Dąbrowski's theory of positive disintegration (TPD and other approaches to personality. In S. Mendaglio (Ed.), *Dąbrowski's Theory of Positive Disintegration* (pp. 249-274). Scottsdale, AZ: Great Potential Press.

CHAPTER 6

Academic Dialogue on Dąbrowski's theory

As with other domains of academic pursuits, differences of opinion abound in the field of gifted education. Of particular importance is divergence of opinions in conceptual foundations of a discipline: its constructs and theories. With respect to constructs, divergence in defining giftedness flourishes. Expressions of differences in definitions of giftedness are typically publications in which proponents argue for their positions. Similarly with theories, advocates of a theory publish their interpretation of it. In neither the case of constructs nor theories do proponents and critics engage in scholarly dialogue to air their differences. By formal academic dialogue, I mean a critic replies to a proponent's position, followed by the proponent's rejoinder to the critic's response. I firmly believe that such dialogue is an essential ingredient to keep a theory—including Dąbrowski's theory—vibrant. For this belief I have been influenced by a statement made by Aronson (1978, p. 215):

> *What kills a theory? Thomas Huxley once identified one of the great tragedies of science as the slaying of a beautiful theory by an ugly fact. Although facts (ugly or otherwise) may slay theories in the* natural *sciences, in the* social *sciences, what generally kills a theory is benign neglect—by its critics as well as by its advocates (italics in original).*

This chapter contains an article that was part of an academic dialogue regarding the theory of positive disintegration. Piechowski's

(2014) commentary on Dąbrowski's theory sparked a reply, coauthored with William Tillier, reproduced in this chapter. Following our reply, Piechowski published a rejoinder (Piechowski, 2015). All three articles appeared in *Roeper Review.*

References

Aronson, E. (1979). The theory of cognitive dissonance: Current perspective. In L. Bekowitz (Ed.), *Cognitive theories in social psychology*, pp. 215-221). NY: Academic Press.

Piechowski, M. M. (2015). A Reply to Mendaglio and Tillier. *Roeper Review, 37*(4), 229–233.

Piechowski, M. (2014). Rethinking Dąbrowski's Theory: I. The Case Against Primary Integration. *Roeper Review, 36*(1), 11–17.

Mendaglio, S., & Tillier, W. (2015). Has the Time Come to Emulate Jung? A Response to Piechowski's Most Recent Rethinking of the Theory of Positive Disintegration: I. The Case Against Primary Integration. *Roeper Review, 37*(4), 219–228. https://doi-org.ezproxy.lib.ucalgary.ca/10.1080/02783193.2015.1077495

Has the Time Come to Emulate Jung?

A Response to Piechowski's Most Recent Rethinking of the Theory of Positive Disintegration:

I. The Case Against Primary Integration

Sal Mendaglio and William Tillier

Disagreements between theorists and their collaborators are as old as the field of psychology itself. The most well-known example of a professional relationship marked by diverging viewpoints in psychology is that of Sigmund Freud and Carl Jung. Theoretical disagreements between them were resolved by Jung's creation of a new theory. In this article, the authors suggest that, in the field of gifted education, there exists a significant theoretical disagreement analogous to that of Freud and Jung, namely, that of Dąbrowski and Piechowski. Though the analogy to Freud-Jung does not hold at the personal relationship level, the authors of this article argue that it is a valid analogy at the theoretical level. Acknowledged by Piechowski, in the context of their genial and collaborative relations, there was a disagreement regarding a key concept of Theory of Positive Disintegration (TPD). That disagreement was discussed orally between Dąbrowski and Piechowski; the other areas of Piechowski's disagreement have been presented in a series of articles. Piechowski (2014) is the most current of these articles. In responding to Piechowski (2014), the authors present both areas of agreement and disagreement with Piechowski's case against primary disintegration. We conclude with the recommendation that Piechowski emulate Jung, not intended as criticism but rather as way of resolving his disagreement with Dąbrowski's original theorizing.

Piechowski (2014) argued against primary integration, a central concept in Dąbrowski's theory of positive disintegration (TPD). This is not the first time that Piechowski articulated his theoretical disagreement with Dąbrowski's theory (e.g., Piechowski, 1978, 2002, 2003, 2008). Given the title of the 2014 article, it seems that he plans to share with us further "rethinkings" of TPD. With a history of and prospect of more disagreements to come, we wonder whether it is time for Piechowski to propose his own theory or version of TPD.

As we prepared our response to Piechowski (2014), we were reminded of another disagreement among scholars working with the same theory. We thought of the theoretical differences between Sigmund Freud and Carl Jung. Drawn together by their commonalities, Freud and Jung had an intense relationship beginning in 1906, lasting until 1913. However, Jung increasingly developed his own interpretations and disagreed with Freud on some major issues; for example, on the nature and role of religion. Jung went on to continue to differentiate and develop his views, producing a large body of his own unique work. We believe that the Freud-Jung analogy is appropriate to illustrate our point of how significant theoretical disagreements can be resolved by a dissenter proposing his or her own theory. In all other respects, the analogy does not hold—unlike Freud and Jung, the personal relationship between Piechowski and Dąbrowski was "close and friendly" (M. Piechowski, personal communication, June 3, 2015).

Piechowski (2008) noted that meeting Dąbrowski in Edmonton in the winter of 1967 made a significant impression on Piechowski, so much so that he left his career as a microbiologist at the University of Alberta and began a "close collaboration," with Dąbrowski, that "continued until 1975" (pp. 45–46). Piechowski undertook the study of counseling, leaving Edmonton in January 1970 to begin work on a doctorate at the University of Wisconsin (Piechowski, 2008). Piechowski worked closely with Dąbrowski for 8 years; their close personal relationship lasted 10 years. Unlike Freud and Jung, during the duration of their collaboration, there appeared to be only one significant theoretical disagreement: Dąbrowski objected to Piechowski equating Level IV with Maslow's concept of self-actualization

(Piechowski, 1978). Piechowski (e.g., 1979, 1986, 1991) went on to promote overexcitability in the gifted education field and to criticize TPD, suggesting a series of changes to it (e.g., Piechowski, 2002, 2008). In the current iteration of his disagreement with Dąbrowski's presentation of TPD, Piechowski continues to take issue with a fundamental construct of Dąbrowski's theory: primary integration.

On the basis of Piechowski's past and continuing publications indicating significant theoretical divergence from TPD, we suggest two alternatives: (a) Piechowski might differentiate his work from that of the originator of the theory as Jung did and propose his own theory under his own name or, alternatively, (b) he could take the approach that Robbie Case did in developing a neo-Piagetian theory (Case, 1985, 1992) and integrate his views in a neo-Dąbrowskian conceptualization, amending TPD to reflect a Piechowskian perspective. We believe that our response provides evidence for our suggestion to Piechowski.

From Agreements to Strong Disagreements

In our reading of Piechowski (2014), we conclude that we can wholeheartedly agree with some points raised and partially agree with other points. However, we strongly disagree with the core of the article. We judge that there is a lack of evidence to support the case against primary integration.

We support Piechowski's call for an examination of TPD in light of accumulated psychological research. We agree with Piechowski (2014) when he states:

> *[L]ittle effort has been directed toward examining its defining concepts (Mendaglio, 2008; Zielinski, 1997). Terms like* developmental potential, disintegration versus integration, levels, dynamisms, and multilevel versus unilevel process *call for examination in the light of accumulated knowledge.... (p. 11, emphasis in original)*

We agree that researchers in the gifted field have shown little interest in these important constructs[1] with the research focused almost exclusively on overexcitability (Pyryt, 2008). This may be

1. These are not concepts; they are constructs (Slaney & Racine, 2013).

due in part to historical reasons. Piechowski's introduction of TPD mainly emphasized the construct of overexcitability in the gifted field (see Piechowski, 2008). The idea was operationalized in the Overexcitability Questionnaire (Lysy & Piechowski, 1983). Falk, Lind, Miller, Piechowski, and Silverman (1999) later developed a revised instrument (the Overexcitability Questionnaire–II). The ready availability of these questionnaires stimulated many studies focused solely on overexcitability. Mendaglio and Tillier (2006) summarized this research.

Though empirical investigation of Dąbrowskian constructs is preferred to refine the theory, given the current state of research on TPD, extant psychological research relating directly or indirectly to TPD must be used. Of course, the selection of research studies to shed new light on a theory depends on the author who is conducting the task. We applaud Piechowski for providing an example of how this strategy may be applied. As the reader will see later, though, we disagree with his interpretation of the psychological research he selected to present his case.

Perhaps the most basic issue raised by Piechowski (2014), which we support, is how to describe Dąbrowski's theory. Dąbrowski called his work the *theory of positive disintegration* to emphasize the necessary and vital role he saw for disintegration in personality development. In general terms, Dąbrowski referred to his theory as describing "personality development" (Aronson, 1964, p. xii). The description of the theory by others often depends on their emphasis and use of theory. For example, William Hague (1986, 1995) used the theory in the study of moral development and therefore emphasized its role in this context. Others have described the theory primarily in the context of the gifted field, for example: "the only psychological theory specific to the development of giftedness and creativity" (Silverman, 1992, p.6).

Related to how to describe the theory is the inconsistent titling of the theory. This has created some confusion because authors use various titles for TPD. For example, Silverman (Silverman, 1983, 1993a, 1993b) used Dąbrowski's theory of emotional development as the title of the theory. Some have used both titles; for example, Piirto (1997, p. 7) referred to "explorations into the Dąbrowski Theory of

Positive Disintegration (as it is called in Canada, or of Emotional Development as it is called in the United States)." Sisk (2008, p. 26) also referred to the theory using both titles: "Dąbrowski's... Theory of Positive Disintegration, also known as the Theory of Emotional Development." In a 2008 lecture given in Calgary, Canada, Piechowski used the title Dąbrowski's theory of *emotional development through positive disintegration.* It is our position that no one author is responsible for this inconsistency; however, we concur with Piechowski's distinction and we ask future authors to use the proper name: *Dąbrowski's theory of positive disintegration.*

We can only partially agree with the section of Piechowski (2014) entitled "Common Errors." That errors are present in some authors' representation of TPD is apparent by a perusal of publications in gifted education. Our support for this part of the article is limited because, ironically, we found that, in attempting to rectify some errors, new errors were created. In the second section, "Misleading Terms," we take issue with the title. *Misleading* may imply *deceptive*, *false*, or *disingenuous*. Perhaps the word was used in the sense of *confusing* or *ambiguous*. We find that a careful reading of Dąbrowski's own words indicates that terms are not misleading in any sense of the word. Admittedly, his books pose a challenge to readers, but those who persevere will find clarity of expression. Having said that, we believe that TPD terms need operationalization and modernization. In addition, similar to other theorists whose work spans decades, we should expect some evolution in Dąbrowski's thinking over time.

Following the section on misleading terms, the remainder of Piechowski's article deals primarily with his case against primary integration. In reading it, we do not find his argument for eliminating or reframing primary integration convincing due largely to our interpretation of the research he used to support his case. For our detailed response to Piechowski's "rethinking," we have chosen to confine our comments to the sections of the article dealing with common errors and the argument against primary integration.

Common Errors

To begin, our use of *error* needs explanation. In our view, authors commit errors when they misrepresent TPD constructs and when they mistakenly attribute ideas or statements to Dąbrowski. The standard by which we identify errors is Dąbrowski's writing: authors' statements are compared to Dąbrowski's presentation of his TPD; errors occur when authors' have diverged from the written record. It is important to note that we differentiate error from *disagreement*. In presenting disagreements with TPD, one should accurately present Dąbrowski's position and then critique it. In his article, Piechowski provides several good examples of how to present disagreements. In the presentation of our disagreements, we, too, follow that procedure: stating Piechowski's claim, often using his words, before we provide our position. We are aware that it is usual practice to use paraphrases rather than direct quotations, which normally should be used sparingly. However, given the nature of the task at hand, the use of Piechowski's and Dąbrowski's own words is required to support our disagreements.

Piechowski (2014) lists six errors that serve to obscure TPD. Describing the first error, Piechowski (2014, pp. 11–12) says, "To refer to the theory of positive disintegration as a stage theory confuses the different meanings of *stage* and *level*" (emphases in original). Dąbrowski and his coauthors often used the words *stage* and *level* interchangeably. However, the term *stage theory* does not appear, to our knowledge, in any of the works, and Dąbrowski (1996) clearly delineated the two constructs, level and stage: "A level is a distinct identifiable developmental structure. It is not a temporal sequence, which makes it distinct from a stage" (p. 17). We agree with Piechowski that to equate level and stage, when stage implies stage theory, is erroneous.

Piechowski (2014) notes that the second error flows from the first error:

> *To refer to the* stages *of positive disintegration as realizable within one lifetime follows hypnotically from Error 1, because stages suggest development through the life span. The mistake is to equate the scale of levels with an ontogenetic sequence. (p. 12, emphasis in original)*

We agree that it is mistaken to view the realization of positive disintegration through a succession of stages and to view it as normal life span development. What we strongly disagree with is what immediately follows these statements—Piechowski accuses Dąbrowski of making this error! He proclaims: "Paradoxically Dąbrowski himself slipped at one point and committed both errors" (Piechowski, 2014, p. 12). To support this allegation, he draws on a hypothesis from a list of hypotheses proposed by Dąbrowski and Kawczak (Dąbrowski, 1970), providing direction for future research on TPD. Ironically, Piechowski himself makes a mistake because he does not quote the entire hypothesis. He comments on hypothesis 2 (Dąbrowski, 1970) as follows:

> *In hypothesis 2 they [Dąbrowski and Kawczak] said: "The full cycle of ontogenetic development of man includes five main stages" and then listed the levels of development through positive disintegration. The two basic errors are: saying that development through positive disintegration goes through stages, and they fit into the stages of life span development.* (Piechowski, 2014,p.12)

However, Dąbrowski (1970) went on in the subsequent sentences to qualify that the hypothesis does not apply to development in general, only to cases displaying *full* potential leading to advanced (and rare) development:

> *This hypothesis [hypothesis 2] should not be interpreted as a classification, a mere typology, but rather as a type of biological generalization, since it refers to every individual* that possesses the full endowment and developmental potential *peculiar to this species. This claim is based on the temporal sequence of the above five stages, their irreversibility, and on already known mechanisms of causal connection.* (Dąbrowski, 1970, p. 132, emphasis added)

As previously mentioned, Piechowski (2014, p. 12) says that Dąbrowski's "mistake is to equate the scale of levels with an ontogenetic sequence." Dąbrowski (1996) explained his approach:

> *Available theories of development appear bound to an ontogenetic approach. It is our contention that a general theory must look at development as a more general sequence of evolving patterns of organization of behavior. This leads to a discovery of developmental sequences which may occur in some ontogenetic paths but be absent from others. The comparison of these paths will then lead to a more extended overall picture of development that can occur but does not always occur.* (p. 7)

Dąbrowski (1970) recognized two qualitatively different types of mental life and development. First, there is a *heteronomous* form governed by biological and or environmental forces. Dąbrowski said that this form, commonly seen in primary integration, follows ontogenetic development. Dąbrowski identified other broad dimensions of mental life and development that also display ontogenetic growth; for example, the development of instincts (Dąbrowski, 1970).

Dąbrowski could not observe an "ontogenetic pattern of stages of emotional growth." He concluded: "Emotional development [is] a nonontogenetic evolutionary pattern of individual growth. This means that the *level* of emotional functioning is not produced automatically in the course of ontogenesis but evolves as a function of other conditions" (Dąbrowski, 1996, p. 9, emphasis in original). The second form of development Dąbrowski described, the *autonomous*, is qualitatively different from the first. This form consists of self-determination and self-consciousness in a new type of self-controlled, volitional mental growth that transcends the biological life cycle. For Dąbrowski, the development of autonomy, expressed through volitional action, must overcome ontogeny: "We think that, as a rule, the act of volition is a serial, chain operation, connected with many conflicts, many resistances, many overcomings on the road to phylogenetic and ontogenetic development" (Dąbrowski, 1967, p. 123). One should note that Piechowski (1974, p. 90) initially endorsed this dual approach to development: "In many individuals their personal evolution is indistinguishable from the sequence of stages of the life cycle (normal development) while others transcend the life cycle; their development proceeds with higher intensity and at a greater pace (accelerated development)."

Regarding Error 3, Piechowski (2014) states: "The concept of *overexcitabilities* is often erroneously called a *theory of overexcitabilities*" (p. 12, emphasis in original). We agree that it is mistaken because overexcitability is only one of numerous constructs that comprise TPD. (We discussed this issue earlier in the article indicating our agreement that authors should use the proper title when referring to TPD.)

As with Error 3, we concur with Piechowski's Error 4, namely, that "to regard with disdain Level II and the process of unilevel disintegration is an error" (Piechowski, 2014, p. 12). Nowhere in Dąbrowski's writings do we encounter an attitude of contempt in his descriptions of unilevel disintegration. To say, as Piechowski does, that "an enormous amount of human suffering and unhappiness is bound here [unilevel disintegration]" (Piechowski, 2014, p. 12) is consistent with Dąbrowski's depiction of this level of development (Dąbrowski, 1996). From the very beginning, Dąbrowski (1929, 1937) was concerned about the possibility of self-destructive behaviors and suicide in those undergoing disintegration. These potential developmental stresses are highest during unilevel disintegration, and Dąbrowski (1972) said that the possibility of progressive development was "the defense (protection) and prophylaxis against serious mental disorders or suicide" (p. 136). The suffering and disharmony experienced in level two are not viewed disdainfully; they are celebrated. The loosening of the mental structures of primary integration enable the opportunity for true development and therefore play a critically important role.

In Error 5, Piechowski (2014) expresses concern over "confabulation" (p. 12) of opinions expressed by Dąbrowski in personal conversations regarding the written corpus of his theory, meaning that what was heard only in conversations was taken as a formal part of TPD. As an example, Piechowski asserts that Dąbrowski's view of sensual and psychomotor overexcitabilities (OEs) as "lower forms" is not a formal part of TPD, simply an opinion expressed in the course of conversations. That sensual and psychomotor OEs are lower forms is part of the written record (Dąbrowski, 1973). Dąbrowski (1996,

p. 16) said: "Great strength of the psychomotor and the sensual forms limits development to the lowest levels only." Negative development or one-sided development is the product of these two OEs when they occur in isolation. However, when combined with the big three OEs (emotional, imaginational, and intellectual), sensual and psychomotor are transformed and serve, among other things, to energize individuals. Piechowski's analysis, suggesting that exemplars of humanity (e.g., Gandhi and Peace Pilgrim) manifest a great deal of energy and that great writers (e.g., Rumi and Omar Khyaam) display heightened sensuality, is not an appropriate critique of Dąbrowski's theory—in fact, this is consistent with TPD: When the other three OEs are present, psychomotor and sensual OEs are harnessed to serve the higher aims of individuals. In exemplars noted by Piechowski, psychomotor and sensual OEs are present but transformed.

According to Dąbrowski, ideal exemplars of development will exhibit strong expressions of all five forms (as Dąbrowski did personally). Dąbrowski (1972) said that in higher development, the *expression* of sensual and psychomotor overexcitabilities will be transformed and they will play an important role:

> *Some forms of overexcitability constitute a richer developmental potential than others. Emotional (affective), imaginational and intellectual overexcitability are the richer forms. If they appear together they give rich possibilities of development and creativity. If these three forms of overexcitability are combined with the sensual and psychomotoric then these latter two are both enriched and enhanced in their positive developmental possibilities.* (pp. 7–8)

Dąbrowski elaborated: "When the psychomotor and sensual overexcitability come under the control of the other three forms of overexcitability they lose their isolated character and leave their single plane of operation" (1972, p. 130). He continued: "Psychomotor overexcitability is transformed into a strong dynamic ability of planning and carrying out one's goals, while sensual overexcitability develops into a hierarchical sensitivity acting towards seeking delights on higher levels of experience" (1972, p. 131). Piechowski also initially included all five forms of OE, saying: "The developmental potential is strong if all, or almost all, forms of overexcitability are present" (1974, p. 91).

The final error, Error 6, refers to the use of *emotional development* to designate Dąbrowski's theory: "To see a generic reference to the theory, *Dąbrowski's theory of emotional development*, as a substitution of its proper name, *theory of positive disintegration* is an error. . . ." (Piechowski, 2014, p. 12). As we have noted earlier, we agree that authors should use the proper name for Dąbrowski's theory of personality.

Our response to this point is composed of a combination of agreements and disagreements with points Piechowski raised. We agree with the need to shed new light on TPD; ideally this should be done through empirical investigations, though in the lack of such evidence, we agree with the use of psychological research findings. Specifically, we support the importance, as Piechowski noted, of investigating other constructs of TPD beyond OE. Consistent use of the proper title of TPD is another point with which we agree. Our reading of the section on common errors resulted in both agreements and disagreements. Regardless, we do appreciate Piechowski's drawing formal attention to the matter that we also have observed: authors have made errors—when compared to Dąbrowski's publications—when referring to and describing TPD. Now, we turn to the core of the Piechowski's article with which we strongly disagree.

Piechowski's Case Against Primary Integration

The bases for his case against primary integration include Piechowski's criticisms of inconsistency in Dąbrowski's descriptions of primary integration, use of both the terms *primary* and *integration*, and its genetic basis.

Lack of Consistency

Piechowski notes that no consistent picture can be found in Dąbrowski's descriptions of primary integration. "They range from psychopathic to normal. . . ."(2014, p. 13). A perusal of Dąbrowski's books reveals, in fact, a consistent picture. There are numerous examples of Dąbrowski's discussion of primary integration in ways that reflect the definition that Piechowski quotes (Dąbrowski, 1970, cited in Piechowski, 2014). For example, in an earlier detailed discussion in which the term *primitive* (a synonym for *primary*) is used, Dąbrowski (1964) stated:

> *Primitive integration is characterized by a compact and automatic structure of impulses to which the intelligence is a completely subordinated instrument. The adaptation to reality in individuals with primitive psychic integration is limited to direct and immediate satisfaction of strong primitive needs. Such individuals either do not possess psychic internal environment or possess it in only its embryonic phase. Therefore, they are not capable of having internal conflicts, although they often have conflicts with their external environment. They are unaware of any qualities of life beyond those necessary for immediate gratification of their primitive impulses, and they act solely on behalf of their impulses.* (p. 4)

Central themes such as impulse gratification, mental functions including intelligence subordinated to primitive drives, and lack of internal conflict are evident in Dąbrowski's various references to primary integration in his English-language books from 1964 to 1996.

Piechowski's impression that the descriptions range from psychopathic to normal is not evidence of inconsistency in the descriptions: Dąbrowski's reference to these terms was to explain subtypes of primitive integration:

> *Psychopaths are among those with primitive integration structure. They are characterized by a stable integration at a low level, and their activities clearly reflect primitive impulses.... Among normal primitively integrated people, different degrees of cohesion of psychic structure can be distinguished.* (Dąbrowski, 1964, p. 66)

(Interested readers should note that Dąbrowski immediately follows this description with illustrative cases.)

Use of the Terms Primary and Integration

Those familiar with the theory know that there is another integration in TPD: secondary integration. In contrast to primary integration, secondary is the apex of human development according to TPD. One could argue with any theorist's choice of terms to label constructs. For example, Piaget used *egocentrism* to refer to a characteristic of early stages of cognitive development. One can argue that it was a misuse because for many of us egocentrism means *selfishness*. Piaget was clear that egocentrism was a cognitive process, not a moral one. Further, would Piechowski's criticism still hold if Dąbrowski consistently used *primitive* integration? We know that Dąbrowski used primary and primitive integration synonymously.

Piechowski takes issue with the use of *integration* because, among other things, integration, according to other theories such as Erikson's (1968), can occur no sooner than adolescence. It is acknowledged that Dąbrowski's theory is not a stage theory, meaning that Dąbrowski did not associate ages or stages of development with his constructs. In fact, it would have been inconsistent for him to associate levels and ages. Had he done that, it would be cause for criticism. To our knowledge, there are only oblique references to age in TPD. For example, OEs may be seen in young children. Puberty and menopause may spark disintegration processes. One may disagree with Dąbrowski's terminology, but his choice of terms and their definitions cannot be a focus of criticism; after all, TPD is his theory!

Genetic Basis of Primary Integration

To critique the genetic basis of primary integration, Piechowski (2014) draws upon some obscure and some well-known works in psychology. He uses these sources to support the crux of his argument that what Dąbrowski terms primary integration is explained by other constructs that have their origins in socialization practices—not genetics.

On the basis of one master's thesis (Schmidt, 1977), Piechowski (2014, p. 13) concluded that primary integration "largely corresponds to the concept of authoritarian personality" and therefore is not genetically inherited; it is the result of social pressures and conformity to authority. He further concludes that failure to develop character is the result of a lack of "love and caring" "in the formative years" and/or the impact of the "physical, sexual, and emotional abuse of children" (Piechowski, 2014, p. 13). We disagree with both assertions, namely, that primary integration corresponds to authoritarian personality and that poor socialization practices produce primary integration.

A comparison of types of primary integration, referred to earlier in this article, and the conceptualization of authoritarian personality serves to illustrate the differences in these terms. Dąbrowski (1964) differentiated primary integration into two subtypes: "A fairly high degree of primary integration is present in the average person; a very high degree of primary integration is present in the psychopath" (p. 121). Psychopaths satisfy their needs without regard for social conventions or for the feelings or welfare of others. Psychopaths can be further differentiated into those who cannot inhibit their behavior and become involved in the criminal justice system, versus a larger group who learn to manipulate the social system, feigning compliance in order to satisfy their wants (Babiak & Hare, 2006). Psychopaths follow internal motivations that reflect lower level instincts and ego desires.

Dąbrowski's approach to the average person was based upon a long history of philosophy starting with Plato's "prisoner" and perhaps reaching an apex in Nietzsche. We concur with Piechowski that no comprehensive description of primary integration appears in Dąbrowski's written works. Therefore, we use Henri Bergson, whose work influenced Dąbrowski, to illustrate his approach. The majority in primary integration constitute the average person. The individual unthinkingly follows the program that society has drawn up for him or her; as Bergson (1935) said, "In the ordinary way, we conform to our [social] obligations rather than think of them" (p. 9). One "goes along, to get along" because it is easier; the path is well traveled and marked. "A road has been marked out by society; it lies open before us, and we follow it; it would take more initiative to cut across country" (Bergson, 1935, p. 10).

As to ideas, Bergson (1935/2001) said that the average person adopts his or her ideas ready-made without any critical examination (Barnard, 2011). Ironically, although we can converse easily using these ideas, and we may defend them vigorously, they do not really belong to us; they are lifeless, external, impersonal, and "float on the surface, like dead leaves on the water of a pond" (Bergson, 1913/2001, p. 135). As Barnard (2011) elaborated, ideas reflecting our true selves and insights are only revealed when we dig deeply below the surface into "the deeper strata of the self" and that this task is extremely difficult and seldom attempted (Bergson, 1913/2001, p. 136). Bergson noted that because the deeper self is seldom experienced, it may be deeply felt emotionally when encountered but may be hard to understand and difficult to articulate and communicate to others. It was Dąbrowski's belief that because the average person primarily follows externally based mores and roles, he or she does not exhibit an authentic and unique personality.

Our reading of TPD suggests that Dąbrowski's conceptualization of psychopathic and average individuals differs significantly from the authoritarian personality. What is the authoritarian personality? During World War II, Nevitt Sanford was studying anti-Semitism and concluded that prejudice arose from deep emotional, personality-based needs (Sanford, 1986). Sanford joined a group of theorists investigating authoritarian potential who were studying American popular culture as fertile ground to create political totalitarianism (Jay, 1973). The team became concerned that the American population could be vulnerable to sympathizing with antidemocratic propaganda and they developed the F (fascist) scale to research the potentially fascistic individual. Their studies were collected and published in 1950 (Adorno, Frenkel-Brunswik, Levinson, & Sanford, 1950). Nine qualities were presented describing the authoritarian personality:

> *conventionalism; submission to in-group authority; authoritarian aggression; opposition to the subjective, the imaginative, the tenderminded; superstition, stereotypy; overemphasis upon the conventionalized attributes of the ego; exaggerated assertion of strength and toughness; destructiveness and cynicism; generalized hostility, vilification of the human; the disposition to believe that wild and dangerous things go on in the world; and an exaggerated concern with sexual "goings-on."* (Adorno et al., 1950, p. 228)

"As postulated, [these] characteristics resembled those of the sado-masochistic character" rooted in the work of Erich Fromm (Jay, 1973, pp. 239–240). Jay (1973) also noted that the term *totalitarian* would have been more accurate than *authoritarian*. Regardless of the severe criticisms of this research (see Martin, 2001; Ray,1990), we find it surprising that Piechowski would draw a comparison between either the psychopath or the average person and the authoritarian personality. Dąbrowski's description of primary integration and the accompanying subtypes, we believe, are significantly different from the concept of authoritarian personality.

Piechowski also cited contemporary authors to support his case. He (2014) cited Bandura's (1986) mechanisms in the "disengagement of one's conscience" leading to "what Dąbrowski saw as *psychopathic* behavior" (emphasis in original). Piechowski (2014) suggested that everyone has an "innate sense of right and wrong" and that "[psychopathic] behavior is not a personality structure but the consequence of a culture that increasingly puts distance between people" (p. 15). This conclusion disregards the large contemporary literature on psychopathy as it relates to personality constructs as well as the neurophysiological substrates that appear to underlie psychopathy. Contemporary research supports Dąbrowski's view of psychopathy (the lower sublevel of primary integration) as a genetic attribute of individuals (Berkout, Gross, & Kellum, 2013; Blair, 2013a, 2013b; Blair, Mitchell, & Blair, 2005; Ermer, Cope, Nyalakanti, Calhoun, & Kiehl, 2013; Herpers, Scheepers, Bons, Buitelaar, & Rommelse, 2014; Patrick, Durbin, & Moser, 2012; Raine, 2013).

Piechowski (2014) invoked Stanley Milgram's (1963) experiments to support the interpretation that primary integration is social in origin: a role, played as a result of the influence of an authority figure. Perry (2013) reviewed Milgram's original audiotapes and reported that Milgram's results were seriously biased and that Milgram acknowledged they were more theater than serious science (see also Brannigan, 2013). Regardless of questions over Milgram's experiments, Piechowski's point was that Milgram could find no means to distinguish those who could resist authority from those who could not. We agree that it is disappointing that psychology has not done more research to provide insight into the question of the possible personality characteristics of resistors (Bocchiaro & Zimbardo, 2010). However, based on this single, meager research strand it seems premature to endorse Piechowski's conclusion that a demanding situation determines behavior, not personality characteristics.

Let us return to Piechowski's (2014) basic question: "Life presents conflict, pressure, and stress. Can personality tests distinguish between individuals who can resist pressure and those who cannot?" (p. 15). Contemporary psychological research now identifies three major outcomes of traumatic events: (a) one can emerge apparently unaffected; (b) one can emerge with long-term stress-related psychopathologies (e.g., anxiety, depression, posttraumatic stress disorder, etc.); or (c) one may report posttraumatic growth (Ramos & Leal, 2013). Although these outcomes will no doubt be determined by complex and multidimensional factors, it is clear that there are large intra-individual differences to which biological and genetic factors contribute (Wu et al., 2013).

Resilience to stress is another individual dimension related to trauma outcomes that is receiving a great deal of research attention. For example, at least 15 research scales measuring resilience are under development (Windle, Bennett, & Noyes, 2011). We cannot review these literatures, but suffice it to say that the articulation of this research should make a major contribution to refining Dąbrowski's theory of how the experience of trauma and crises may relate to psychological development through the process of positive disintegration. This research will also help identify the personality factors underlying either positive or negative outcomes of trauma.

To summarize, we disagree with Piechowski's contention that descriptions of primary integration lack consistency. *Primary* and *integration* are logically used in TPD. Finally, we find Piechowski's interpretation of selected citations to argue against primary integration unconvincing. In fact, we believe that some contemporary research on psychopathy and trauma lends some support for primary integration and TPD in general.

Agree to Disagree

Piechowski's argument against primary integration is not new. Based on what appears to be a philosophical position, Piechowski (2003) has previously rejected a genetic basis of primary integration, saying:

> *Although Dąbrowski viewed primary integration as a rigid [genetic] personality structure, it makes more sense to see it as the outcome of socialization.* If people are operating at Level I it is because this is the condition of the world, not because their psyche is constituted that way. (p. 289, emphasis in original)

We respect both Piechowski's interpretation of a social etiology to primary integration and Da˛browski's view of primary integration as a genetically based personality structure.

To compare and contrast these different interpretations, especially in terms of philosophy and contemporary psychological research, is beyond the scope of our current response.

In calling for the elimination of primary integration, Piechowski's argument appears to be more philosophical than one based upon any research data. His conclusion that primary integration is inconsistent with the theory is illogical—primary integration is integral to Dąbrowski's overall approach. Dąbrowski's observations and description of different levels represent either lower or higher integration or, on the other hand, different types and degrees of disintegration. Dąbrowski's whole theory is predicated on the view that the initial level of integration represents lower, rigid structures guided by primitive instincts and drives. Advanced growth toward autonomy requires the disintegrative processes Dąbrowski described, followed by a gradual reintegration, reflecting the creation of one's personality ideal and its achievement in a second, ultimate, integration.

Piechowski (2014, p. 14) said because "primary integration has a developmental potential so limited that inner transformation…is out of reach…the theory makes it clear that primary integration is not where development can start under any conditions." In his discussion of developmental potential, Piechowski does not acknowledge the possibilities of insufficient positive or negative developmental potential. Piechowski (2014) rejects the construct of primary integration because for multilevel development, "a multilevel development potential must be present" (p. 14). As Dąbrowski made clear, not everyone in primary integration will display sufficient developmental potential for multilevelness to arise; they live in a unilevel reality. "'Normal' and one-sided development lack universality and the more potent multi-level developmental factors, and, therefore, do not reach the highest levels, i.e. organized multilevel disintegration and secondary integration" (Dąbrowski, 1996, p. 20). As well, an individual at level I can be influenced by strong negative developmental potential, possibly leading to psychopathy or mental illness.

There is no contradiction in Dąbrowski's thinking: when *sufficiently strong* developmental *potential* is present, developmental processes may be triggered. *Through* the process of positive disintegration, the structures of primary integration can begin to break down, creating the *opportunity* for volitionally reconstructed, autonomous development to higher levels. Advanced development proceeds *from* primary integration *to* secondary integration. This developmental process is dependent upon one's level of intrinsic (genetic) developmental potential. Those with negative potential, or insufficient positive potential, likely will not progress out of primary integration. The environment an individual is exposed to will greatly influence the outcome of development if his or her potential is equivocal/borderline. Those with strong development potential are good candidates for advanced development (but with no guarantees). As students of TPD, we see Piechowski's position on TPD so divergent from Dąbrowski's written expression of it that we and he must agree to disagree on TPD.

Conclusion

Having carefully considered Piechowski's case against primary integration, we have reached the following verdict: Dismiss the case due to insufficient evidence. Dąbrowski's theory is simply a theory and therefore is subject to criticism and disagreement. However, neither process can strip the theory of its fundamental concepts and continue to refer to it as Dąbrowski's theory. When criticisms and disagreements reach the magnitude evident in Piechowski's treatment of primary integration, we believe that it is time for him to emulate Carl Jung or Robie Case.

References

Adorno, T. W., Frenkel-Brunswik, E., Levinson, D. J., & Sanford, N. (1950). *The authoritarian personality*. New York, NY: Harper.

Aronson, J. (1964). Introduction. In K. Dąbrowski (Ed.), *Positive disintegration* (pp. ix–xxvii). Boston, MA: Little Brown.

Babiak, P., & Hare, R. D. (2006). *Snakes in suits: When psychopaths go to work*. New York, NY: HarperCollins.

Bandura, A. (1986). *Social foundation of thought and action*. Englewood Cliffs, NJ: Prentice-Hall.

Barnard, G. W. (2011). *Living consciousness: The metaphysical vision of Henri Bergson*. Albany, NY: SUNY Press.

Bergson, H. (1935). *The two sources of morality and religion* (R.A. Audra & C. Brereton, with assistance from W. H. Carter, Trans.). London, England: Macmillan.

Bergson, H. (2001). *Time and free will: An essay on the immediate data of consciousness* (3rd ed., F. L. Pogson, Trans.). Mineola, NY: Dover. (Original work published 1913)

Berkout, O. V., Gross, A. M., & Kellum, K. K. (2013). Behaving badly: A perspective on mechanisms of dysfunction in psychopathy. *Aggression and Violent Behavior*, 18, 620–629. doi:10.1016/j.avb.2013.07.013

Blair, R. J. R. (2013a). The neurobiology of psychopathic traits in youths. *Nature Reviews in Neuroscience*, 14, 786–799. doi:10.1038/nrn3577

Blair, R. J. R. (2013b). *Psychopathy: Cognitive and neural dysfunction. Dialogues in Clinical Neuroscience*, 15, 181–190. Retrieved from http://www.ncbi.nlm.nih.gov/pmc/articles/PMC3811089/

Blair, R. J. R., Mitchell, D., & Blair, K. (2005). *The psychopath: Emotion and the brain*. Malden, MA: Blackwell.

Bocchiaro, P., & Zimbardo, P. G. (2010). Defying unjust authority: An exploratory study. *Current Psychology*, 29, 155–170. doi:10.1007/s12144-010-9080-z

Brannigan, A. (2013). Stanley Milgram's obedience experiments: A report card 50 years later. *Society*, 50, 623–628. doi:10.1007/s12115-013-9724-3

Case, R. (1985). *Intellectual development: Birth to adulthood.* New York, NY: Academic Press.

Case, R. (1992). *The mind's staircase: Exploring the conceptual underpinnings of children's thought and knowledge.* Hillsdale, NJ: Erlbaum.

Dąbrowski, K. (1929). *Les conditions psycholopique du suicide* [The psychological conditions of suicide]. Geneva, Switzerland: Imprimerie du Commerce.

Dąbrowski, K. (1937). Psychological basis of self mutilation (W. Thau, Trans.). *Genetic Psychology Monographs*, 19, 1–104.

Dąbrowski, K. (1964). *Positive disintegration.* Boston, MA: Little Brown.

Dąbrowski, K. (1967). *Personality-shaping through positive disintegration.* Boston, MA: Little Brown.

Dąbrowski, K. (with Kawczak, A., & Piechowski, M. M.). (1970). *Mental growth through positive disintegration.* London, England: Gryf.

Dąbrowski, K. (1972). *Psychoneurosis is not an illness.* London, England: Gryf.

Dąbrowski, K. (with Kawczak, A., & Sochanska, A.). (1973). *The dynamics of concepts.* London: Gryf.

Dąbrowski, K. (1996). *Multilevelness of emotional and instinctive functions: Part 1. Theory and description of levels of behavior.* Lublin, Poland: Towarzystwo Naukowe Katolickiego Uniwersytetu Lubelskiego.

Erikson, E. H. (1968). *Identity: Youth and crisis.* New York: Norton.

Ermer, E., Cope, L. M., Nyalakanti, P. K., Calhoun, V. D., & Kiehl, K. A. (2013). Aberrant paralimbic gray matter in incarcerated male adolescents with psychopathic traits. *Journal of the American Academy of Child & Adolescent Psychiatry*, 52, 94–103.e3. doi:10.1016/j.jaac.2012.10.013

Falk, R. F., Lind, S., Miller, N. B., Piechowski, M. M., & Silverman, L. K. (1999). *The Overexcitability Questionnaire–Two (OEQ II): Manual, scoring system, and questionnaire.* Denver, CO: Institute for the Study of Advance Development.

Hague, W. J. (1986). *New perspectives on religious and moral development.* Edmonton, Canada: University of Alberta.

Hague, W. J. (1995). *Evolving spirituality.* Edmonton, Canada: University of Alberta, Department of Educational Psychology.

Herpers, P. C. M., Scheepers, F. E., Bons, D. M., Buitelaar, J. K., & Rommelse, N. N. J. (2014). The cognitive and neural correlates of psychopathy and especially callous–unemotional traits in youths: A systematic review of the evidence. *Development and Psychopathology,* 26, 245–273. doi:10.1017/S0954579413000527

Jay, M. (1973). *The dialectical imagination: A history of the Frankfurt School and the Institute of Social Research,* 1923–1950. London, England: Heinemann.

Lysy, K. Z., & Piechowski, M. M. (1983). Personal growth: An empirical study using Jungian and Dąbrowskian measures. *Genetic Psychology Monographs,* 108, 267–320.

Martin, J. L. (2001). The authoritarian personality, 50 years later: What questions are there for political psychology? *Political Psychology,* 22, 1–26. doi:10.1111/0162-895X.00223

Mendaglio, S., & Tillier, W. (2006). Dąbrowski's theory of positive disintegration and giftedness: Overexcitability research findings. *Journal for the Education of the Gifted,* 30, 68–87.

Milgram, S. (1963). Behavioural study of obedience. *Journal of Abnormal and Social Psychology,* 67, 371–378.

Patrick, C. J., Durbin, C. E., & Moser, J. S. (2012). Reconceptualizing antisocial deviance in neurobehavioral terms. *Development and Psychopathology,* 24, 1047–1071. doi:10.1017/S0954579412000533

Perry, G. (2013). *Behind the shock machine: The untold story of the notorious Milgram psychology experiments* (2nd ed.). New York, NY: The New Press.

Piechowski, M. M. (1974). Two developmental concepts: Multilevelness and developmental potential. *Counseling and Values,* 18, 86–93. doi:10.1002/j.2161-007X.1974.tb01053.x

Piechowski, M. M. (1978). Self actualization as a developmental structure: A profile of Antoine de Saint Exupéry. *Genetic Psychology Monographs,* 97, 181–242.

Piechowski, M. M. (1979). Developmental potential. In N. Colangelo & R. Zaffrann (Eds.), *New voices in counseling the gifted* (pp. 25–57). Dubuque, Iowa: Kendall Hunt.

Piechowski, M. M. (1986). The concept of developmental potential. *Roeper Review,* 8, 190–197. doi:10.1080/02783198609552971

Piechowski, M. M. (1991). Emotional development and emotional giftedness. In N. Colangelo & G. Davis (Eds.), *Handbook of gifted education* (pp. 285–306). Boston, MA: Allyn & Bacon.

Piechowski, M. M. (2002). How well do we understand Dąbrowski's theory? In N. Duda (Ed.), *Positive disintegration: The theory of the future. 100th Da̜browski anniversary program on the man, the theory, the application and the future* (pp. 177–184). Ft. Lauderdale, FL: Fidlar Doubleday.

Piechowski,M.M. (2003). From William James to Maslow and Da̜browski: Excitability of character and self-actualization. In D. Ambrose, L. M. Cohen, & A. J. Tannenbaum (Eds.), *Creative intelligence: Toward theoretic integration* (pp. 283–322). Cresskill, NJ: Hampton Press.

Piechowski, M. M. (2008). Discovering Dąbrowski's theory. In S. Mendaglio (Ed.), *Dąbrowski's theory of positive disintegration* (pp. 41–77). Scottsdale, AZ: Great Potential Press.

Piechowski, M. M. (2014). Rethinking Dąbrowski's theory: I. The case against primary integration. *Roeper Review*, 36, 11–17. doi:10.1080/02783193.2013.856829

Piirto, J. (1997, November). *Twelve issues: Implications of post-modern curriculum theory for the education of the talented.* Paper presented at the meeting of the National Association for Gifted Children Conference, Little Rock, AR. Retrieved from http://www.ashland.edu/~jpiirto/public/postmodweb.html

Pyryt, M. C. (2008). The Da̜browskian lens: Implications for understanding gifted individuals. In S. Mendaglio (Ed.), *Dąbrowski's theory of positive disintegration* (pp. 175–182). Scottsdale, AZ: Great Potential Press.

Raine, A. (2013). *The anatomy of violence: The biological roots of crime.* New York, NY: Pantheon.

Ramos, C., & Leal, I. (2013). Posttraumatic growth in the aftermath of trauma: A literature review about related factors and application contexts. *Psychology, Community & Health*, 2, 43–54. doi:10.5964/pch.v2i1.39

Ray, J. J. (1990). The old-fashioned personality. *Human Relations*, 43, 997–1013. doi:10.1177/001872679004301004

Sanford, N. (1986). A personal account of the study of authoritarianism: Comment on Samelson. *Journal of Social Issues*, 42, 209–214.

Schmidt, M. (1977). *The pebble in song and legend: Primary integration in studies of personality and development* (Unpublished master's thesis). University of Illinois, Urbana–Champaign, Champaign.

Silverman, L. K. (1983). Personality development: The pursuit of excellence. *Journal for the Education of the Gifted,* 6, 5–19.

Silverman, L. K. (1992). Counseling the gifted individual. *Counseling and Human Development*, 25, 1–16.

Silverman, L. K. (Ed.). (1993a). *Counseling the gifted and talented.* Denver, CO: Love.

Silverman, L. K. (1993b). Counseling needs of the gifted. In K. Heller, F. Monks, & A. H. Passow (Eds.), *The international handbook of research and development of giftedness and talent* (pp. 631–647). Oxford, England: Pergamon Press.

Sisk, D. (2008). Engaging the spiritual intelligence of gifted students to build global awareness in the classroom. *Roeper Review,* 30, 24–30. doi:10.1080/02783190701836296

Slaney, K. L., & Racine, T. P. (2013). What's in a name? Psychology's ever evasive construct. *New Ideas in Psychology*, 31, 4–12. doi:10.1016/j.newideapsych.2011.02.003

Windle, G., Bennett, K. M., & Noyes, J. (2011). A methodological review of resilience measurement scales. *Health and Quality of Life Outcomes,* 9, 1–18. doi:10.1186/1477-7525-9-8

Wu, G., Feder, A., Cohen, H., Kim, J. J., Calderon, S., Charney, D. S., & Mathé, A. (2013). Understanding resilience. *Frontiers in Behavioral Neuroscience*, 7, 10. doi:10.3389/fnbeh.2013.00010

Author Bios

Salvatore (Sal) Mendaglio, PhD, is a professor in the Werklund School of Education, University of Calgary. Sal's primary interest is the psychology of giftedness with particular emphasis on Dąbrowski's theory of positive disintegration. He is a licensed psychologist with many years of experience counseling gifted individuals. E-mail: mendagli@ucalgary.ca

William (Bill) Tillier, MSc, is a psychologist with the Ministry of the Solicitor General and Public Security, Alberta, Canada. William received a bachelor of science degree from the University of Calgary and went on to complete a master of science degree at the University of Alberta. It was there that he met Dr. Dąbrowski and became his student. Upon graduation, he worked as a forensic psychologist for over 20 years before developing a neuromuscular disorder. Over the years, William has maintained his interest in Dąbrowski, creating a web page, promoting and distributing Dąbrowski's original works, and helping with many Dąbrowski conferences.

Part II
Commentaries on Research

Chapter 7

Overexcitability Research: Conceptual Analysis

This chapter is comprised of an article coauthored with William Tillier examining overexcitability research undertaken since Piechowski (1979) introduced the theory of positive disintegration to the field of gifted education. While referring to the theory, the publication focused on developmental potential and its major component, overexcitability. It was not long after its introduction that practitioners and educators began applying overexcitability to interpreting various aspects of giftedness and researchers began to explore the relationship between the two constructs. Prescriptive literature outpaced empirical literature initially; soon after, there was an increase in research productivity with the availability of a measure of overexcitability. By the mid-1980s, the Overexcitabilities Questionnaire (OEQ) was created, facilitating some research beyond that of the original devotees of Dąbrowski's theory. However the OEQ, an open ended questionnaire, required expert raters for scoring. It was the availability of the revised version, the Overexcitability Questionnaire 2 (OEQ II), a Likert type scale, that sparked greater interest by researchers. By the early 2000s, a body of literature reporting research investigations was available.

As participant observers in the application of Dąbrowski's theory in gifted education, my co-author, William Tillier and I regularly perused the literature on this topic. We both were aware of Dąbrowski's approach to research with gifted youth published in his books. It was clear to us that the approach to research manifested in publications differed significantly from Dąbrowski's investigation of the relationship between giftedness and his own theory. We decided to review the empirical literature to determine to whether our inference about the literature was correct. That decision led to our conceptual analysis of the research literature, contrasting research on overexcitabilities with Dąbrowski's theorizing.

References

Mendaglio, S. & Tillier, W. (2006). Dąbrowski's theory of positive disintegration and giftedness: Overexcitabilities research findings. *Journal for the Education of the Gifted, 30*, 68-87.

Dąbrowski's Theory of Positive Disintegration and Giftedness: Overexcitability Research Findings

Sal Mendaglio, University of Calgary
William Tillier, Solicitor General, Alberta

During the past 20 years, a significant body of Literature has emerged focusing on the application of Dąbrowski's theory of positive disintegration (TPD) to the study of gifted individuals. Although much of this literature is prescriptive, some research reports spanning this time period are available. A perusal of research on TPD's applicability to gifted individuals indicates that the focus has been Dąbrowski's notion of overexcitability (OE). This article reviews OE research, contrasts it with Dąbrowski's approach to research with gifted individuals, and argues that researchers should emulate Dąbrowski's approach in future investigations.

Introduction

Since the 1980s, the theory of positive disintegration (TPD; Dąbrowski, 1964, 1967, 1970, 1972) has been applied to understanding various giftedness, especially within the social-emotional domain. For example, TPD has been used to explore gifted persons' emotional sensitivity and intensity (Fiedler, 1998); to make a case for the misdiagnosis of gifted persons' traits as (e.g., slash hyperactivity disorder [Flint, 2001] or high-functioning autism[Cash, 1999]}; to describe social and emotional needs of adolescents (Tieso, 1999); to identify creative personality characteristics (Schiever, 1985); to assess social and emotional needs (Gust, 1996); to propose an interplay between developmental potential and spiritual development

(Morrissey, 1996); to counsel gifted persons (Hazell, 1999; Mendaglio, 1998; Ogburn Colangelo, 1989); and to conceptualize suicide (Gust-Brey & Cross, 1999). Overexcitability (OE) has been the Dąbrowskian concept of choice in the application of TPD to giftedness and gifted education. Interest in OE has extended to researchers seeking empirical support for the application of TPD to gifted individuals. The purpose of this article is twofold: to explore research literature in this area, including Dąbrowski's (1967, 1972) research with gifted youth and to encourage future researchers to emulate Dąbrowski by conceptualizing OE within the larger context of developmental potential (DP).

Overexcitability: Conceptual and Operational Definitions

In Dąbrowski's theory, OE is a heightened physiological experience of sensory stimuli resulting from increased sensitivity of the neurons. Dąbrowski (1972) used the phrase *psychic overexcitability* and defined it as "higher than average responsiveness to stimuli, manifested either by psychomotor, sensual, emotional (affective), imaginational, or intellectual excitability, or the combination thereof" (p. 303). Piechowski (1975) stated, "Overexcitability means that the response exceeds the stimulus input" (p. 270). Piechowski (1991) noted that Dąbrowski used the term psychic overexcitability to "underline the enhancement and intensification of mental activity much beyond the ordinary" (page 287). The five manifestations of overexcitability, commonly called the five OEs, underlie the conceptual and operational definitions used by researchers.

Dąbrowski's theory describes five different levels of personality development that he observed in human populations. These different levels reflect differences in the psychological characteristics of individuals that, in turn, reflect the potential for advanced development of personality. Dąbrowski used the term *developmental potential* to refer to the constellation of psychological features that he believed were associated with advanced personality development. These characteristics include three main features: (1) special abilities and talents (like athletic or unique musical ability), (2) the five forms of overexcitability, and (3) a strong autonomous drive to achieve individuality. Dąbrowski also advanced the idea that the major process of development involves a breakdown of the existing psychological structures, allowing the individual to examine his or her own values, emotions, behavior, and other personality characteristics consciously. This breakdown takes the form of nervousness and psychoneuroses (essentially strong anxieties and depressions). Development resolves these internal conflicts and results in a strong, unique, autonomous, and authentic value and personality structure.

Conceptual Definition Evident in OE Research

Perusal of the empirical literature on OE reveals a consensus on its conceptual definition. Piechowski's (1975, 1979, 1986, 1991) elaboration of OE forms the conceptual basis. Tucker and Hafenstein's précis of Piechowski's elaboration on the topic typifies how researchers conceptually define OE:

> **Psychomotor Overexcitability.** The manifestations of psychomotor excitability are essentially of two kinds: surplus of energy and nervousness. In nervousness, the emotional tension is translated into psychomotor activity such as tics, nail biting, or impulsive behavior... The surplus of energy can be observed in animated gestures and taking on self-improvement tasks....
>
> **Sensual Overexcitability**. Sensual overexcitability is expressed in heightened experiencing of sensory pleasures and then seeking sensual outlets for inner tension... other manifestations of sensual overexcitability include marked interest in clothes and appearance, fondness for jewelry and ornaments...
>
> **Intellectual Overexcitability.** The manifestations of intellectual overexcitability are associated with an intensified and accelerated activity of the mind. Its strongest expressions have more to do with striving for understanding, probing the unknown, and love of truth

> than with learning per se or academic achievement...
>
> **Imaginational Overexcitability.** The presence of imaginational overexcitability can be inferred from frequent distractions, wandering attention, and daydreaming. These occur as consequence of free play of the imagination. Here, too, belong illusions, animistic thinking, expressive image and metaphor, invention and fantasy...
>
> **Emotional Overexcitability.** Among the five forms of psychic overexcitability, the manifestations of emotional overexcitability are the most numerous. They include certain characteristic and easily recognizable somatic expressions, extremes of feeling, inhibition, strong affective memory, concern with death, anxieties, fears, feelings of guilt, and depressive and suicidal moves.... (p. 68, boldface and ellipses in original)

Operational Definitions

Similar to the conceptual view of OEs, there is agreement on the operational definition of OE. With some exceptions, OE is assessed with the Overexcitability Questionnaire (OEQ; Lysy & Piechowski, 1983). Bouchet and Falk (2001) used the OEQ II (Falk, Lind, Miller, Piechowski, & Silverman, 1999), Bouchard (2004) developed her own measure (ElemenOE), while Tucker and Hafenstein (1997) used qualitative case-study methods, and Dąbrowski (1970, 1972) used medical-psychological evaluation. These operational definitions are described below.

1. OEQ consists of 21 open-ended questions designed to assess the presence and intensity of the five OEs. Respondents are asked to provide written answers to questions designed to elicit descriptions of personal experiences that are theoretically related to OEs. Regarding its administration, there are no time limits and no supervision of the respondents. Scoring of the OEQ requires trained

raters who assign numerical values to responses indicating whether there is evidence of the presence of a particular OE and, if so, it's intensity (see Lysy & Piechowski, 1983).

2. The OEQ II is a 50-item self-report questionnaire asking participants to provide their responses to items using a Likert scale. The items were the result of a process of item selection, which began with the use of data from hundreds of participants responses to the OEQ. Scoring for each OE is based on a total score of the items related to each OE (Bouchet & Falk, 2001)
3. ElemenOE is a 30-item observation checklist designed for use by teachers to rate OEs in elementary school children. Teachers use a Likert scale to rate children's behaviors, presumed to be indicative of OEs, in terms of frequency and intensity (Bouchard, 2004).
4. Qualitative case study methods include purposeful sampling, analysis of documents, observation, and interviewing. Tucker and Hafenstein's (1997) application of these methods began with teacher nominations of children who manifested all OEs. These children were randomly selected to participate. They examined their school records and conducted nonparticipant observations of the children and semistructured interviews with their teachers (Tucker and Hafenstein, 1997).
5. Medical-psychological evaluation designates a combination of assessment strategies. These include psychiatric, neurological, and psychological testing; history taking; interviewing; and case study (see Dąbrowski, 1967, 1972).

Overexcitabilities: Research Findings

Review of research on OE and giftedness is presented in chronological order beginning with the older reports to illustrate how research on the topic has evolved. The notable exception is Dąbrowski's research. It is presented last so that researchers' approaches and findings can be contrasted with his work in this area.

Silverman and Ellsworth (1981) designed a study to assess to hypotheses; namely, gifted individuals have higher developmental potential, as manifested by greater OEs than nongifted individuals, and gifted individuals have higher intellectual, emotional, and imaginational than sensual and psychomotor OEs. As a preliminary test of these hypotheses, Silverman and Ellsworth analyzed the data of 31 identified gifted adults' (i.e., artists, members of Mensa or eligible members based on test scores, and former students in gifted education programs) responses to the OEQ, designed to assess overexcitability, and the Definition Response Instrument (DRI; Gage, Morse & Piechowski, 1981), developed to assess levels of development (Lysy & Piechowski, 1983). Silverman and Ellsworth also compared their sample's responses with Lysy's (1979) data on counselors and noncounselors. Findings included elevated OE scores among the intellectually gifted adults, with scores on emotional and intellectual OEs being equal. Further, the intellectually gifted adult groups scored substantially higher than Lysy's sample on intellectual, imaginational, and emotional OEs.

Lysy and Piechowski (1983) were primarily interested in studying the process of development. The participants of the study included counselors because the researchers reasoned that counselors have a significant interest in personal growth and development. Noncounselors formed a comparison group. Secondarily, the investigators were interested in validating two measures of psychological growth, namely the OEQ and the DRI. The DRI consists of six open-ended items created to assess for Dąbrowskian levels of development. Both instruments were administered to the participants, 20 in the counseling group and 22 in the noncounseling group. Both groups consisted of adult participants who were either graduate students or employed in counseling and other professions. Significant differences between groups were found for OEs but not for levels of development. Counselors scored higher than noncounselors on sensual and imaginational OEs. However, they scored lower on the intellectual OE. There were no significant differences found on the groups' scores on the DRI.

Piechowski and Cunningham (1985) attempted to uncover patterns of OEs in 13 artists. These participants shared a "serious involvement with artistic or creative work at professional, vocational or long-standing avocational levels" (p. 158). Data were collected by using the OEQ and interviews. The researchers derived three patterns of OE constellations using the amount of interaction among the OEs and the amount of emotional OE to construct the patterns. In Pattern A, the OEs were highly interactive with similar amounts of emotional OE and imaginational OE. In Pattern B, emotional OE was particularly strong, overshadowing the other OEs. In Pattern C, emotional OE was lower, with psychomotor and sensual OEs higher. The researchers described Pattern A as balanced and integrated, Pattern B as emotionally vulnerable, and Pattern C as polarized and restless.

Piechowski and Cunningham (1985) also compared their participants' responses with those of the intellectually gifted adult participants in Silverman and Ellsworth's (1981) study. Imaginational OE was found to be the most significant difference between the artist group and the intellectually gifted group, with the artists scoring higher. In addition, the artists scored higher on emotional OE.

Piechowski, Silverman, and Falk (1985), in a comparative study, explored the mental functioning of intellectually and artistically gifted adults. Their sample consisted of two groups: 37 intellectually gifted adults and 23 artists. Data gathered in a previous study (Lysy & Piechowski, 1983) whose sample consisted of 42 graduate students were also used in the analyses. Participants in both studies completed the OEQ. The artist group scored significantly higher than graduate students on all five OEs and higher than the intellectually gifted group on emotional and imaginational OEs. The intellectually gifted group scored higher than the graduate students on emotional, imaginational, and intellectual OEs.

Schiever (1985) compared OE profiles of students in a gifted education program on a measure of creativity. Her sample consisted of 21 seventh-grade students. Participants completed the OEQ and the Something About Myself (SAM) part of the Khatena Torrance Creative Perception Inventory (Khatena & Torrance, 1976). Using the scores on the SAM, Schiever grouped her participants into high- and low-creativity groups. The high-creativity groups scored significantly higher on imaginational, emotional, and intellectual OEs. There were no group differences on psychomotor and sensual OEs.

Gallagher (1986) investigated the possibility of a significant difference in OEs when comparing groups of children high and low on creativity, gifted children, and children who are not gifted. Her participants were 24 sixth-grade students attending the same school; 12 children were in the school's program for gifted students, and 12 were selected randomly. There were no significant correlations found between the scores on Torrance Tests of Creative Thinking and OEQ data. When participants were split into high- and low-creativity groups using Verbal Subtest scores, the scores of the highly creative group or higher on imaginational OE. When the Figural Subtest scores were used to create high- and low-creativity groups, the highly creative group scored higher on psychomotor OE. When comparing gifted students and students not identified as gifted, significant differences were found on intellectual, imaginational, and emotional OEs in favor of the gifted group. No differences were found on the other OEs.

Lewis and Kitano (1992) investigated affective characteristics of academically gifted adults using a concept of psychological intensities and a mixed-research design (quantitative and qualitative methods). Psychological intensity was constructed by combining Clark's (1983) notion of concomitant problems, associated with Clark's work on characteristics of gifted children, and Dąbrowski's concept of overexcitabilities (Piechowski, 1979). The researchers developed a questionnaire to assess intensity characteristics. The sample consisted of 31 academically high-achieving adults. The achievement criterion was operationally defined as admission to a doctoral program in education. The primary purpose of the study was to determine whether, and to what extent, high-achieving adults are characterized by psychological intensities. The researchers analyzed the quantitative data obtained by the use of their questionnaire with the entire sample and the qualitative data gathered from 11 students who participated in focus groups. The purpose of this aspect of the study was to explore perceptions of psychological intensities. Statistical analyses of the questionnaire data provided support for the concomitant-problems model rather than the Dąbrowskian model. Qualitative analyses of the focus-group data provided most support for psychological intensities in the realms of intellectual and emotional intensities; some support was found for imagination and sensual intensities. However, there was no support for psychomotor intensity.

Miller, Silverman, and Falk (1994), in a comparative study, hypothesized that intellectually gifted adults measured OEs and level of development would be higher than OEs of a group of graduate students; that there would be no gender differences; and that developmental potential as measured by OEs—specifically intellectual, imaginational, and emotional—would predict level of development. Participants consisted of 41 intellectually gifted adults recruited for the study and data on 42 graduate students retrieved from a previous study (Lysy & Piechowski, 1983). All participants completed the OEQ and the DRI. The hypothesis that intellectually gifted adults would score higher on OEs than graduate students was partially supported by the finding that the intellectually gifted group scored higher on emotional and intellectual OEs than the comparison group. Regarding the second hypothesis, some gender differences were found on OEs: Women scored higher on emotional OE and men scored higher on intellectual OE. No gender differences were reported on the other OEs. On the DRI, women scored significantly higher than did men. The third hypothesis was not supported: There was no difference between the intellectually gifted group and graduate students on the DRI. The gifted group did not manifest a higher level of development, despite having a higher scores on the OEs.

Ackerman (1997) conducted an exploratory study aimed at assessing the use of OEs as an alternate means of identifying gifted students. Seventy-nine high school students, 42 of whom were identified gifted, formed the sample. Participants completed the OEQ. Findings indicated that the identified gifted group's OE profile contained higher scores on psychomotor, intellectual, and emotional OEs. Psychomotor OE contributed most to the differentiation between groups.

Falk, Manzanero, and Miller (1997) conducted a cross-cultural study attempting to add further validity to previous findings that artists exhibit high intellectual, imaginational, and, emotional OEs.

Participants were recruited through a Venezuelan school of fine arts. The sample consisted of both professional and amateur artists. Twenty-seven Venezuelan artists completed a Spanish translation of the OEQ. Twenty-three American artists from a previous study (Piechowski, et al., 1985) constituted a comparison group. The OE profile of the Venezuelan artists was virtually the same as the American artists: emotional, imaginational, and intellectual OEs were substantially higher than the sensual and psychomotor OEs. American artists scored significantly higher on psychomotor OE than did the Venezuelans.

Tucker and Hafenstein (1997) used a qualitative, multiple case-study design to describe the manifestations of OEs in young gifted children. Early childhood teachers were asked to nominate children whom the teachers believed manifested all of the OEs. From the pool of nominees, the researchers randomly selected five children. Tucker and Hafenstein used several data sources, including classroom observations, school documents, and interviews with the children's teachers. Findings indicated that all five children manifested behaviors Tucker and Hafenstein associated with intellectual, imaginational, and emotional OEs. Two of the children also manifested behaviors associated with psychomotor and sensual OEs.

Bouchet and Falk (2001) tested two hypotheses: (1) university students who attended gifted education programs have greater emotional, intellectual, and imaginational OEs than those who did not, and (2) gender differences exist in OE scores, such that women score higher on emotional and sensual and men score higher on intellectual and psychomotor OEs. The sample consisted of 562 undergraduate university students. The OEQ II (Falk et al., 1999) was administered to assess participants' OEs. A second questionnaire asked participants to indicate whether they participated in gifted education, Advanced Placement courses, or standard programs in high school. Results provided partial support for the hypothesis that those students who attended gifted education programs have higher emotional, imaginational, and intellectual OEs. Specifically, when compared to the other two groups, the gifted group did score significantly higher on two of the three OEs, namely, emotional and intellectual. Gender differences were also found. Females scored higher on emotional and sensual, and males scored higher on intellectual, Imaginational, and psycho motor OEs.

Bouchard (2004), similar to Ackerman (1997), was interested in using the OEs as a means of identifying gifted students. She detailed the development of an instrument with the goal of using it to identify elementary school children. The ElemenOE is a Likert-scaled checklist designed for use by teachers to select children for gifted education programs. Teacher ratings were obtained on 96 identified gifted children and 75 nonidentified gifted children. Analyses of the teacher ratings indicated that the two groups differed only on intellectual and psychomotor OE scores in favor of the gifted group. As with Ackerman's finding, psychomotor ratings contributed most to distinguishing between the two groups.

Summary

Taken as a group, findings indicate partial support for the predicted OE profile. The greatest support for the claim that gifted persons manifest the profile of elevated imagination or, intellectual, and emotional OEs–the Big Three—with depressed sensual and psychomotor OEs is found in the studies with adult participants. Further, the strongest support is found in studies that use creativity as a criterion, particularly when this was demonstrated in artistic productions.

Of the eight studies where adults constituted the samples, research with artists lend the greatest support for the OE profile associated with multilevel development. Piechowski et al. (1985) reported elevated scores on all OEs for the American artists they studied. Venezuelan artists' profile, similar to American artists, in the Falk et al. (1997) study manifested the elevated scores on emotional, intellectual, and imaginational OEs. Piechowski and Cunningham's (1985) study with artists also provided support.

With one exception, when intellectually gifted adults constituted the samples, partial support is found. Silverman and Ellsworth (1981) found that their sample of intellectually gifted adults scored substantially higher on the three critical OEs than nonidentified gifted adults. Four studies (Lewis & Kitano, 1992; Lysy & Piechowski,

1983; Miller et al., 1994; Bouchet & Falk, 2001) provide varying levels of partial support.

Of the four studies with children or adolescents as participants, two studies provide support for the expected OE profile. In Tucker and Hafenstein's (1997) qualitative study, the five gifted children nominated by their teachers manifested behaviors associated with all OEs. Gallagher's (1986) identified gifted group scored higher than the nongifted group on the three key OEs.

Research with larger samples of adolescents and children, however, did not lend significant support. In fact, both Ackerman (1997) and Bouchard (2004) found that psychomotor OE contributed most significantly to differentiating between gifted and nongifted groups, with gifted participants scoring higher on this OE.

Dąbrowski's Research with Gifted Individuals: Beyond OEs

Dąbrowski (1967, 1972) reported his research with gifted youth in two places. The accounts are substantially the same, with minor differences. For example, Dąbrowski used the term "outstanding abilities" (p. 251) in 1967, whereas he used "superior abilities" (p. 204) in 1972. Both terms referred to abilities that allow an individual to achieve at a level surpassing significantly the standard accepted for those of similar age and education. The more recent account is the basis for this summary.

Dąbrowski's stated purpose was to investigate the relationship between two sets of characteristics: superior abilities and psychoneuroses. Dąbrowski (1972) defined superior abilities as "abilities (in any field), which permit an individual to achieve results considerably surpassing the average accepted as standard for individuals of the same age and the same level of education" (p. 204). Superior abilities were divided into two types: general and special. Superior general abilities were ascribed to the elementary school children in his sample and were grouped into humanistic, mathematical, and scientific. Superior special abilities, said to characterize students attending art school, including drama, dance, art, and music. Psychoneurosis is defined as "a more or less organized form of growth through positive disintegration" (p. 303).

The sample consisted of 80 youth (aged 8 to 23). Thirty participants were intellectually gifted elementary school children; 50 participants attended art schools, studying ballet, theatre, and art. A comparison group of 30 developmentally delayed youth was also included in the sample. Participants were assessed using a combination of medical and psychological procedures. Neurological and psychiatric examinations were conducted on all participants. Psychological assessment was conducted using the Wexler-Bellevue (Wexler, 1939); the Rorschach (Rorschach, 1921); the Thematic Apperception Test (Murray, 1943), a questionnaire designed to assess for the presence of psychoneurotic traits and signs of forces associated with positive disintegration; interview; and case study.

Dąbrowski (1972) reported that "[e]very one of the children investigated showed considerable psychomotor, sensual, affectional [emotional], intellectual mental overexcitability" (p. 205). Dąbrowski concluded that there is a relationship between superior abilities and psychoneuroses. He noted that his sample's various interests and abilities coincided with complex psychoneurotic manifestations, that is, with signs of potential for advanced development.

It is evident from the description of his research that Dąbrowski assessed more than his participants' OEs. He assessed the developmental potential (DP). Dąbrowski (1972) defined DP as the

> *constitutional endowment, which determines the character and the extent of mental growth possible for a given individual. The developmental potential can be assessed on the basis of the following components: psychic overexcitability..., special abilities and talents, and autonomous factors (notably the third factor).* (p. 293)

In addition to OEs and special abilities and talents, DP includes autonomous forces that are called *dynamisms* in TPD. Dynamisms are defined as a "[b]iological or mental force controlling behavior and its development. Instincts, drives, and intellectual processes combined with emotions are dynamisms (Dąbrowski, 1972, p. 294).

Dąbrowski (1972, 1973) noted that in a few dynamisms, including the third factor, were the sine qua non of the developmental process. (The third factor will be discussed in detail below.)

Piechowski (1975) also emphasize the importance of dynamisms in his definition of developmental potential:

> *Developmental potential is the original endowment which determines what level of development a person may reach if the physical and environmental conditions are optimal. Developmental potential has certain defining characteristics which allow us to detect its presence and measure its strength. The defining characteristics of DP are forms of overexcitability and developmental dynamisms. Dynamisms [italics in original] are intrapsychic processes of positive disintegration which shape development and the expression of behavior. Each level of development has a different set of dynamisms.* (p. 250)

In a similar vein to Dąbrowski, Piechowski (1975) is emphatic about the centrality of dynamisms (e.g., self-awareness, dissatisfaction with self, and empathy) in positive disintegration: For Piechowski, dynamisms are not forces carrying out disintegration, they "*are* [italics in original] the disintegration" (p. 277).

The third factor is a particularly important dynamism that appears only after other dynamisms such as subject-object in oneself and inner psychic transformation are well established. As such, the third factor is evident at a high level of mental development. Dąbrowski (1973) admitted that this dynamism is particularly difficult to define. Although connected to one's heredity and environment, it transcended these two factors. The third factor does not appear in a prefabricated form—it arises gradually in certain individuals who, as a result of their inner struggles, develop sustained self-consciousness. Such individuals become controlled by their inner voices and values rather than by their heredity and environment. Increased consciousness, self-determination, authenticity, and autonomy are the hallmarks of the third factor. Dąbrowski (1973) defined it as follows:

> The third factor is a dynamism active at the stage of organized multilevel disintegration. Its activity is autonomous in relation to the first (hereditary) and the second (environmental) factor. It consists in a selective attitude with regard to the properties of one's own character and temperament, as well as to environmental influences. This dynamism paves the way for the impact of the ideal of personality upon the individual. (p. 80)

Developmental Potential and Dynamisms in Dąbrowski's Research With Gifted Students

References to developmental potential and specific dynamisms are evident in Dąbrowski's (1972) discussion of research findings. Developmental potential is discussed in a case that Dąbrowski used to illustrate his findings:

> *His [8-year-old grade-three boy]* ***developmental potential*** [bold italics added] *can be seen in the combination of his fairly high excitability with inhibition, in the combination of his sensitivity, impatience and anger with states of anxiety, and above all his sensitivity to unjust treatment, his strong relationship with mother, a feeling of inferiority in respect to himself, and his feeling of responsibility and systematic approach to his schoolwork.* (p. 208)

Dynamisms, including the third factor, are noted in discussing the role of creative abilities and development in his sample:

> *Among older youths the majority of creative abilities was displayed by individuals with a very advanced development (i.e., multilevel disintegration) of their internal psychic milieu. We have assessed in these individuals their enhanced emotional overexcitability and initial activity of such* ***dynamisms like subject-object in oneself, the third factor, forms of periodical self-control*** [bold italics added]. (p. 218)

Although Dąbrowski was studying the relationship of special abilities and indicators of positive disintegration, he assessed the DP of his participants. This approach to researching his theory suggests that Dąbrowski believed that components of DP operate in an integrated manner. Those interested in applying TPD to giftedness and gifted education should consider emulating Dąbrowski's approach.

Research findings on the application of TPD may be reflective of the exclusive focus on OEs. The findings with adult artists—the samples that provide consistent support for elevated OEs, especially the Big Three—add support to this possibility. In addition to elevated OEs, adult artists possess superior talents (superior special abilities). They have had the opportunity to engage in experiences leading to inner struggles and the birth of self-consciousness (evidence of dynamisms). Other samples of adults and children alike may not have had other components of DP, which may explain the findings. In other words, individuals meeting criteria for gifted programs may be intelligent and may even have elevated OEs, but may be lacking in other aspects of DP. Intellectual giftedness may be a prerequisite for the potential for advanced development, but it may not be sufficient for multilevel development. (Mendaglio & Pyryt, 2004; Nixon, 2005; Silverman & Ellsworth, 1981). By using all components of DP in applying TPD to gifted individuals, we should be in a better position to confirm or disconfirm claims regarding the applicability of TPD to giftedness and gifted education.

Conclusion

For both Dąbrowski and Piechowski, OEs represent only a partial view of DP. OEs are inextricably bound to the other components of DP. To provide empirical support for a Dąbrowskian view of development, special abilities, dynamisms, and the quality of the environment also need to be considered. Using DP and not solely OEs will prove challenging to researchers and others who are interested in the application of TPD to giftedness and gifted education. For researchers, the prospect of creating operational definitions of the other components of DP, especially dynamisms, may appear daunting. The work on the development of the now-taken-for-granted OEQ, spearheaded by Michael Piechowski, should be a source of inspiration for the work ahead. Piechowski and his associates rose to the challenge of operationalizing overexcitability; similarly, we need to confront other aspects of Dąbrowski's theory in our continuing efforts to apply it to the field of giftedness.

References

Ackerman, C. (1997). Identifying gifted adolescents using personality characteristics: Dąbrowski's overexcitabilities. *Roeper Review*, 19, 229-236.

Bouchard, L. L. (2004). An instrument for the measure of Dąbrowskian overexcitabilities to identify gifted elementary students. *Gifted Child Quarterly*, 48, 339-350.

Bouchet, N., & Falk, R. F. (2001). The relationship among giftedness, gender, and overexcitability. *Gifted Child Quarterly*, 45, 260-267.

Cash, A. B. (1999). A profile of gifted individuals with autism: The twice-exceptional learner. *Roeper Review*, 22, 22-27.

Clark, B. (1983). *Growing up gifted* (2nd ed.). Columbus, OH: Charles E. Merrill.

Dąbrowski, K. (1964). *Positive disintegration*. Boston: Little, Brown.

Dąbrowski, K. (1967). *Personality-shaping through positive disintegration*. Boston: Little, Brown.

Dąbrowski, K. (1970). *Mental growth through positive disintegration*. London: Gryf.

Dąbrowski, K. (1972). *Psychoneurosis is not an illness*. London: Gryf.

Dąbrowski, K. (1973). *The dynamics of concepts*. London: Gryf.

Falk, R. F., Manzanero, J. B., & Miller, N. B. (1997). Developmental potential in Venezuelan and American artists: A cross-cultural validity study. *Creativity Research Journal* 10, 201-206.

Falk, R. R., Lind, S., Miller, N. B., Piechowski, M. M., & Silverman, L. K. (1999). *The Overexcitability Questionnaire—Two (OEQII): Manual scoring system, and questionnaire*. Denver, CO: Institute for the Study of Advanced Development.

Fiedler, E. D. (1998). Denial of anger/denial of self: Dealing with the dilemmas. *Roeper Review*, 20, 158-161.

Flint, L. J. (2001). Challenges of identifying and serving gifted children with ADHD. *Teaching Exceptional Children*, 33, 62-69.

Gage, D. F., Morse, P.A., & Piechowski, M. M. (1981). Measuring levels of emotional development. *Genetic Psychology Monographs*, 103, 129-152.

Gallagher, S. A. (1986). A comparison of the concept of overexcitabilities with measures of creativity and school achievement in sixth grade students. *Roeper Review*, 8, 115-119.

Gust, K. L. (1996). Assessing the social and emotional needs of the gifted: Using the Children's Self-Report and Projective Inventory as a potential tool. *Gifted Child Today*, 19, 38-40.

Gust-Brey, K., & Cross, T. (1999). An examination of the literature base on the suicidal behaviors of gifted students. *Roeper Review*, 22, 28-35.

Hazell, C. G. (1999). The experience of emptiness and the use of Dąbrowski's theory in counseling gifted clients: Clinical case examples. *Advanced Development: A Journal on Adult Giftedness*, 8, 31-46.

Khatena, J., & Torrance, E. P. (1976). *Manual for Khatena-Torrance Creative Personality Perception Inventory*. Chicago: Stoelting.

Lewis, R. B., & Kitano, M. K. (1992). Psychological intensities in gifted adults. *Roeper Review*, 15, 25- 31.

Lysy, K. Z. (1979). Personal growth in counselors and noncounselors: A Jungian and Dąbrowskian approach. Unpublished doctoral dissertation, University of Illinois, Urbana-Champaign.

Lysy, K. Z., & Piechowski M. M. (1983). Personal growth: An empirical study using Jungian and Dąbrowskian measures. *Genetic Psychology Monographs*, 108, 267-320.

Mendaglio, S. (1998). Counselling gifted students: Issues and recommendations for teachers and counselors. *AGATE*, 12, 18-25.

Mendaglio, S., & Pyryt, M. C . (2004, June). The role of intelligence in Dąbrowski's theory of positive disintegration. In W. Tillier (Ed.), *Developmental potential-from theory to practice: Educational and therapeutic perspectives*. Unpublished manuscript. (Proceedings from the Sixth International Congress of the Institute for Positive Disintegration in Human Development, Calgary, Alberta, Canada.)

Miller, N. B., Silvern1an, L. K., & Falk, R. F. (1994). Emotional development, intellectual ability, and gender. *Journal for the Education of the Gifted*, 18, 20-38.

Morrissey, A. M. (1996). Intellect as prelude: The potential for higher level development in the gifted. *Advanced Development: A Journal on Adult Giftedness*, 7, 101-116.

Murray, H. A. (1943). *Thematic Apperception Test manual.* Cambridge, MA: Harvard University Press.

Nixon, L. (2005). Potential for positive disintegration and IQ. *The Dąbrowski Newsletter*, 10(2), 1- 5.

Ogburn Colangelo, M. K. (1989). Giftedness as multilevel potential: A clinical example. *Advanced Development: A Journal on Adult Giftedness*, 1, 87-100.

Piechowski, M. NL (1975). A theoretical and empirical approach to the study of development. *Genetic Psychology Monographs*, 92, 231-297.

Piechowski, M. M. (1979). Developmental potential. In N. Colangelo & R. T. Zaffrann (Eds.), *New voices in counseling the gifted* (pp. 25-57). Dubuque, IA: Kendall Hunt.

Piechowski, M. NL (1986). The concept of developmental potential. *Roeper Review*, 8, 190- 197.

Piechowski, M. M. (1991). Emotional development and emotional giftedness. In N. Colangelo & G. Davis (Eds.), *Handbook of gifted education* (pp. 285-306). Boston: Allyn & Bacon.

Piechowski, M. M., & Cunningham, K. (1985). Patterns of overexcitability in a group of artists. *Journal of Creative Behavior*, 19, 153- 174.

Piechowski, M. M., Silverman, L., & Falk, F. (1985). Comparison of intellectually and artistically gifted on five dimensions of mental functions. *Perceptual and Motor Skills*, 60, 539-549.

Rorschach, H. (1921). *Psychodiagnostics: Diagnostic perception.* New York: Grune & Stratton.

Schiever, S. W. (1985). Creative personality characteristics and dimensions of mental functioning in gifted adolescents. *Roeper Review*, 7, 223-226.

Silverman, L. K., & Ellsworth, B. (1981). The theory of positive disintegration and its implications for giftedness. In N. Duda (Ed.), *Theory of positive disintegration: Proceedings of the third international conference* (pp. 179-194). Miami, FL: Xerox.

Tieso, C. L. (1999). Meeting the socio-emotional needs of talented teens. *Gifted Child Today*, 22, 38- 43.

Tucker, B., & Hafenstein, N. (1997). Psychological intensities in young gifted children. *Gifted Child Quarterly,* 41, 66-75.

Wechsler, D. (1939). *The measurement of adult intelligence.* Baltimore: Williams & Wilkins.

Chapter 8

Overexcitability Research: Methodological Analysis

This chapter's article is a reflection on overexcitability research. I was motivated to write this particular critique of research on the topic because of the rise of publications, driven by the ease of administration and scoring of the OEQ II. As I note in the article, I saw the increase in research interest as double edged: word about Dąbrowski's theory was reaching international realms; however, research assumptions and methods were inconsistent with my understanding of the theory. While Mendaglio & Tillier (2006) analyzed the literature strictly from a conceptual perspective, for this entry I examined research on overexcitability and giftedness by critiquing research assumptions and methods based upon them. Data analysis used by researchers requires assuming that overexcitability is a continuous variable, normally distributed in a population. I argue that the assumptions required to perform selected statistical analyses yielded by the OEQ II disregard the essence of Dąbrowski's overexcitability.

Readers need to understand that I am not blinded by my passion for the theory of positive disintegration. Researchers are free to do as they wish. My point is simply: If researchers investigate a construct, they should not approach the task by "surgically removing it" from the theory from which it comes. It should not be assumed that overexcitability is an atheoretical construct that can be investigated as can be many other psychological constructs, without consideration for the complex, highly integrated conceptual whole from which it is drawn, Dąbrowski's theory of positive disintegration.

References

Mendaglio, S. (2012). Overexcitabilities and Giftedness Research: A Call for a Paradigm Shift. *Journal for the Education of the Gifted*, 35(3), 208–219. https://doi-org.ezproxy.lib.ucalgary.ca/10.1177/0162353212451704

Overexcitabilities and Giftedness Research: A Call for a Paradigm Shift

Research investigating overexcitability (OE) and giftedness has increased in recent years. Although the number of recent research publications is not voluminous, the increase is noteworthy, given the history of research on the topic. Michael Piechowski's introduction of OE to the field of gifted education in 1979 generated research investigations conducted largely by a small group of American researchers. In addition to Piechowski, Linda Silverman, Nancy Miller, and Frank Falk pioneered research in this area. Research on OE (e.g., Miller & Silverman, 1987; Piechowski, Silverman, & Falk, 1985) was facilitated by the construction of the OE Questionnaire (OEQ; Lysy & Piechowski, 1983). The OEQ is an open-ended, self-report questionnaire designed to assess the five forms of OE: sensual, psychomotor, imaginational, intellectual, and emotional. Administration of the OEQ is straightforward, but scoring requires training.

Whereas the OEQ sparked some research, the rate of publications has increased with the development of the OEQ Two (OEQ II; Falk, Lind, Miller, Piechowski, & Silverman, 1999). The OEQ II is a Likert-type self-report questionnaire designed to measure the five OEs. It is reasonable to assume that the ease of administration and scoring of the OEQ II has influenced research in the area, increasing the number of publications and the diversity of participants used in studies. Samples used in recent published investigations of OE include, for example, Chinese (Siu, 2010) and Korean participants (Hyeyoung & Montgomery, 2010). The preponderance of early and recent research concerns itself with the investigation of OE as measured by the OEQ II and giftedness as assessed by some indicator of intelligence (see Mendaglio, 2010; Mendaglio & Tillier, 2006).

At first glance, increase in the research on OE and giftedness seems encouraging for those of us interested in the entire theory of positive disintegration (TPD; Dąbrowski, 1964, 1967), from which OE is derived. Studies clearly represent OE as a concept in Dąbrowski's theory of personality and not as an isolated psychological construct (e.g., Piirto, Montgomery, & May, 2008; Rinn & Reynolds, 2012; Siu, 201 O; Tieso, 2007). Therefore, an increase in the number of studies and the advent of new researchers bode well for the dissemination of the theory. However, with the ease of data collection, I see increased reason for concern. It seems to me that researchers, although they acknowledge the theoretical underpinnings of OE, approach their investigations of OE and giftedness as if it were an atheoretical psychological construct. In psychological research using Likert scales, for example the OEQ II, it is common practice to view psychological constructs as continuous variables, normally distributed in a population. Such assumptions are necessary to justify the use of the parametric statistics commonly used in OE and giftedness research, such as analysis of variance. Without such assumptions, it is not possible to use analysis of variance with categorical variables such as the Likert scales of the OEQ II.

Another common practice relates to the investigation of the relationship among variables. When the relationship between two variables is the subject of investigations, a positive relationship is frequently the focus of hypotheses or research questions. Researchers typically use intelligence or cognitive ability as the main, if not sole, criterion to classify gifted and nongifted participants. When researchers hypothesize that gifted individuals, those participants with above-average or higher level of intelligence, will score higher on the OEQ II than nongifted individuals, those participants with average level of intelligence, it seems to me that there is an assumption of a positive relationship between OE and intelligence. In this article, I argue that these assumptions underlying current OE and giftedness research may be acceptable for general research purposes, but they are contrary to the conceptualization of OE and its relationship to intelligence in Dąbrowski's theory. After discussing the assumptions noted above, I present a Dąbrowskian view of the variables of interest and conclude with some recommendations for future research.

Analysis of OEQ II Data: From Categorical to Continuous Variables

The OEQ II was designed to measure the five forms of OE: psychomotor, sensual, imaginational, intellectual, and emotional (Falk et al., 1999) The OEQ II consists of 50 self-report items using a 5-point Likert scale with responses ranging from 1 (not at all like me) to 5 (very much like me). High scores indicate higher levels of OE. Each OE subscale was made up of 10 items. An example from the Psychomotor OE subscale is "When I have a lot of energy, I want to do something really physical." A sample item for the Sensual OE subscale is "Viewing art is a totally absorbing experience." The Intellectual OE subscale includes items such as "Theories get my mind going," and an example from the Imaginational OE subscale is "Things that I picture in my mind are so vivid that they seem real to me." A sample item for the Emotional OE subscale is "I can be so happy that I want to laugh and cry at the same time." Total scores are calculated for each OE (Bouchet & Falk, 2001).

Researchers analyze OEQ II data using parametric statistics. For example, Bouchet and Falk (2001) and Tieso (2007) used multivariate analysis of variance, whereas Siu (2010) used a univariate and two-way analysis of variance. Strictly speaking, parametric statistics should be used only with continuous variables, that is, with interval and ratio data (Peers, 1996). Likert scales, such as the OEQ II, yield ordinal data, a type of categorical variable, which also includes nominal data. Arithmetic operations used in parametric statistics cannot be used with ordinal data because the numbers in Likert items are simply labels of categories, a means of ordering the categories but lacking the properties of numbers. Furthermore, ordinal data do not satisfy the assumption of normality needed in statistical procedures such as analysis of variance (Harwell & Gatti, 2001). Pasta (2009) describes how researchers mentally transform categorical into continuous variables to rationalize use of parametric statistics:

> *Researchers, for the purposes of statistical analyses, treat these as continuous variables enabling them to use parametric statistics such as analysis of variance. Treating ordinal data in this manner suggests that researchers assume that the variable is a measurement of an underlying continuous value and the differences between values (e.g., between not like me and somewhat like me; very much like me and like me) are equal.* (p. 3)

Those who argue that parametric statistics are robust with respect to the violations of assumptions relating to the level of measurement and normal distribution support the recasting of Likert scales into continuous variables (Carifio & Perla, 2008; Norman, 2010). Although this may be acceptable for analytical purposes, conceptualizing OE as a continuous variable with a normal distribution is inconsistent with Dąbrowski's theorizing.

Giftedness as Intelligence

Although there are various conceptions of giftedness available, some of which resonate with TPD (e.g., Columbus Group), researchers use a conception of giftedness anchored to intelligence or cognitive ability. In some cases this is done directly, for example, by using a test of cognitive ability; in other cases, it is done indirectly by utilizing the criterion of attendance at a program for gifted students. Examples of studies using tests of cognitive ability to operationalize giftedness are Siu (2010), Wirthwein, Becker, Loehr, and Rost (2011), and Yakmaci-Guzel and Akarsu (2006). Siu (2010) used the scores on the Test of Nonverbal Intelligence-III to "confirm whether participants were in the correct group, that is, gifted and nongifted groups" (p. 7 5). Wirthwein et al. (2011) used scores of "three well-established standardized intelligence tests" (p. 147). Furthermore, for the purposes of their study, they equated giftedness with intelligence: "In the present study, we adopted the definition of 'intellectual giftedness' as being characterized by a high level of intelligence…" (p. 147). Yakmaci-Guzel and Akarsu (2006) used scores on the Raven Advanced Progressive Matrices Test "to group students in terms of their intellectual abilities" (p. 46) and to assign participants to a gifted (high intellectual ability) group or nongifted (low intellectual ability) group.

Studies using enrollment at programs for gifted students (including summer programs) as a criterion for giftedness include Bouchet and Falk (2001); Miller, Falk, and Yinmei (2009); and Rinn and Reynolds (2012). Bouchet and Falk (2001) designated college student participants as gifted if they reported participating in a "program for gifted and talented children" (p. 262). Miller et al. (2009) also identified university students in their sample as gifted if they reported having been "in a gifted program at some time in their educational career" (p. 164). Rinn and Reynolds' (2012) participants were recruited "from a summer program for intellectually gifted students…To qualify for this summer program, students must have been eligible to attend talent search summer programs" (p. 41). I assume that identification of gifted students for participation in a program for gifted students usually includes the criterion of intelligence because tests of cognitive ability are commonly used for the selection of students for participation in programs for the gifted including education programs and talent searches:

> *In the typical school's gifted program, students are identified and selected for a program that offers greater challenge than provided in the regular classroom setting. A primary method of identification includes the administration of group-administered tests such as the Iowa Tests of Basic Skills (Hoover et al., 2003) and/or the Cognitive Abilities Test* (CogAT; Lohman &Hagen, 2001).

Similar to many K-12 identification methods for gifted education programs, the procedures for implementing the Talent Search model commence with gradelevel, group-administered, standardized tests (e.g., the *Iowa Tests of Basic Skills*), which are usually administered as part of the school district's regular testing program. (Assouline & Lupkowski-Shoplik, 2012, p. 48)

As gifted and nongifted participants are so designated using intelligence or cognitive ability, studies investigating OE and giftedness may be interpreted as studying the relationship of OE and intelligence.

Research findings indicating that the gifted sample scored higher on one or more OE(s) than the nongifted sample may be interpreted as supporting association of OE(s) with above-average or higher level of intelligence. An examination of Dąbrowski's theorizing regarding OE in the broader context of TPD reveals a more complex relationship between OE and intelligence.

Current research on OE and giftedness, then, treats OE as a continuous variable, normally distributed across the population, associated with a high level of intelligence. An examination of OE in the broader context of TPD identifies inconsistencies between conceptualization of OE for research purposes with Dąbrowski's theorizing.

OE, Advanced Development, and Developmental Potential

Dąbrowski used OE and *hyperexcitability psychic OE* as synonyms, whereas current literature uses OEs. OE is a heritable property of the central nervous system that produces greater than expected responses to internal and external stimuli. Dąbrowski (1972) defined OE as heightened physiological experience of sensory stimuli caused by increased sensitivity of neurons. OE is depicted as a "higher than average responsiveness to stimuli, manifested either by sensual, psychomotor, emotional (affective), imaginational, or intellectual excitability, or the combination thereof" (Dąbrowski, 1972, p. 303). Not all forms of OE are inherently beneficial. Individuals with Sensual OE are described by Dąbrowski as possessing a superficial sensitivity to beauty, as being suggestible and being more exposed to the difficulties of life. Sensual OE is manifested in a cycle of intense sensual hunger and excessive satiation of drives. Individuals with Psychomotor OE are described as restless, curious, and incapable of sitting still. Individuals with this OE are said to have an insatiable need for change and of "wandering into space" (p. 7). Dąbrowski stated that psychomotor is "the main cause of violent reactions, motor unrest and the need for action" (p. 7). Individuals with Intellectual OE manifest at an early age analytic and synthetic reasoning abilities. Early in life they tend to ask probing questions and demand logical answers. Dąbrowski noted that Intellectual OE "causes a whirl, a stream of problems, thoughts, multidimensional mental attitudes, and a richness of associations and methods of work" (p. 7). Individuals with Imaginational OE are "[s] ensitive toward 'imaginational realities,"' (p. 7). Such individuals are often creative, capable of generating many ideas, fantasies, and dreams, which are often expressed in artistic products such as poetry, music, and paintings. Individuals who possess the final OE, Emotional, are described as being sensitive, often taking life events to heart, and creating intense experience of emotions in self and others. Individuals with Emotional OE are empathic. Attuned to the suffering of others, they develop attitudes of compassion, pity, and worry toward others. Emotional OE is also manifested in the need for exclusive and lasting relationships.

Advanced Development and Developmental Potential

Advanced development—transformation from a lower to a higher way of being—requires the presence of certain forms of OE. Dąbrowski presented forms of OE hierarchically, that is, some are higher and others are lower with respect to the developmental process. He made it clear that the higher forms of OE—intellectual, imaginational, and emotional—are a *sine qua non* of the developmental force. He noted that these three forms serve to transform the lower forms: sensual and psychomotor (Dąbrowski, 1972). Dąbrowski used OE to distinguish between two types of developmental potential: the presence of all forms of OE, which he termed *positive developmental potential* and the presence of only psychomotor and sensual, which he termed *negative developmental potential.*

Positive developmental potential. Developmental potential is positive when the five forms of OE are present. Such OE sparks the process of development by provoking

> *Conflicts, disappointments, suffering in family life, in school, in professional life. In short, interaction of all forms of OE leads to external conflicts with the social environment. Overexcitability also provokes inner conflicts as well as the means by which these conflicts can be overcome.* (Dąbrowski, 1970, p. 38)

All five forms of OE are necessary for producing the type of interpersonal and intrapersonal conflict essential for development in the TPD. Individuals' development begins with experiences of such conflicts and evolves when individuals transcend the dictates of the social environment and biological drives.

Negative developmental potential. According to Dąbrowski's descriptions, the sensual and psychomotor forms have a dark side to them. When all five forms are present, the higher forms transform psychomotor and sensual such that their energy is harnessed in the service of the developmental process. When occurring by themselves, psychomotor and sensual forms constitute negative developmental potential (Dąbrowski, 1972). Under certain conditions, the combination of psychomotor and sensual leads to serious negative outcomes: "When enhanced psychomotor and Sensual overexcitability is combined with strong ambition, tendency to showing off and lying, it constitutes a nucleus of psychopathy with some neuropathic components" (Dąbrowski, 1972, p. 11).

Developmental Potential and Environmental Influence

For both types of developmental potential discussed in this article, the social environment has little influence (Dąbrowski, 1972). In the case of positive developmental potential, the influence of the environment is negligible—even a negative social environment will not impede the growth of individuals. Individuals' biological endowment is sufficient to propel them toward advanced development. Similarly, social environmental influence has no significant effect on negative developmental potential. The presence of only psychomotor and sensual is not deemed sufficient to spark the developmental process. Transformation, that is, transcending the influence of biology and the social environment, is not possible with negative developmental potential, regardless of the most favorable environmental conditions. It must be remembered, however, that I am discussing development in a Dąbrowskian sense, not the commonly used psychological sense.

OE and Factors of Development

Dąbrowski's propositions regarding OE are clarified in the context of his factors of development. Dąbrowski used an ordinal way of labeling these factors. Biology is the First Factor, social environment is the Second Factor, and a set of autonomous forces constitute the Third Factor. The First Factor represents the constitutional makeup of individuals. As an uncommon heritable characteristic, OE may or may not be part of an individual's biological endowment. However, instincts, such as self-preservation, and drives, such as hunger, are universal. The Second Factor refers to the social environment in which individuals find themselves. This includes the values, norms, and prescriptions associated with that environment. The Third Factor of development is a concept Dąbrowski considered difficult to define (Dąbrowski, 1973). In TPD, this factor of development is present only in those individuals who have positive developmental potential, that is, all forms of OE. The Third Factor arises from the interaction of the five forms of OE as they come in contact with the demands of the social environment. Internal and external conflicts are the products of these interactions. As individuals with positive developmental potential experience crises sparked by interactions in the social environment, autonomous forces, termed *dynamisms*, are triggered. In time, a super dynamism, which serves to coordinate other dynamisms emerges—the Third Factor. As a result, the developmental process is in the hands of individuals themselves and not directed by the demands of the other two factors.

An indication of whether individuals are developing can be found by answering the question: Which factor(s) is (are) influencing individuals' daily living? Individuals who are primarily influenced by the First and/or Second Factors are not on the path of advanced development. Influence of these factors represents what Dąbrowski termed biological development (Dąbrowski, 1972). Individuals who are primarily influenced by the Third Factor represent *autonomous development* (Dąbrowski, 1972). The presence of only the lower forms of OE is associated with biological development. We can see support for this association in Dąbrowski's description and his definition of negative developmental potential. Specifically, Sensual OE is preoccupied with satiation of instincts and drives (First Factor) and is suggestible, conforming to societal expectations (Second Factor). Autonomous development is the result of the influence of the Third Factor, requiring positive developmental potential, that is, all five forms of OE.

In sum, OE is a heritable property of the central nervous system. As such, individuals may inherit all forms of OE, one or more, or none at all. When all five forms are present (positive developmental potential), development is described as autonomous. When only sensual and psychomotor are present (negative developmental potential), development is described as biological. OE and the type of development are described in the context of the three factors of development. Autonomous development represents the influence of the Third Factor; biological development represents the influence of the First and Second Factors. Dąbrowski's theory regarding OE does not support the conceptualization of OE as a continuous variable, normally distributed across the population.

Intelligence

In his research and clinical work, Dąbrowski (1972) measured intelligence by using a test of cognitive ability, namely, contemporary versions of the Wechsler scales, the Wechsler Intelligence Scale for Children (WISC; Wechsler, 1949) and the Wechsler Adult Intelligence Scale (WAIS; Wechsler, 1955). When he made references in his writing to below average, average, above-average, or high level of intelligence, it is reasonable to assume that he was referring to intelligence as measured by an intelligence test. It is important to note, however, that he distinguished between Intelligence and Intellectual OE; his caution to readers: "intellectual overexcitability should not be confused with intellectual functioning and intelligence. Under the term intellectual overexcitability we put those forms of enhanced reactivity which are expressed in logical and causal cognition focused on finding answers to probing questions" (Dąbrowski, 1996, p. 182).

Dąbrowski relegated intelligence to a subservient role in daily functioning. Intelligence, regardless of level, is simply a tool individuals use to achieve aims and goals. What an individual does with his or her intelligence depends on the type of development involved. In what Dąbrowski described as biological development, intelligence is in the service of individuals' gratification of instincts, drives, and needs. In the extreme negative version of biological development, *one-sided development*, intelligence is directed by sociopathic and, at times, criminal aims and goals. In contrast, in autonomous development, intelligence serves higher aims and values, such as altruism and authenticity. Different levels of intellectual functioning are associated with all three types of mental development. Dąbrowski attributed average level of intelligence to biological development. However, he attributed above-average level of intelligence to one-sided and autonomous forms. Above-average intelligence, then, cannot be associated exclusively with one particular type of development. Above-average intelligence itself cannot be used to differentiate between development that is manifested by a lack of empathy "emotional coldness, unlimited ruthlessness and craving for power [one sided development]" (Dąbrowski, 1970, p. 30) and development that is manifested in "individual differentiation, autonomy in relation to the laws of biology, authenticity, creativity [autonomous development]" (p. 29).

A conclusion drawn from Dąbrowski's postulates regarding the role of intelligence and advanced development is that a high level of intelligence is a required but insufficient condition for advanced development (Mendaglio & Pyryt, 2004). Further support for this contention is found in our experiences and Dąbrowski's writings. If we reflect for a moment, we can conjure up not only public and historical figures but also some individuals that we may encounter in our daily life who are, by all accounts, highly intelligent but are far from being exemplars of humanity. Regarding Dąbrowski's writings, in addition to the general comments I noted above, comments about the complex relationship between intelligence and development abound (Nixon, 2005). His discussions of intelligence in the context of developmental levels make the point emphatically (see Dąbrowski, 1996). For example, he states that individuals may make great contributions in scientific and scholarly fields—requiring high levels of intelligence-without concomitant growth in other areas, indicated by a lack of consideration for others, a need for self-aggrandization, and a hunger for power. In such cases, there is a very high level of intelligence coupled with an absence of positive developmental potential—a lack of OE or the presence of some but not all forms of OE. In such individuals, intelligence is a self-serving instrument. From a Dąbrowskian perspective, then, above-average intelligence—the way researchers define giftedness—may be associated with autonomous or biological development. That is, above-average intelligence may be associated with all forms of OE or only with some forms.

In sum, intelligence is not synonymous with Intellectual OE. Above-average intelligence is theoretically associated with autonomous and biological development. That is, above-average intelligence not only occurs with the five forms of OE but it is also associated with the presence of only sensual and psychomotor OEs. TPD does not predict a positive relationship between giftedness (as operationally defined in current research) and OE.

Researching TPD Concepts: Need for a Paradigm Shift

Research methodology currently used to investigate giftedness and OE seems to assume that OE is an atheoretical construct that can be treated like many other psychological constructs. Research methods seem to me to be in stark contrast with the depiction of OE in the introductory sections of research publications. There is a consensus in such articles that OE is an integral part of Dąbrowski's TPD, his theory of personality. Such acknowledgment of the conceptual source of OE, however, does not seem to permeate the research process.

Students of TPD are aware of its uniqueness and the demands it makes particularly when one first encounters it: TPD requires us to understand paradoxical-sounding terms and to reframe our understanding of virtually all common psychological terms. OE, positive disintegration, and positive maladjustment are only a few terms that pose challenges to new students of the theory. Furthermore, TPD requires us to reconsider the meaning of terms such as intelligence, development, and personality. Intelligence plays a subordinate role in development, whereas emotions are primary; development, in short, means the movement from a life being driven by biological and social forces to one motivated by higher aims and values; and personality is an achievement, not a given human attribute (Mendaglio, 2008). Most important of all is that TPD is a comprehensive theory of personality with a multitude of assumptions, propositions, and concepts highly integrated into a conceptual whole. As such, it is difficult to investigate one concept without reference to other aspects of the theory. The phrase *paradigm shift* may suffer from overuse, but it strikes me as the perfect phrase to describe the task facing researchers who wish to test hypotheses based on TPD concepts.

A general suggestion for making this shift is the use of related TPD concepts to interpret research findings on OE. To illustrate, I use findings reported by several studies. Some studies (e.g., Siu, 2010) have reported that participants who are gifted score higher on the OEQ II than their nongifted counterparts on all five forms of OE. However, this is not the case with all studies. Some studies found that giftedness is associated with only some forms of OE (e.g., Bouchet & Falk, 2001), whereas others reported that psychomotor is the best form of OE to distinguish between gifted and nongifted individuals (e.g., Bouchard, 2004). Inconsistent research findings may in fact be reinterpreted as lending some support for Dąbrowski's conception of the relationship between above-average intelligence and OE: above-average intelligence is not automatically associated with the presence of all or some forms of OE. In other words, the findings may indicate that the participants who are gifted vary in terms of the developmental trajectory they are currently experiencing, biological or autonomous.

To avoid inconsistency with Dąbrowski's theoretical framework, I recommend the following for researchers interested in exploring giftedness and OE:

- Consider using other conceptions of giftedness, ideally those that resonate with TPD.
- Use nonparametric statistics for analyzing OEQ II data.
- Design large-scale studies using a measure of intelligence, not to identify giftedness but rather to test the Dąbrowskian view of OE and intelligence.
- Avoid references to TPD if the study treats OE as an atheoretical construct.

Conclusion

Research on OE and giftedness is on the increase, which benefits the dissemination of Dąbrowski's TPD. The increase also highlights the need for a cautionary note regarding assumptions underlying research methodology. A close examination of Dąbrowski's theorizing is needed to ensure that researchers are assessing OE as represented in TPD. If giftedness is defined as intelligence, then we need to understand the relationship between intelligence and OE as described in TPD. A major challenge confronting researchers interested in TPD concepts is the theory itself. Its uniqueness does require a paradigm shift for researchers steeped in investigating concepts from other theories in psychology.

To conclude, it is important to emphasize that my sole interest lies in refining not reifying the TPD. Theories will not endure if their tenets are perceived as written in stone. If research methodology accurately reflects TPD concepts and we find, for example, that OE is in fact quite common, such information can be used to revise the theory. Negative findings arising from methodology reflective of theorizing, in my mind, are as useful as positive results. However, researchers need to ensure that they are, in fact, investigating concepts such as OE as represented in the theory; otherwise, it is not possible to use their findings to refine Dąbrowski's TPD.

Declaration of Conflicting Interests

The author declared no potential conflicts of interest with respect to the research, authorship, and/or publication of this article.

Funding

The author received no financial support for the research and/or authorship of this article.

References

Assouline, S. G., & Lupkowski-Shoplik, A. (2012). The talent search model of gifted identification. *Journal of Psychoeducational Assessment,* 30, 45-59.

Bouchard, L. L. (2004). An instrument for the measure of Dąbrowskian overexcitabilities to identify gifted elementary students. *Gifted Child Quarterly,* 48, 339-350.

Bouchet, N., & Falk, R. F. (2001). The relationship among giftedness, gender, and overexcitability. *Gifted Child Quarterly*, 45, 260-267.

Carifio, J., & Perla, R. (2008). Resolving the 50 year debate around using and misusing Likert scales. *Medical Education,* 42, 1150-1152.

Dąbrowski, K. (1964). *Positive disintegration.* Boston, MA: Little Brown.

Dąbrowski, K. (1967). *Personality-shaping through positive disintegration.* Boston, MA: Little Brown.

Dąbrowski, K. (1970). *Mental growth through positive disintegration.* London, England: Gryf.

Dąbrowski, K. (1972). *Psychoneurosis is not an illness.* London, England: Gryf.

Dąbrowski, K. (1973). *The dynamics of concepts.* London, England: Gryf.

Dąbrowski, K. (1996). *Multilevelness of emotional and instinctive functions. Part 1: Theory and description of levels of behavior.* Lublin, Poland: Towarzystwo Naukowe Katolickiego Uniwersytetu Lubelskiego.

Falk, R. R., Lind, S., Miller, N. B., Piechowski, M. M., & Silverman, L. K. (1999). *The Overexcitability Questionnaire-Two (OEQ II): Manual, scoring system, and questionnaire.* Denver, CO: Institute for the Study of Advanced Development.

Harwell, M. R., & Gatti, G. G. (2001). Rescaling ordinal data to interval data in educational research. *Review of Educational Research,* 71, I 05-132.

Hyeyoung, B., & Montgomery, D. (2010). Exploring Korean and American teachers' preferred emotional types. *Roeper Review,* 32, 176-188.

Lysy, K. Z., & Piechowski M. M. (1983). Personal growth: An empirical study using Jungian and Dąbrowskian measures. *Genetic Psychology Monographs,* 108, 267-320.

Mendaglio, S. (2008). Dąbrowski's theory of positive disintegration: A personality theory for the 21st century. In S. Mendaglio (Ed.), *Dąbrowski's theory of positive disintegration* (pp. 13-40). Scottsdale, AZ: Great Potential Press.

Mendaglio, S. (2010). Overexcitabilities and Dąbrowski's theory. In F. Preckel, W. Schneider, & H. Holling (Eds.), *Diagnosis of giftedness. Series: Yearbook of the pedagogicalpsychological diagnosis.* Tests and Trends (Vol. 8, pp. 169-196).

Mendaglio, S., & Pyryt, M. (2004). The role of intelligence in the theory of positive disintegration. In W. Tillier (Ed.), *Developmental potential—From theory to practice: Educational and therapeutic perspectives* (pp. 64-181). Proceedings from the Sixth International Congress of the Institute for Positive Disintegration in Human Development Calgary, Alberta, Canada.

Mendaglio, S., & Tillier, W. (2006). Dąbrowski's theory of positive disintegration and giftedness: Overexcitabilities research findings. *Journal for the Education of the Gifted*, 30, 68-87.

Miller, N. B., Falk, R., & Yinmei, H. (2009). Gender identity and the overexcitability profiles of gifted college students. *Roeper Review*, 31, 161-169.

Miller, N. B., & Silverman, L. K. (1987). Levels of personality development. *Roeper Review*, 9, 221-225.

Nixon, L. (2005). Potential for positive disintegration and IQ. *Dąbrowskian Newsletter*, 10(2), 1-5.

Norman, G. (2010). Likert scales, levels of measurement and the "laws" of statistics. *Advances in Health Education*, 15, 625-632.

Pasta, D. J. (2009). Learning when to be discrete: Continuous vs. categorical predictors. *Proceedings of the SAS Global Forum*, USA. (Paper No. 248-2009).

Peers, I. S. (1996). *Statistical analysis for education and psychology researchers.* London, England: Routledge.

Piechowski, M. M., Silverman, L., & Falk, F. (1985). Comparison of intellectually and artistically gifted on five dimensions of mental functions. *Perceptual & Motor Skills*, 60, 539-549.

Piirto, J., Montgomery, D., & May, J. (2008). A comparison of Dąbrowski's overexcitabilities for American and Korean high school gifted students. *High Abilities Studies*, 19, 141-153.

Rinn, A. N., & Reynolds, M. J. (2012). Overexcitabilities and ADHD in the gifted: An examination. *Roeper Review*, 34, 38-45.

Siu, A. F. Y. (2010). Comparing overexcitabilities of gifted and nongifted school children in Hong Kong: Does culture make a difference? *Asia Pacific Journal of Education*, 30, 71-83.

Tieso, C. L. (2007). Overexcitabilities: A new way to think about talent? *Roeper Review*, 29, 232-239.

Wechsler, D. (1949). *Wechsler Intelligence Scale for Children: Manual.* New York, NY: Psychological Corporation.

Wechsler, D. (1955). *Wechsler Adult Intelligence Scale: Manual.* New York, NY: Psychological Corporation.

Wirthwein, L., Becker, C. V., Loehr, E.-V., & Rost, D. H. (201 J). Overexcitabilities in gifted and non-gifted adults: Does sex matter? *High Abilities Studies*, 22, 145-153.

Yakmaci-Guzel, B., & Akarsu, F. (2006). Comparing overexcitabilities of gifted and non-gifted 10th grade students in Turkey. *High Ability Studies,* 17, 43-56.

Chapter 9
Overexcitability Research: International Focus

This chapter is my contribution to a handbook of gifted education relevant to the Asia-Pacific geographic region. In examining the available research on the theory of positive disintegration and giftedness, I found that the state of research related to the theory was similar to that in North America—limited to overexcitability. The chapter includes an overview of the theory of positive disintegration presented informally but retaining the essence of it. My suggestions for educators wishing to apply the theory in their work with gifted students conclude the chapter.

Reference

Mendaglio S.S. (2019) Overexcitability and Giftedness Research: Whose Constructs Are Being Investigated and How? In: Smith S. (ed.) *Handbook of Giftedness and Talent Development in the Asia-Pacific.* Springer International Handbooks of Education. Springer, Singapore.

Overexcitability and Giftedness Research: Whose Constructs Are Being Investigated?

What began as the fascination of a handful of American proponents and researchers in the 1980s, overexcitability (OE) has risen to prominence in the field of gifted education (Bailey, 2011). The global popularity of OE is manifested in publications by researchers from numerous countries outside the USA: Turkey, Spain, Germany, France, Venezuela, and more recently, Malaysia, Taiwan, Hong Kong, Korea, New Zealand and Australia. Presentations at national and international conferences, popular literature and countless websites make OE in its five forms—sensual, psychomotor, imaginational, intellectual and emotional—accessible to educators, practitioners and parents of gifted children. With the intense attention OE receives, novices can be forgiven if they conclude that OE is a theory unto itself, rather than one component of a comprehensive, complex theory; namely, the theory of positive disintegration (TPD; Dąbrowski, 1967, 1970, 1972). Scholars investigating OE in gifted education often show a similarity to individuals who are new to the construct. Though researchers typically include reference to TPD in their reports, noting that OE is part of TPD, their assumptions and methodology create the impression that they share neophytes' perception of the construct.

In my reviews of the literature, I have criticised the research on both conceptual and methodological grounds. In my most recent commentary on OE research (Mendaglio, 2012), I called for a paradigmatic shift in research. I observed that recent research investigating OE and intellectual giftedness, including that by a number of

Asian-Pacific investigators, continues to use the old pattern (e.g. see Alias, Rahman, Majid, & Yassin, 2013). Researchers state that OE is part of TPD, then approach it as an atheoretical construct separate from the TPD (Tillier, 2009; Vuyk, Kerr, & Krieshok, 2016). After presenting a critique of current research, I discuss OE in the context of Dąbrowski's TPD.

OE and Intellectual Giftedness Research

The established pattern of exploring the relationship between OE and giftedness is to conduct studies that investigate differences between gifted and non-gifted samples or explore profiles of OE among gifted samples. Use of the Overexcitability Questionnaire Two (OEQII), which has all but replaced the Overexcitability Questionnaire (OEQ), is part of the research methodology. The descriptions of the two questionnaires immediately explain why OEQII has supplanted the original version.

OE Questionnaires

The OEQ (Lysy & Piechowski, 1983) is designed to assess the five over-excitabilities. It consists of a 21-item open-ended self-report questionnaire with no space or time limits. The OEQ may be completed in groups or individually with the researcher either present or absent. The questions are intended to facilitate individuals' self-analyses and reflections. Responses are scored by trained raters who make judgements regarding the absence, or the presence and intensity, of an overexcitability in a participant's written answers. Questions were originally intended to identify a particular OE, but later the procedure was amended to examine each response for indications of any one of the five OEs. Sample items include: 'Do you ever feel incredibly happy? Describe your feelings. When do you feel the most energy and what do you do with it? What do you like to concentrate on most? If you ask yourself "who am I" what is the answer? When you read a book, what attracts your attention the most?' (see Piechowski & Miller, 1995 for the entire list of questions). Indices of reliability and validity of the OEQ are reported as respect-able with test-retest reliability of 0.65, 3–6 weeks apart, for a group of adults. Construct validity was established by studies using practising artists who scored significantly high on emotional, imaginational and intellectual OEs (see Silverman, 2008). While the OEQ yields rich material regarding OE, it is complicated and time-consuming to use in research. Piirto and Fraas (2012) illustrate this point: 'The OEQ is cumbersome to score and analyze. Just scoring and entering the data for [our] small study took months' (p. 29).

The OEQII (Falk, Lind, Miller, Piechowski, & Silverman, 1999) is an adaptation of the original OEQ. The OEQII is a 50-item Likert-type self-report questionnaire also designed to measure the five overexcitabilities. Participants respond to the items using a 5-point scale ranging from 1 (not at all like me) to 5 (very much like me). Each OE is assessed by ten items. Sample items for each OE include: When I have a lot of energy, I want to do something really physical (psychomotor). Viewing art is a totally absorbing experience (sensual). Theories get my mind going (intellectual). Things that I picture in my mind are so vivid that they seem real to me (imaginational). And, I can be so happy that I can laugh and cry at the same time (emotional). For each OE, total scores are calculated. The higher the score, the greater the presence of the OE. Using normative sample data, Falk et al. (1999) reported high Cronbach alphas for each set of the OE items: psychomotor (0.86), sensual (0.89), imaginational (0.85), intellectual (0.89) and emotional (0.84).

While the OEQ sparked the investigation of OE and giftedness, it is the OEQII that is responsible for a dramatic increase in OE research productivity over the years. As can be seen in the descriptions of the two questionnaires, they are both easy to administer, but that is where the similarity ends. With the OEQII's easily accessible scores, data entry and analyses are readily conducted. The OEQII not only facilitates data analysis, but also has a particular advantage to researchers. Similar to investigating other constructs using Likert-type scales, researchers need not concern themselves with the conceptual basis of the construct. All that is required in the current research approach is minimal mention of TPD and review of previous empirical findings. Using the OEQII does not require researchers to have any actual knowledge of Dąbrowski's conception of the construct they investigate. Therein lies the problem. An understanding of the nature of OE, as an integral part of TPD, is essential. In my view, the use of the OEQII is conceptually problematic. From a TPD perspective, OE is a heritable property of the central nervous system which is not evenly distributed across a population. Accordingly, some individuals inherit no OE, others inherit one or more and, finally, the rare individual inherits all five forms. Using Likert-type scales to assess OE suggests most if not all individuals have some level of OE (Mendaglio, 2012).

The OEQII has been criticised by others on psychometric grounds. Warne (2011) conducted a reliability generalisation (RG) of the measure: 'RG is a specific type of meta-analysis in which reliability coefficients are meta-analyzed instead of effect sizes' (p. 674). Warne's extensive analyses of the reliability of scores in 16 studies provided a great deal of information to guide future researchers in designing their studies with the OEQII. However, it was one of his concluding remarks regarding limitations of his study that is relevant to my discussion of the measure:

> *Finally, although this study constitutes the most thorough examination of the reliability of OEQII scores, it provides little—if any—information about the validity of the OEQII score interpretations. It has never been clear what exactly the OEQII measures and evidence of any sort of validity has been meager (Miller et al., 2009) or unfavorable for the OEQII (Warne, 2011). Further psychometric studies on the instrument should be conducted before the instrument gains widespread acceptance.* (Warne, 2011, p. 688)

Winkler and Voight (2016) also meta-analysed the scores of 12 studies to investigate the relationship between giftedness and OE. They reported medium and small effect sizes for the five forms of OE, suggesting some support for relating OE and giftedness. However, they note that a number of considerations complicate the interpretations of results. For one thing, there is the dispute regarding psycho-metric and theoretical merits: 'If the OEQII were a psychometrically flawed instrument as some have claimed (Warne, 2011), then this would make this meta-analysis at least partially invalid' (p. 251). Winkler and Voight conclude that the findings, given the controversy over the OEQII, should not be taken as support for the relationship between OE and giftedness. One suggestion they make is that it may be used by practitioners with individual gifted students and patients.

These meta-analyses support the conceptual reviews by Mendaglio and Tillier (2006) of studies from the 1980s to the early 2000s. The 14 studies reviewed generally lent partial support for the association of OE and giftedness. Greater support was found in studies that used adult participants. The greatest support was found in a few studies that used creativity as a criterion for giftedness, particularly when the participants were practising artists. While there was consensus on assessing the OE variable, the OEQ, this was not the case with assessing the giftedness variable. The samples of gifted individuals included elementary school children who had been assessed, counsellors, and graduate students, practising artists, students in gifted programmes, and children who scored high on tests of creativity.

In more recent studies concerned with comparing gifted and non-gifted and exploring gifted individuals' OE profiles, there is a greater agreement among researchers regarding the method of assessing both constructs (Mendaglio, 2012). The OEQII replaces the OEQ. Giftedness is determined by the use of intelligence, estimated directly or indirectly. In rare instances, researchers identify their gifted participants by administering a test of intelligence. More commonly, researchers use the criterion of enrollment in a school for the gifted or that of attendance at a summer camp for gifted youth. In the latter method, intelligence is assumed since it is the major criterion used for selecting gifted students. Technically, researchers are investigating the relationship between OE and intellectual giftedness.

Mendaglio and Tillier (2006) and Mendaglio (2012) identified theoretical issues that led to their questioning the validity of the studies. They noted researchers' disregard of Dąbrowski's conception of OE and its boundedness to his TPD. Researchers mistakenly represented OE as a positive construct with no negative aspects, assumed that giftedness necessarily means possession of all five forms of OE, and implied that OE and intelligence are correlated, since giftedness is often assessed in terms of intelligence. In some cases, the belief in the relationship between giftedness and OE is such that researchers expect that OE should predict giftedness. These misconceptions appear in many articles published over the years and they persist today. Not surprisingly, they have been exported to Asia-Pacific investigators.

Brief Overview of the Usage of the OE Questionnaire in Some Asia-Pacific Nations

Interest in researching OEs took about 40 years to extend from America to Asian-Pacific countries, such as Australia (e.g. Harper, Cornish, Smith, & Merrotsy, 2017), Hong Kong, China (e.g. Siu, 2010); Korea (e.g. Yoon & Moon, 2009), Taiwan (e.g. Chang & Kuo, 2009) and Malaysia (e.g. Alias et al., 2013) to name a few. It is not surprising that the design of studies is similar to the American approach in their underlying assumptions and data collection methods. To illustrate, I first briefly describe a sample of publications, followed by discussion of one study in depth to elaborate on my perspective regarding the current research approach to OE. Yoon and Moon (2009), using a Korean translation of OEQII, examined gender differences in OE scores within a large sample of gifted and non-gifted Korean students. They reported that the gifted sample scored higher than the nongifted on all OEs, with intellectual OE scores discriminating the most between gifted and nongifted participants. Findings included gender differences. Yoon and Moon concluded that the best predictor of giftedness is the intellectual OE, with the best predictor of giftedness among girls being imaginational OE.

Siu (2010) claimed to be the first to introduce Dąbrowski's theory and overexcitabilities into the Chinese literature and use the OEQ for Hong Kong students. Siu explicitly stated that the purpose of the study was to find alternate, non-IQ methods of identifying gifted students. Similar to Yoon and Moon, Siu used a translation of the OEQII to examine group and gender differences among gifted and non-gifted Chinese school children in Hong Kong. Gifted children's scores were higher than non-gifted on all OEs. Interestingly, both gifted and non-gifted female students scored significantly higher on emotional OE than males. Further, gifted females scored significantly higher on sensual OE than gifted males. He and Wong (2014) were also interested in gender differences, including whether there was greater variability with respect to the five OEs. Using a Chinese translation of the OEQII, they surveyed a large number of adolescent students. The male pattern of scores indicated greater variability on the sensual, imaginational and intellectual OE than females. Males scored significantly higher on psychomotor; females scored significantly higher on emotional.

He, Wong, and Chan (2017) investigated the prediction of creativity among Hong Kong students using overexcitabilities. The Chinese translation of OEQII and a measure of creativity were administered to a large sample of Hong Kong adolescent students. The sample consisted of students with a wide range of academic abilities. Results indicated significant, but low correlations among the five OEs and creativity. The most significant predictor of creativity was imaginational. The studies described above demonstrate similar concerns identified by Mendaglio and Tillier (2006).

In order to illustrate my perspective, I discuss a Malaysian study specifically. Alias, Rahman, and colleagues (2013) investigated the OE profiles of gifted Malaysian students using a Malay translation of the OEQII. The sample consisted of 335 students, aged 10–15 attending a summer camp specifically for gifted students. In the rationale for the study, the researchers clearly acknowledge that OE is part of Dąbrowski's theory. They also express the belief that OE can be used by teachers to identify gifted students' strengths. Examples are provided for each form of OE. The following lengthy quotation is necessary to convey how the forms of OE are generally presented as exclusively positive in nature, contrary to OE in TPD (discussed in detail later in this chapter):

> *[O]verexcitabilities can be used to identify the gifted students' potentials based on their domains of Overexcitabilities. For example, gifted students who show the following characteristics have potentials in the respective fields: i) psychomotor overexcitability would bring out potential in the field of sports or extreme and challenging*

> *sports; ii) sensual overexcitability with high sensitivity to taste buds reflects the potential in the field of culinary arts; iii) imagination overexcitability shows potential in the field of performing or visual arts or creatively produce outstanding inventions; iv) intellectual overexcitability is essential in developing potentials academic fields such as science and technology; and finally v) emotional overexcitability would bring out the sensitivity towards potentially in the of social activities that concerns with the wellbeing of the human civilisation.*

Therefore, overexcitabilities should be accepted as part of the gifted students' personalities that should be understood, stimulated, and also supported to ensure a healthy development of their potentials (Daniels & Meckstroth, 2009), rather than being labelled and punished as behavioural or problematic problems. (Alias et al., 2013, p. 121)

Initially, the researchers presumed that all gifted students possess OEs, which can be used to identify their potentials. On the first half of this point, assuming that all gifted students have OEs is problematic when contrasted with TPD, which indicates that some individuals are bereft of OE. Later in interpreting their findings, the authors created four profiles, one of which seemed to contradict this position. Of interest is Profile 4 in which 88 students had low scores on all forms of OE. Citing Piirto (2010), the authors interpreted the low scores as indicating an absence of OE. To their credit, in so doing, they illustrated the Dąbrowskian perspective that not everyone, gifted or not, has OE. With respect to the second half of the presumption, Dąbrowski's interest in OE was in its relationship to human development, not the actualisation of specific potentials. Citing other scholars, the authors claim that 'Dąbrowski had stated that an individual who possesses more than one over-excitability characteristic is a gifted and talented individual' (p. 122). This illustrates one of a number of common misconceptions about OE and intelligence. An implication of this erroneous statement is that OE can be used to identify giftedness. In a broader sense, because researchers' beliefs about OE influence their interpretation of their findings, it is essential that all scholars become familiar with all aspects of TPD. Generally, studies investigating the relationship between giftedness and OE and profiles of OE among gifted students have some commonalities. Their results indicate various levels of correlation among one or more OE, as measured by the OEQII, and giftedness as measured by intelligence scores. Similarly, OE profiles of gifted students vary from those having high scores on all forms of OE to those having low scores. The studies generally represent assumptions that are inconsistent with Dąbrowski's theorising. Lastly, their use of the OEQII has rendered findings that may be interesting, but which cannot be interpreted as testing TPD constructs.

OE and Intelligence in the Theory of Positive Disintegration

Overexcitabilities

Dąbrowski (1972) defined OE as heightened physiological experience of sensory stimuli caused by increased sensitivity of neurons. OE is depicted as a 'higher than average responsiveness to stimuli, manifested either by sensual, psychomotor, emotional (affective), imaginational, or intellectual excitability, or the combination thereof' (Dąbrowski, 1972, p. 303). Dąbrowski initially used psychic over-excitability to emphasise that the five forms represent the magnification and enhancement of cognitive processes. While many descriptions appear in original sources of TPD, the description provided in a posthumously published book (Dąbrowski, 1996) captures the essence of the five forms. Given the variations appearing in the literature, it is important to review Dąbrowski's original conceptualisation.

Sensual overexcitability is a function of a heightened experiencing of sensory pleasure. It manifests itself as need for comfort, luxury, aesthetics, fashions, superficial relations with others, frequent changes of lovers, etc. As with the psychomotor form it also may, but, need not be, a manifestation of a transfer of emotional tension to sensual forms of expression of which the most common examples are overeating and excessive sexual stimulation. In children, sensual overexcitability manifests itself as a need for cuddling, kissing, clinging to mother's body, early heightened interest in sexual matters, showing off, and need to be with others all the time.

Psychomotor overexcitability is a function of an excess of energy and manifests itself, for example, in rapid talk, restlessness, violent games, sports, pressure for action or delinquent behaviour. It may either be a 'pure' manifestation of the excess of energy, or it may result from the transfer of emotional tension to psychomotor forms of expression such as those mentioned above.

Imaginational overexcitability in its 'pure' form manifests itself through association of images and impressions, inventiveness, use of image and metaphor in verbal expression, as well as strong and sharp visualisation. In its 'impure' form, emotional tension is transferred to dreams, nightmares, mixing of truth and fiction, fears of the unknown, etc. Imaginational overexcitability leads to an intense living in the world of fantasy, predilection for fairy and magic tales, poetic creations, or invention of fantastic stories.

Intellectual overexcitability in contrast to the first three does not distinctly manifest the transfer of emotional tension to intellectual activity under specific forms. This does not mean that intellectual and emotional processes of high intensity do not occur together. They do, but they do not appear to take on such distinct forms. Intellectual overexcitability is manifested as a drive to ask probing questions, avidity for knowledge, theoretical thinking, reverence for logic, preoccupation with theoretical problems, etc.

Emotional overexcitability is a function of experiencing emotional relationships. The relationships can manifest themselves as strong attachment to persons, living things, or places. From the developmental point of view presented here, intensity of feelings and display of emotions alone are not developmentally significant unless the experiential aspect of relationship is present. This distinction is very important. For example, when a child is refused candy he may throw a temper tantrum just to show his anger. Or, he may go away sad thinking he is not loved (Boldface in original; Dąbrowski, 1996, pp. 72–73).

In TPD, not all forms of OE are inherently beneficial. Dąbrowski specifically identified sensual and psychomotor as lower forms of

OE (Dąbrowski, 1972). Sensual is manifested in a cycle of intense sensual hunger leading to preoccupation with satisfaction of drives. Psychomotor is manifested in a need for novelty, rest-lessness, hyperactivity and impulsivity. The higher forms—imaginational, intellectual and emotional—serve to attenuate the lower forms. The naturally occurring manifestations are sublimated into higher forms of expression and serve to energise the individuals' quest for higher functioning.

It is important to note that individuals may inherit no OE, one or more forms, or all forms. These various combinations have implications for development or lack of development. It is important to remember that development has a unique meaning in this theory. Simply stated, it refers to a nonlinear progression from a civilised animal-like existence to a highly aware, autonomous, altruistic, values-driven living. All five forms are required for individuals to be on that journey. A lack of OE suggests that individuals may lead a good life being solid citizens but with little awareness or autonomy, living under the influence of biology and society. Dąbrowski was clear about the negative outcomes associated with the presence of only the lower forms: 'When enhanced psychomotor and sensual overexcitability is combined with strong ambition, tendency to showing off and lying, it constitutes a nucleus of psychopathy with some neuropathic components' (1972, p. 11). (This statement is worth recalling when research findings claim to indicate that psychomotor assessment is the best form to differentiate gifted from non-gifted individuals.)

Intelligence. TPD's lexicon is replete with unique terminology (overexcitability, dynamisms; see Harper et al., 2017 for definitions), unexpected juxtapositions (positive disintegration, negative adjustment) and reframing of common terms (development, personality). *Intelligence* is an exception. In his clinical work, writing and research, Dąbrowski retained the mainstream conception of the term. This is manifested in his use of Wechsler scales to assess intelligence in his patients and research participants (Dąbrowski, 1967). In his discussions, he refers to below average, average, above average or high level of intelligence. However, Dąbrowski reframed the role of intelligence in development in general. According to Mendaglio (2014), Dąbrowski relegated intelligence to a subservient role in daily functioning. Intelligence, regardless of level, is simply a tool that individuals use to achieve aims and goals. What an individual does with his or her intelligence depends on the type of development involved. In what Dąbrowski described as biological development, intelligence is in the service of individuals' gratification of instincts, drives and needs. In the extreme negative version of biological development, one-sided development, intelligence is directed by sociopathic and, at times, criminal aims and goals. In contrast, in autonomous development, intelligence serves higher aims and values, such as altruism and authenticity.

Thus, it is not the level of intelligence that is critical; it is how it is used by individuals. Intelligence, including high level—that is, giftedness—may be used for good or evil purposes, depending on the individual's level of development. Interestingly, Dąbrowski attributes average intelligence to both one-sided and autonomous development. Giftedness, as defined in research on OE, cannot be used to differentiate between one-sided development (associated with, for example, cold-ness, cruelty, and lust for power) and autonomous development (associated with empathy, altruism, and personal responsibility). Therefore, it can be concluded that above average intelligence is a necessary, but not sufficient condition for autonomous development (Mendaglio & Pyryt, 2004). Of the two constructs, it is not intelligence that determines type of development, but rather OE, which is the expression of a larger factor in TPD developmental potential and will be discussed later in this chapter.

Dąbrowski did not use giftedness as part of his theory, though he included significant commentary on intelligence. In fact, in TPD, there is a relationship between OE and intelligence. However, the relationship between these two constructs is not a positive correlation in which the higher the intelligence the more OE. The role Dąbrowski attributes to intelligence is what makes the relationship complicated. Moreover, at first glance, it may seem appropriate to view intelligence as similar to intellectual OE. However, Dąbrowski cautioned against this association because the intellectual form of OE, as described above, includes several factors which differ from simple cognitive ability. Unless researchers understand the Dąbrowskian perspective on

OE and intelligence, they cannot claim that they are investigating OE as a construct of TPD. In my reviews of research investigating OE and giftedness (Mendaglio, 2012, 2014), I have concluded that, in essence, OE is treated as if it were atheoretical, that it has meaning in and of itself. However, like virtually all of the Dąbrowskian constructs, OE is qualitatively different from mainstream psychological constructs, and must be understood and investigated with respect to the theory in which it originated.

OE in Context

It is acknowledged here that parts of this section appeared in German in Preckel, Schneider, and Holling (2010). Permission to publish it here has been granted.

In his conception of OE, Dąbrowski (1967, 1970) noted that individuals vary in their inheritance of overexcitability: some inherit none, other individuals, one or two or more, and some inherit all five forms. As noted earlier, OE is essential for development. OE creates inner conflict, which Dąbrowski postulated was essential for his conception of human development (Dąbrowski, 1972). It is important to note again, however, that not all forms of OE are of equal importance for development. Individuals who inherit only psychomotor and sensual forms, according to Dąbrowski, may become successful in life but they will be motivated by self-interest, with little genuine concern for others; that is, they limit development to the lowest level (Dąbrowski, 1996). Dąbrowski stipulated that the emotional, intellectual and imaginational forms are required for development (Dąbrowski, 1972). Unlike common psychological perspectives, in Dąbrowski's usage, development is not equivalent to the progression of life span stages, from infancy to old age; nor is it equated with Piagetian cognitive development (Piaget & Inhelder, 1969). It does have a superficial similarity to Kohlberg (1970) because both Kohlberg and Dąbrowski were interested in moral development. However, unlike Kohlberg, Dąbrowski focussed on moral *behaviour* not moral reasoning. OE is fundamental to individuals' attainment of the highest level of human functioning characterised by moral-ethical living.

Although OE is a prerequisite for advanced development, how development occurs is a complex process which Dąbrowski explained by numerous interrelated concepts (Dąbrowski, 1973). Dąbrowski's presentation of his theory is replete with idiosyncratic use of language (see Mendaglio, 2008a). To present a synopsis of the theory of positive disintegration, I have taken the liberty of replacing some original terminology with my own terms. Specifically, I use my terminology to represent in general Dąbrowski's view of development. Based on my knowledge of the theory, I have elected to discuss Dąbrowskian development as a progression from living an egocentric-robotic life to living an altruistic-autonomous one.

In an egocentric-robotic life, individuals use their resources—intelligence, skills and talents—for the gratification of biological needs and drives such as self-preservation, self-promotion, and sexuality, which are expressions of Dąbrowski's (1964) *primary integration.* The more common of two subtypes of the egocentric-robotic approach to living are the individuals who gratify biological urges and needs by complying with societal prescriptions. Such individuals, often motivated by social approval, may become very successful in societal terms but lack development from a Dąbrowskian sense. A less common subtype of the egocentric-robotic are the individuals who become very successful in gratifying their biological urges by disregarding societal norms and by using other people for their own purposes. These two subtypes represent a lack of development because, for Dąbrowski, such individuals are self-serving, which is most obvious in the second, antisocial subtype. Though not as apparent, the egocentrism is also active in the socialised subtype: when such individuals, for example, make a financial contribution to a charitable organisation, they do so because it is socially appropriate, not because they have thoughtfully considered the organisation's cause and concluded that it was the right thing to do. Their contribution is seen as altruistic; however, their rationale is egocentric. The three subtypes represent a lack of development which Dąbrowski defines as 'the movement toward higher and higher levels of personality functions in the direction of the personality ideal' (Dąbrowski, 1964, p. 112). Further, Dąbrowski proposes that the approaches to life described above as three subtypes represent the absence of mental health (Dąbrowski, 1964).

In an altruistic-autonomous life, individuals use their resources in the process of development. The more common of the two subtypes of the altruistic-autonomous are the individuals who are successful in breaking the bonds of biology and society, through the process of positive disintegration (Dąbrowski, 1967), placing such individuals on a developmental trajectory. Unfortunately, the bonds are extremely difficult to break requiring a great deal of mental energy. The energy required generally comes from experiences of developmental milestones, such as puberty, or environmental crises such as the death of a loved one (Mendaglio, 2008b). Natural milestones and environmental events trigger a disruption in the established mental organisation (how individuals construe their world and themselves) that individuals use to guide their day-to-day behaviour. Such disruptions result in individuals' becoming aware of how their lives have been focussed on gratifying their urges and conforming to societal expectations, while rarely reflecting on oneself and the world. Growing awareness creates inner conflict where none existed previously. The inner conflict stems from their growing awareness of the discrepancy between the ways the world and themselves are and the way the world and they ought to be (Dąbrowski, 1973). For example, intense emotions are created by the growing awareness of poverty, war and disease in the world and world leaders' apparent disinterest in dealing with these issues. Similarly, emotions such as disappointment, anger and anxiety arise from a growing dissatisfaction with oneself as one becomes aware of the way he or she should behave and how she or he actually behaves. While unseen by others, such individuals spend their lives in an ebb and flow of intense negative emotions as they experience themselves succeeding and failing in their battles over their biological urges and the need for social approval. Individuals in this subtype experience recurring inner conflicts with periods of calm throughout life, which Dąbrowski (1972) termed psychoneurotics. The second and rare subtype consists of individuals who achieve the ultimate goal of behaving in an altruistic and autonomous way; they are living what Dąbrowski termed their *personality ideal* (Dąbrowski, 1967). Such individuals no longer experience inner conflict of the type described above because their daily behaviours are consistent with their ideals—they are their brothers' and sisters' keepers and not bound by societal norms but by their reflective moral approach to life. These individuals are exemplars of the phrase 'truly human' (Dąbrowski, 1967). Both subtypes represent development because, for Dąbrowski, human development is equated with a transcendence of one's biology and socialisation; in the first subtype, the transcendence is partial; in the second, it is complete.

That maturational and environmental events trigger development in some individuals and not others is not a chance occurrence: advanced development is possible only in individuals who possess more than the psychomotor and sensual forms of OE (Dąbrowski, 1996). In rare cases when individuals possess high levels of all five forms of OE, the interaction among the forms themselves (without the need for environmental contribution) provide energy and internal psychic conflict that are necessary for advanced human development (Dąbrowski, 1972). Through inner conflict and the negative emotions associated with it, particularly the experiencing of dissatisfaction with self, lower-level mental structures are destroyed—disintegrated—and replaced by new mental structures. When the outcome contributes to development, the process is termed *positive disintegration*, the phrase Dąbrowski chose to name his theory. Disintegration, however, may be negative as well. Persistent, intense emotions associated with OE-generated internal conflict and the presence of a toxic social environment may result in negative outcomes such as suicide and psychoses (Dąbrowski, 1970). OE is an essential element in the process of development, but OE is the expression of a larger hereditary factor in the theory of positive disintegration, that is, developmental potential.

Dąbrowski (1972) defined developmental potential as the 'constitutional endowment, which determines the character and the extent of mental growth possible for a given individual' (p. 293). There are four components of developmental potential: OE, special abilities, talents and autonomous forces. Special abilities and talents include, for example, mathematical ability and musical talent. Autonomous forces, termed *dynamisms* in TPD, drive development. Dynamisms seem to be triggered by overexcitable individuals' interaction with their social environments. At the early stages of development, these forces serve to disintegrate the lower mental structures, and in later stages, autonomous forces direct individual course of development. For example, dissatisfaction with oneself is one such *disintegrating* autonomous force. In more advanced development, autopsychotherapy, a *developmental* autonomous inner force, enables individuals to become their own therapists by analyzing and treating their own psychological issues (for a detailed account, see Mendaglio, 2008b). OE serves to create inner conflict; the disintegrating forces do the actual work of disintegration. Dąbrowski assessed the level of developmental potential by the presence or absence of its four components and their relative strengths. Researchers have focussed almost exclusively on OE as a measure of developmental potential, ignoring its complexity.

The synopsis of Dąbrowski's theory discussed above presents only what I consider critical to the question of whether the focus of research on OEs, independent of the many other concepts and principles comprising TPD, is appropriate or likely to contribute value to the field of gifted education.

Conclusion

Application of OE in Practice

Educators and counsellors search for information to guide their work with gifted students. Of increasing concern is social-emotional functioning of these students not simply their cognitive-academic performance. Dąbrowski's theory has grown in popularity among practitioners because scholars in gifted education have interpreted it as explaining the non-cognitive aspects of giftedness despite the fact that Dąbrowski himself termed TPD as his theory of personality. Additionally:

> *OEs separated from TPD become a problem, as in TPD OEs interact with dynamisms to achieve personality or advanced development (Pyryt, 2008) and should not serve merely as descriptive constructs. However, in gifted education OEs are presented mostly out of the context of TPD*

> *as if they were stable personality traits, thereby creating inconsistencies in the application of the original theory.* (Vuyk et al., 2016, p. 60)

Hence, applying Dąbrowski's theory to gifted students has meant using OE to reframe students' behaviours. Some common recommended applications of OE misrepresent the meaning of OE, creating a disservice to professionals eager to find means of assisting gifted students. Misrepresentation of OE is most commonly apparent in the application of psychomotor and emotional overexcitabilities. Psychomotor is used to reframe attention deficit hyperactivity disorder (ADHD). When discussing dual exceptionality of gifted and ADHD, there is a tendency to reframe it as gifted and psychomotor OE. However, a close reading of symptoms of ADHD and Dąbrowski's psychomotor suggests that psychomotor and ADHD overlap. With respect to emotional OE, any intense emotional expression reframed as emotional OE is inconsistent with it in the TPD.

When applying OE, practitioners, first, should be aware of its meaning in TPD, and second, they should uncover the rationale for students' behaviour. The key is to understand why students are behaving the way they do. As indicated in the description of emotional OE presented earlier, a child may cry for a myriad of reasons some of which may indicate emotional OE; other reasons may be manipulative. Implicit in using OE is the requirement that we have more than a superficial knowledge of the student. We cannot accurately identify students' motivation underlying their behaviours without a relationship with them.

Adults' responding to children's expressions of OE should ensure that their responses reflect Dąbrowski's conception of OE. As can be seen from the OE descriptions presented earlier in this chapter, sensual and psychomotor include some manifestations that are clearly negative in nature, requiring differentiated responses. Sensual OE is a heightened experiencing of sensory pleasure. A child's need for cuddling with mother suggests that an accepting response is appropriate. However, manifestation of overeating tends to require a response aimed at correcting the behaviour. Psychomotor OE is a function of excessive energy. Manifestations tend to be negative ranging from rapid speech to delinquent behaviours. The negative manifestations of excessive energy are transformed when the higher forms of OE are present. However, unless that occurs, parents' responses should be aimed at eliminating the negative behaviours.

Imaginational, intellectual and emotional are the higher forms of OE; their manifestations are generally positive in nature, though they may challenge parents and teachers. Imaginational OE, as the name implies, is a function of imagination and fantasy. When children exhibit inventiveness, use of metaphors or sharp visualisations, parents should admire their children's creativity. More challenging manifestions are imaginary playmates and nightmares. These manifestations tend to worry parents. They need to transcend their own anxiety in order to respond effectively. In both cases, parents should avoid denying children's realities. With nightmares, children also need reassurance from parents. Intellectual OE is a function of enthusiasm for learning coupled with theoretical thinking. A manifestation that may challenge parents and teachers is asking probing questions. Adults may misinterpret expressions of curiosity as questioning or challenging their authority. Such misinterpretations lead to defensiveness in parents and teachers, with inappropriate, at times, punitive responses. The challenge posed by the feature of asking probing questions is that adults have to decipher the motivation underlying the questions. Young children asking why they should go to bed and questioning parents' reasoning are not manifestations that need to be nurtured. In a different vein, parents should not feel that they must be able to answer any question that children's OE generates. Rather, parents should encourage children to engage in independent research. Emotional OE is a function of experiencing emotional relationships—not simply being intensely emotional. Emotions are experienced and expressed in the context of relationships. A strong attachment to people and living things is a context in which manifestations of emotions occur. Experiencing a connection with other people's suffering creates intense emotions such as sadness. The challenge for parents is to inhibit the natural inclination to use logical explanations to reduce children's negative emotions, such as sadness in response to another person's plight. Such parental responses, though well-intentioned attempts to alleviate children's distress, in actuality, serve to deny children's emotions. Children need ackowledgement and acceptance when expressing emotions produced by emotional OE.

Research Implications when Using OE

While there are opposing views to overexcitabilities in the gifted education literature, opponents appear to be showcasing their own theories and recommendations for pragmatic services for gifted students as alternatives to OE, rather than advancing the benefits of OE within the TPD (e.g. see Vuyk et al., 2016). Nonetheless, there is a push for more empirical research associated with giftedness and overexcitabilities that recognise OE within the larger and more complex TPD (e.g. see Harper et al., 2017). Viewing giftedness through a Dąbrowskian lens may provide new opportunities for designing more meaningful empirical research (e.g. Pyryt, 2008). There is little doubt that TPD has the potential to contribute significantly to our understanding of giftedness; the challenge is how we can take full advantage of Dąbrowski's creation.

Overexcitability is a compelling component of TPD but we cannot treat its five forms as discrete variables, nor should we assume that OE correlates with intellectual giftedness. However, if researchers wish to continue an exclusive focus on OE, I suggest we reconceptualise the five forms as factors, not variables. In operationalising OE, a step closer to the Dąbrowskian view is to emulate the Five Factor Model (FFM) of personality. The FFM consists of factors and facets, neuroticisim, extroversion, openness, agreeableness and conscientiousness, which are each composed of several facets (Mendaglio, 2008c). For example, agreeableness includes facets such as trust, altruism, compliance and modesty. A measure of OE reflecting the factor-facet approach, using Dąbrowski's manifestations of each form, is a closer quantitative approximation of OE than the available questionnaires.

A better approach would be to study the five forms in the broader component of TPD, in which it is located. As we know, OE is one part of developmental potential, which also includes special abilities and talents, as well as dynamisms. Research exploring all components of developmental potential should yield more meaningful results than simply tables of scores revealing various profiles of specific forms. Taking into account the degree to which OE is accompanied by special abilities and talents would likely support Dąbrowski's firm contention that a high level of intelligence alone represents a prerequisite for OE, not a guarantee. Decidedly operationalising developmental potential is more difficult than creating a Likert-type measure. Whether investigating OE as isolated concepts or in the broader context of developmental potential, I recommend the use of qualitative methodology. Engaging participants in conversations and using Dąbrowski's formulations to interpret the data would more likely enhance our understanding of the relationship between OE and giftedness. Qualitative methodology has an additional benefit: it would not have an 'a priori belief that gifted persons were more overexcitable than nongifted persons' (Winkler & Voight, 2016, p. 252), which appears to underline the current OEQ questionnaires.

OE is a complex construct that is an integral part of the theory of positive disintegration. It cannot be investigated as an independent construct. The current approach to research is not reflective of or informed by Dąbrowski's theory. OE is inextricably bound to developmental potential, which is integral to human development. Researchers interested in studying Dąbrowski's OE ought to accept that it cannot be assessed by exclusively using questionnaires of any kind, especially not those composed of Likert-type scales. Simply acknowledging that OE is part of TPD is not sufficient; TPD, in its fullness, must permeate researchers' assumptions and methodology. Until researchers design their studies of OE and giftedness with Dąbrowski's TPD in mind, the question remains: Whose constructs are being investigated?

References

Alias, A., Rahman, S., Majid, R. A., & Yassin, S. F. M. (2013). Dąbrowski's Overexcitabilities profile among gifted students. *Asian Social Science, 9*(16), 120–125. https://doi.org/10.5539/ass.v9n16p120

Bailey, C. L. (2011). An examination of the relationships between ego development, Dąbrowski's theory of positive disintegration, and the behavioral characteristics of gifted adolescents. *The Gifted Child Quarterly*, 55, 208–222. https://doi.org/10.1177/0016986211412180

Chang, J. J., & Kuo, C. C. (2009). Overexcitabilities of gifted and talented students and its related researches in Taiwan. *Asia-Pacific Journal of Gifted and Talented Education*, 1(1), 41–74.

Dąbrowski, K. (1964). *Positive disintegration.* Boston, MA: Little Brown.

Dąbrowski, K. (1967). *Personality-shaping through positive disintegration.* Boston, MA: Little Brown.

Dąbrowski, K. (1970). *Mental growth through positive disintegration.* London, England: Gryf.

Dąbrowski, K. (1972). *Psychoneurosis is not an illness.* London, England: Gryf.

Dąbrowski, K. (1973). *The dynamics of concepts.* London, England: Gryf.

Dąbrowski, K. (1996). *Multilevelness of emotional and instinctive functions. Part 1: Theory and description of levels of behavior.* Lublin, Poland: Towarzystwo Naukowe Katolickiego Uniwersytetu Lubelskiego.

Daniels, S. & Meckstroth, E. (2009). Nurturing the sensitivity, intensity, and developmental potential of young gifted children. In Daniels, S. & Piechowski, M. (Eds.), *Living with intensity: Understanding the sensitivity, excitability, and emotional development of gifted children, adolescents and adults.* (pp. 33–56). Scottsdale, AZ: Great Potential Press.

Falk, R. R., Lind, S., Miller, N. B., Piechowski, M. M., & Silverman, L. K. (1999). *The overexcitability questionnaire–two (OEQII): Manual, scoring system, and questionnaire.* Denver, CO: Institute for the Study of Advanced Development.

Harper, A., Cornish, L., Smith, S., & Merrotsy, P. (2017). Through the Dąbrowski Lens: A fresh examination of the Theory of Positive Disintegration. *Roeper Review*, 39(1), 37–43. https://doi.org/10.1080/02783193.2016.1247395

He, W., & Wong, W. (2014). Greater male variability in overexcitabilities: Domain-specific patterns. *Personality and Individual Differences*, 66, 27–32. https://doi.org/10.1016/j.paid.2014.03.002

He, W., Wong, W., & Chan, M. (2017). Overexcitabilities as important psychological attributes of creativity: A Dąbrowskian perspective. *Thinking Skills and Creativity*, 25, 27–35. https://doi.org/10.1016/j.tsc.2017.06.006

Kohlberg, L. (1970). Moral stages and moralization: The cognitive-developmental approach to socialization. In T. Kickona (Ed.), *Moral development and behaviour: Theory, research and social issues* (pp. 31–43). New York, NY: Holt, Rinehart & Winston.

Lysy, K. Z., & Piechowski, M. M. (1983). Personal growth: An empirical study using Jungian and Dąbrowskian measures. *Genetic Psychology Monographs,* 108, 267–320.

Mendaglio, S. (Ed.). (2008a). *Dąbrowski's theory of positive disintegration.* Scottsdale, AZ: Great Potential Press.

Mendaglio, S. (2008b). Dąbrowski's theory of positive disintegration: A personality theory for the 21st century. In S. Mendaglio (Ed.), *Dąbrowski's theory of positive disintegration* (pp. 13–40). Scottsdale, AZ: Great Potential Press.

Mendaglio, S. (2008c). The theory of positive disintegration (TPD) and other approaches to personality. In S. Mendaglio (Ed.), *Dąbrowski's theory of positive disintegration* (pp. 227–248). Scottsdale, AZ: Great Potential Press.

Mendaglio, S. (2012). Overexcitabilities and giftedness research: A call for a paradigm shift. *Journal for the Education of the Gifted,* 35(3), 207–219.

Mendaglio, S., (2014). Dąbrowski on intelligence: Dethroning a venerable construct. *International Journal for Talent Development and Creativity,* 15, 30–45

Mendaglio, S., & Pyryt, M. C. (2004). The role of intelligence in Dąbrowski's theory of positive disintegration. In W. Tillier (Ed.). *Developmental potential: From theory to practice: Educational and therapeutic perspectives.* Proceedings from the sixth international congress of the Institute for Positive Disintegration in Human Development. Calgary, AB.

Mendaglio, S., & Tillier, W. (2006). Dąbrowski's theory of positive disintegration and giftedness: Overexcitabilities research findings. *Journal for the Education of the Gifted,* 30, 68–87.

Miller, N. B., Falk, R. F., & Huang, Y. (2009). Gender identity and the overexcitability profiles of gifted college students. *Roeper Review,* 31, 161–169.

Piaget, J., & Inhelder, B. (1969). *The psychology of the child.* New York, NY: Basic Books.

Piechowski, M. M., & Miller, N. B. (1995). Assessing developmental potential in gifted children: A comparison of methods. *Roeper Review,* 17, 176–180.

Piirto, J. (2010). 21 Years With the Dąbrowski Theory: An Autoethnography. *Advanced Development*, 12, 70–92.

Piirto, J., & Fraas, J. (2012). A mixed-methods comparison of vocational and identified-gifted high school students on the Overexcitability Questionnaire. *Journal for the Education of the Gifted,* 35(1), 3–34. https://doi.org/10.1177/0162353211433792

Preckel, F., Schneider, W., & Holling, H. (Eds.). (2010). Diagnostic von hodchbegabung. Gottingen, Germany: Hogrefe. [Mendaglio, S. *Overexcitabilities and Dąbrowskis Theorie der Positiven Desintegration*, pp. 169–196.].

Pyryt, M. (2008). The Dąbrowskian lens: Implications for understanding gifted individuals. In S. Mendaglio (Ed.), *Dąbrowski's theory of positive disintegration* (pp. 175–182). Tucson, AZ: Great Potential Press.

Silverman, L. K. (2008). The theory of positive disintegration in the field of gifted education. In S. Mendaglio (Ed.), *Dąbrowski's theory of positive disintegration* (pp. 157–173). Scottsdale, AZ: Great Potential.

Siu, A. F. Y. (2010). Comparing overexcitabilities of gifted and non-gifted school children in Hong Kong: Does culture make a difference? *Asia Pacific Journal of Education*, 30(1), 71–83.

Tillier, W. (2009). Dąbrowski without the theory of positive disintegration just isn't Dąbrowski. *Roeper Review*, 31, 123–126. https://doi.org/10.1080/02783190902737699

Vuyk, M. A., Kerr, B. A., & Krieshok, T. S. (2016). From overexcitabilities to openness: Informing gifted education with psychological science. *Gifted and Talented International,* 31(1), 59–71. https://doi.org/10.1080/15332276.2016.1220796

Warne, R. T. (2011). A reliability generalization of the Overexcitability Questionnaire-Two. *Journal of Advanced Academics*, 22, 671–692.

Winkler, D., & Voight, A. (2016). Giftedness and overexcitability: Investigating the relationship using meta-analysis. *The Gifted Child Quarterly*, 60(4), 243–257.

Yoon, Y. H., & Moon, J. H. (2009). A comparison of the overexcitabilities: In gifted and non-gifted Korean primary-school children. *Journal of Gifted/Talented Education*, 19(3), 585–602.

Part III

Recent Words on Dąbrowski's Theory and Giftedness

Chapter 10
Interview on TPD

The entry in the final chapter includes an interview with me conducted by the current co-editors of the Journal of Advanced Academics, Todd Kettler and Anne Rinn. I appreciated the opportunity to share my concerns about the portrayal of the theory in a venue other than a formal article. I responded to excellent questions on the theory and its relation to the psychology of giftedness. Of particular interest to me was the opportunity to address a call for the replacement of overexcitability with concepts from the Five Factor Model of personality. Attempts to replace Dąbrowskian constructs, in my view, are simply another way of manifesting a lack of understanding of his theory.

Reference

Mendaglio, S., Kettler, T., & Rinn, A. N. (2019). Psychology of giftedness and the theory of positive disintegration: A Conversation With Sal Mendaglio. *Journal of Advanced Academics*, 30(4), 500–507. https://doi-org.ezproxy.lib.ucalgary.ca/10.1177/1932202X19869010

Psychology of Giftedness and the Theory of Positive Disintegration: A Conversation With Sal Mendaglio

Salvatore "Sal" Mendaglio is Professor of Education in the Werklund School of Education at the University of Calgary in Calgary, Alberta, Canada. He also serves as Chair of Educational Studies in Counseling Psychology and the Graduate Program Director for the Educational Psychology Program. His primary area of research and scholarship is the psychology of giftedness and the theory of positive disintegration, with special emphasis on counseling gifted individuals. Born in Italy, Dr. Mendaglio spent his youth in Canada. He earned his PhD in Counseling Psychology at the University of Toronto in 1976. Shortly thereafter, he joined the Counseling Psychology program at University of Calgary and in 1995 began teaching in the School of Education where he currently offers courses in leadership and gifted education. This interview took place in the spring of 2019.

JoAA: How would you describe your initial interest in Dąbrowski's theory of positive disintegration?

Mendaglio: To appreciate my initial interest in the theory of positive disintegration (TPD), you need to know how I was first introduced to it. My introduction to it was the result of necessity—through serendipity I began counseling gifted individuals in a small independent practice. Though I had no academic background in giftedness/gifted education, I received referrals of identified gifted students considered academic underachievers.

Necessity led me to TPD. During the early 1980s, there were virtually no resources in Calgary for education of gifted children and no resources at all for counseling gifted individuals. With no previous background knowledge in giftedness or counseling gifted individuals, I, of course, did what any professional should do—I went searching the literature. I was very disappointed because, in the voluminous literature, there were only a handful of titles that had counseling in the title. To be frank, those resources contained information related to counseling but nothing that I felt could help me direct a counseling process. Ultimately, I discovered TPD through secondary sources, most notably the works of Michael Piechowski and Linda Silverman. Subsequently, I began studying Dąbrowski's English book made available by my friend and occasional collaborator William Tillier.

My interest in the theory was sparked by Dąbrowski's privileging emotion over intelligence, in human behavior and development. Prior to encountering TPD, I had developed my own theorizing to guide my counseling with clients. A key element in my emerging theory was the importance of emotion in daily living. I developed a rallying cry: "It's all about emotion." Applying it to counseling, I concluded that the actual reason for clients' seeking counseling and psychotherapy is their inability to handle intense negative emotions, regardless of their presenting problems. As I learned more about TPD from original sources, I found it fascinating how Dąbrowski explained—not simply described—that negative emotions propelled some individuals toward the highest level of human development. Dąbrowski's theory initially helped me deepen my understanding of my rallying cry. By explaining that negative emotions may lead to higher levels of functioning, Dąbrowski taught me that for some clients the goal of counseling is not to eliminate those emotions but celebrate them as signs of development.

JoAA: In what ways might the theory of positive disintegration contribute to understanding the psychology of giftedness?

Mendaglio: That is a great question. To answer the question, we need to consider existing conceptions of giftedness. As you know, authors have proposed an increasing number of definitions, especially since the 1970s. While there is a lack of consensus on how to define giftedness, I see a few themes evident in these definitions. There are implicit or explicit critiques of Terman's exclusive focus on intelligence: it is too narrow and conservative resulting in identifying a rather small percentage of a population. Sydney Marland dealt with that by expanding the areas in which giftedness may be manifested and thereby identified. Gagné followed Marland's multidimensional approach while providing a more detailed and theoretical rationale for his numerous categories of gifts and talents. Renzulli proposed replacing giftedness as trait preferring the notion of gifted behavior in his famous three ring conception. Renzulli's focus on productivity appears to have influence subsequent conceptions. In recent years, there is a greater focus by proponents such as Sternberg, Subotnik, and others on productivity as the major component of giftedness. Others such as Annemarie Roeper and the Columbus group focus more on such matters as processes of awareness and asynchrony. Despite the diversity of approaches, one constant is apparent: the criterion of high intelligence, at times referred to as cognitive ability. Dąbrowski's conceptualization of intelligence contributed to my psychology of giftedness.

It must be said that TPD is not a theory of giftedness. The term gifted appears here and in Dąbrowski's English language books but there is no explicit definition. His approach to giftedness is illustrated in a study he reported. He conducted a comparative study with gifted and developmentally delayed youth to explore certain facets of his theory. He used the Wechsler test of intelligence to select his sample. In effect, Dąbrowski used Terman's definition of giftedness—a high score on an intelligence test. In his use of gifted in his books, it is clear to me that he is referring to well-above-average intelligence.

If we view giftedness solely in terms of intelligence (as I do), then, TPD has a great deal to offer to the psychology of giftedness. One implication is that giftedness is neutral in nature: intelligence may be used for positive or negative ends. Intelligence, in and of itself, is subordinate to emotion. A high level of intelligence is no guarantee of developing a highly functioning human being. Dąbrowski stated that well above average intelligence is necessary but not enough for moral development. A high level of intelligence coupled with Dąbrowskian developmental potential creates internal conflict that is the essence of positive disintegration—the process of development—to occur. A high level of intelligence—giftedness—in such circumstances provides the keen aware-ness of self and the world that creates negative emotions (disintegrating dynamisms) that are driving forces of development.

Giftedness can also be used for self-serving, narcissistic, and outright evil purposes. Dąbrowski noted that high intelligence with limited developmental potential with high ambition leads to very dangerous uses of intelligence. He illustrated this by describing well-known historical figures who committed heinous acts on humanity. Criminal behavior and bullying are other less extreme examples of how high intelligence can be manifested.

The TPD perspective on intelligence convinced me to view giftedness as neutral in nature. This contrasts with the positive bias in most current conceptions of giftedness.

JoAA: What are some ways that the theory of positive disintegration could be helpful for educators or researchers working in gifted education and other advanced academic programs?

Mendaglio: For those interested in applying TPD, it is essential to understand what it is not and what it is. TPD is not a theory of giftedness. TPD is not a theory of overexcitability (OE). Not all TPD concepts are applicable to all gifted individuals. TPD is Dąbrowski's explanation of the full range of human functioning from the worst to the best of humanity. TPD is a theory that emphasizes biological bases of human functioning, which some find problematic. It uses terms (e.g., disintegration, development, personality) idiosyncratically, differing significantly from their general psychological usage. TPD is a theory containing assumptions, propositions, and constructs, tightly knitted together such that it is challenging to consider a construct in isolation.

Regarding its application, Dąbrowski advises that TPD should not be used to justify or condone disruptive behavior. In my experience, the challenge for teachers and parents of all children is responding to their emotion expressions. Not all expressions are of equal value! Children and adolescents are known to use emotions to manipulate adults. A young child's crying when reminded that it is bedtime is an example of attempt to derail parents and allow the child to stay up longer. Using emotions to manipulate occurs in various forms, some subtle, some aggressive. Clearly this is the type of emotion expression that adults should discourage.

Children and adolescents possessing all forms of OE tend not to behave in manipulative, aggressive ways. They tend to present more emotional expressions than other children. Presence of OEs manifests in children's expressions of concern for other, social withdrawal, awareness of global issues, altruistic behaviors, intellectual curiosity, and asking probing questions. Dąbrowski stated that OE may be manifested young children, such as 2 or 3 years of age.

Whenever adults interpret emotion expression in all children and adolescents, my advice is to ignore it and avoid being distracted from the task at hand. On the contrary, when emotions are the result of altruism or genuine questioning, adults should encourage youth to express them in an accepting atmosphere. Naturally, the context is important, for example, teachers or parents cannot be expected to drop everything and attend to children's emotion. Adults should invite children to discuss their experiences at a more opportune time.

I think that most parents and educators know how to appropriately respond to children's emotions. To my mind, what is more important for educators and others is to avoid misuse TPD. A situation that I have witnessed is teachers and parents familiar with OE excusing disruptive behavior: "It's just the manifestation of OEs."

JoAA: What are your thoughts on the way overexcitabilities are seen from the point of view of teachers and parents versus researchers?

Mendaglio: I see no difference among those three groups in terms of how they perceive overexcitabilities. There tends to be confusion regarding the nature of Dąbrowski's OEs. It is a property of the central nervous system that is not a universal endowment. OE is not learned, it is the product of heredity—some people have no OE, others have some, and few have all five forms (psychomotor, sensual, intellectual, imaginational, and emotional). Bearing in mind that giftedness is equated with high intelligence, giftedness is not synonymous with inheritance of all forms of OE.

Furthermore, the possession of all five forms is essential for advanced development by contributing to inner conflict. The interaction of the lower forms (psychomotor, sensual) and the higher forms (imaginational, intellectual, emotional) and the social environment is responsible for inner conflict.

Teachers, parents, and researchers tend to assume that all gifted individuals possess all forms of OE and that OE is generally positive. Giftedness, as high intelligence, is not synonymous with possession of OE. While high intelligence is a prerequisite for OE, it is not a guarantee. Some gifted individuals may possess no form, some forms, or all forms. Of course, if one were to define giftedness using Dąbrowski's OE, then all gifted individuals would possess all forms of OE.

As I noted earlier, the possession of all forms of OE results in inner conflict. This means that such individuals are prone to experience existential anxiety, depression, and guilt. Such negative emotions arise as they become aware of the discrepancy between the way the world is and the way it ought to be—between the ideal and real.

JoAA: Teachers and parents can be quick to point out the overexcitabilities of their students and children, but researchers remain skeptical of their existence. How can we reconcile these differing viewpoints?

Mendaglio: Parents, typically, do not concern themselves with scholarly research; they are likely most affected by opinions of authors and practitioners. Overexcitabilities are likely the most accessible TPD construct. Unlike positive disintegration, dynamism, and inner conflict, OEs have a positive flavor to them. Rarely are parents presented with the full TPD picture of OEs. Parents observe boundless energy (psychomotor), enjoyment of certain foods (sensual), children's imaginary playmates (imagination), asking questions (intellectual), or emotional expressions (emotional). OEs may be also used to explain negative behaviors—attributing the cause to OEs no other reasons (e.g., egocentrism, impulsivity, poor parenting). Parents can't be blamed for not reading research findings, when experts provide readily accessible information in books or websites.

On the contrary, researchers have a different agenda—they need to scrutinize construct and theories examining them in dispassionate ways. I think that some—not all—researchers are skeptical. This is evidenced by a growing number of researchers globally (from Denver to Hong Kong) who investigate the relationship between giftedness and OE.

I am not concerned about researchers' remaining skeptical of the existence of OE. That is their prerogative. Dąbrowski's TPD is simply a theory after all. In my view, it is a theory akin to the theories of Freud, H.S. Sullivan, and Rogers. Psychoanalysis, interpersonal theory of psychiatry, and self-theory were created by clinicians who were astute observers, producing theories, manifesting their creativity. Similarly, Dąbrowski created a theory based on his interpretation of observations he made in life and in clinics. I would be concerned when skepticism is based on limited knowledge of TPD.

If skepticism of OE is based on published research, I fully understand. I have written a couple of articles critiquing the approach to research on OE and giftedness. Current questionnaires, for example, do not accurately reflect Dąbrowski's view which is far more complex that can be captured in a Likert-type questionnaire.

But let's face it, whether it is OE, anxiety, perfectionism, we are dealing with constructs. By definition, constructs have no empirical referent in the world. We cannot see anxiety. The nature of constructs encourages skepticism, not to mention numerous definitions for the same construct.

JoAA: Vuyk, Krieshok, and Kerr (2016) found evidence to suggest Openness to Experience, one of the Big Five factors of personality, actually encompasses and explains overexcitabilities: "Individuals

who are open to new experiences enjoy both outer and inner worlds, are curious, and hold novel ideas. They have high aesthetic sensitivity, intellectual curiosity, vivid imagination, and evolving value systems. This description appears extraordinarily analogous to descriptions of OEs [overexcitabilities], which describe active imaginations, enjoyment of sensory pleasures such as art and beauty, intensity of feelings, love of learning, and a pull for action" (p. 192). Botella et al. (2015) found the same results using French versions of the OEQ-II and a measure of the Big Five. What do you make of these findings?

Mendaglio: I am quite familiar with those findings. The conclusion of their findings, as Vuyk et al.'s title suggests, is that gifted education should replace OE with open-ness to experience. I completely disagree with that proposal. That two measures correlate is not enough rationale to abandon OEs. I cannot, with authority, comment on the appropriateness of the measure used to operationalize openness to experience. With my background knowledge of TPD, I am, however, in a position to critique the OE measure, which I have done elsewhere. The OEQ-II cannot capture the complexity of Dąbrowski's definition and description of the five forms of OE. If one reads TPD in the original, it would be apparent that a Likert-type scale cannot adequately reflect the construct of OE. Having said that, I understand that researchers like the OEQ-II is because of its ease of administration and scoring.

Beyond my issues with the questionnaire, I disagree with the conclusion to abandon OE on conceptual grounds. Let's look at the two conceptualizations in which openness and OE appear. The five-factor model has its origin in the lexical approach used by Cattell (1957) as well as Allport and Odbert (1936). They read numerous dictionaries looking for descriptors of personality. They found literally thousands of words. Cattell used a subset to create a taxonomy of traits. Such is the origin of the five-factor model. In contrast, Dąbrowski began in the 1930s creating his theory based on, among other things, observations of human functioning and his clinical practice. The five-factor model describes traits; TPD explains the range of human functioning. The five-factor model is not a theory; it is an empirically derived categorization of human traits. TPD is a theory replete with assumptions, principles, propositions, and constructs that create a coherent whole.

What is missing in the case made by the two cited articles is the nature and role of OE. The forms of OE are not simply standalone traits—they are processes which interact to create an intensification of experience and inner conflict which contribute to individual's transcending lower forms to higher forms of functioning; from a life motivated by needs and drives to one motivated by universal positive values. My comments approximate Dąbrowski's view of OE. I am not aware of how openness to experience, rather than constructs with which it is correlated, is proposed as transformational human functioning. If openness to experience is proposed as a factor, which is said to transform primitive level of human functioning, based on such matters as self-preservation to higher levels of functioning manifested in exemplars of humanity, then I would agree with replacing OE. The two articles provide evidence of how OE, which is only valid in the context of TPD, is not fully represented in research.

JoAA: What are some ways the theory of positive disintegration has been studied or applied beyond studies on the psychology of giftedness?

Mendaglio: It is rare to encounter studies that do not investigate OE in the context of giftedness. There are rare studies investigating gender differences on OE and its effects on creativity. The paucity of studies of OE beyond giftedness is not surprising because TPD is only widely known in the fields of giftedness/gifted education.

JoAA: How do you see the future of the theory of positive disintegration?

The increase in research investigating OE and giftedness that I have witnessed over the years will continue. Overexcitability is an intriguing construct and it has become inextricably bound by many authors with giftedness. The increase in research in this area is the result of the availability of a questionnaire that is easily administered and scored by researchers. Despite my critique of such research, I have noticed that researchers have begun elaborating on the TPD context of OE in their articles. This is good news and bad news from my perspective. It is good news because research helps in the dissemination of TPD. It is bad news because increased popularity of the current approach to research reinforces inaccurate representation of TPD.

Though I predict the increase in such research, I do not think it will last. To be frank, I cannot see how the current research on OE and giftedness is sustain-able. I wonder how long readers interested in Dąbrowski's theory will tolerate publications noting that the gifted sample scores (3.2) were significantly higher than the nonidentified sample (2.8) on a form of OE. Given its complexity and association with other TPD constructs, I suggest that it is better to use qualitative rather than quantitative methods to investigate it.

References

Allport, G. W., & Odbert, H. S. (1936). Trait-names: A psycholexical study. *Psychological Monographs*, 47(1), i-171.

Botella, M., Furst, G., Myszkowski, N., Storme, M., Pereira Da Costa, M., & Luminet, O. (2015). French validation of the Overexcitability Questionnaire 2: Properties and factorial structure. *Journal of Personality Assessment*, 97, 209-220. doi:10.1080/00223891.2014938750

Cattell, R. B. (1957). *Personality and motivation structure and measurement.* Yonkers, NY: World Book.

Vuyk, M. A., Krieshok, T. S., & Kerr, B. A. (2016). Openness to experience rather than over-excitabilities: Call it like it is. *Gifted Child Quarterly,* 60, 192-211. doi:10.1177/00169 86216645407

CPSIA information can be obtained
at www.ICGtesting.com
Printed in the USA
FSHW022004090222
88209FS

9 781953 360090